The Global Pantry Cookbook

The Global Pantry Cookbook

TRANSFORM YOUR EVERYDAY COOKING
with TAHINI, GOCHUJANG, MISO, and
OTHER IRRESISTIBLE INGREDIENTS

Ann Taylor Pittman
Scott Mowbray

———

Photography by Kevin Miyazaki

Workman Publishing
New York

Library of Congress Cataloging-in-Publication Data is available.

ISBN 978-1-5235-1685-8

Design by Becky Terhune
Food photography by Kevin Miyazaki
Product photography by Spring Rd. Studios
Food styling by Erica McNeish
Props by Tina Gill
Hand-made Japanese ceramics by Kazu Oba, obaware.com
Additional props by Anuschka Pashel, bloomdenver.com
Additional copyediting by Susan Roberts McWilliams
Additional photos: **Getty Images:** Tomohiro Ohsumi/Bloomberg p. 7, Mehmet Akif Parlak/
Anadolu Agency p. viii. **Shutterstock.com:** AmyLv p. 14, Angorius p. 14, EvgeniiAnd p. 23,
manbo-photo p. 25, New Africa p. 18, Vitals p. 11.

Workman books are available at special discounts when purchased in bulk for
premiums and sales promotions as well as for fundraising or educational use.
Special editions or book excerpts can also be created to specification.
For details, please contact special.markets@hbgusa.com.

Workman Publishing Co., Inc.,
a subsidiary of Hachette Book Group, Inc.
1290 Avenue of the Americas
New York, NY 10104

workman.com

WORKMAN is a registered trademark of Workman Publishing Co., Inc.,
a subsidiary of Hachette Book Group, Inc.

Printed in China on responsibly sourced paper.
First printing August 2023

10 9 8 7 6 5 4 3 2 1

For Patrick, Connor, and Daniel
—Ann

For my enthusiastic eaters,
Kate, Rosa, Emily, Annie, and Emmy.
In memory of Kay Mowbray and Anne Eisen
—Scott

Contents

Pomegranate molasses is made the traditional way—slow reduction of bright juice to syrupy goodness—by villagers in the province of Gaziantep in southern Turkey, near the Mediterranean sea (tragically, Gaziantep was devastated by the 2023 earthquake). The result is tart, tannic, fruity, and delicious. It's easily found in Middle Eastern food stores and good supermarkets.

Discovering the Treasures of the Global Pantry

The ancient alchemists who fancied that they could turn lead into gold never managed the trick. But wondrous transformations had been happening nearby, and pretty much everywhere since pretty much forever. Food, under the sway of biological processes, was being cured, salted, sugared, dried, spiced, smoked, and fermented by cooks and artisans. As it was preserved, flavors concentrated and transmuted. From the Mekong Delta to the cacao-bean forests of the Olmec people in present-day Mexico, a global pantry of fantastic treasures marked the long, slow rise of the great cuisines. These treasures, the heritage of hundreds or thousands of years of food knowledge, survived to become ingredients that, today, can imbue anyone's cooking with their flavor magic. They are, as our friend chef Keith Schroeder put it, "the gift of time in a bottle."

For decades, these pantry treasures poured into American "ethnic" shops and markets, powered by immigration and the trade that flowed in its wake. Most were sold to their immigrant communities, although any curious cook in a midsize city could find a good number of them. Then, accelerating as the 20th century progressed, came a great awakening to flavors that had been hiding in plain sight all along. Millions of Americans tasted dishes in restaurants and markets that were made delicious, in part, by the global pantry. The American palate has expanded remarkably since then, and today the foods and flavors of Thailand, Korea, China, India, Mexico, Israel, Lebanon, and so many more cuisines that Americans go nuts for in restaurants can be brought into the home—easily, cheaply, deliciously.

But these foods and flavors are *not* brought home, many of them, usually. Partly this is because they're intimidating or assumed to be useful only in the dishes they're associated with, rather than understood as powerful and versatile new tools for the cook's toolbox. And partly because, however mall-ubiquitous Thai and other restaurants have become, ingredients like makrut lime leaves are rarely seen or explained in chain supermarkets. For every thoroughly mainstreamed elixir, like sriracha or balsamic vinegar, a hundred other pantry products, often much more tasty, are still mostly used by cooks who know and love them because their mothers or fathers did: fermented fish sauces from Vietnam, fruity chile pastes from Peru, salted lemons from Morocco, gochujang from Korea. Yet these flavor bombs represent some of the easiest ways to elevate anyone's cooking. The secrets of the global pantry are there for anyone to borrow.

This is the idea behind *The Global Pantry Cookbook*—embracing a broad and playful flavor inclusiveness through global pantry exploration.

Of course, the products we celebrate in these pages have long been essential to "American cooking," when the phrase is used to mean *all the cooking in American kitchens,* whether in homes or restaurants, and not some narrower slice of the pie. But these global pantry products may not yet be used in *your* kitchen. To shop widely, to trip joyfully down all the aisles of the global pantry, sampling its treasures, is an adventure and education for any cook.

The variety of products is astonishing. There are 300-plus jars of chile pastes and related mixtures on just *one side of one aisle* in the pan-Asian supermarket, H Mart, a few miles from Scott's Colorado home (there are almost 100 outlets of this wonderful chain nationwide—look for one near you). There are more than 50 masala spice mixtures at a tiny Indian store 3 miles away. Nine sour creams in a local Latin supermarket. The number of such products that have been creeping into Whole Foods, Costco, and Walmart is heartening. When local shops don't provide, there's the infinitely expanding array of global pantry shelves that is the internet. For those living in small towns or rural areas, the web *is* the global pantry, the delivery truck the last-mile version of a 16th-century ship just in from the Malabar Coast, bearing cardamom, cloves, and nutmeg.

Of course, as cooks we're interested in what these products can do for us, tonight, for dinner. Fascinated by and respectful of traditional uses, we are always looking for something new. This is the American way, one supposes, until one eats in a Tokyo spaghetti shop, with its uni and pasta and mozzarella, everything quick-cooked in a wok, and realizes that cross-cultural mash-ups define the history of much global cooking. When we brush fish sauce onto ribs before grilling, we're mindful that we're deploying an artisanal food whose roots go back thousands of years. The ancient oceanic umami of the fish sauce lifts and concentrates the beefiness of the beef. And that is often the role of global pantry ingredients in our recipes: to blend into a dish, to tie threads together and sing a background melody. They boost flavors, add depth or heat or fragrance or acidic zing, improve texture, or finish dishes on an elusive, delicious note. This is their alchemical power. One slice of Allan Benton's profoundly smoked Tennessee Mountain bacon does the flavor work of six slices of boring factory stuff. By the time the sweet wine of Banyuls, France, has spent years lounging in barrels to become Banyuls vinegar, a spoonful generates an ethereal loveliness in a salad dressing or a sauce that no industrial balsamic or red wine vinegar comes close to matching. A dab of shrimp paste from Indonesia brings a platter of sweet, slippery fried noodles to a place of gorgeous flavor. A glug of oyster sauce makes the meatiest pot roast ever.

Yes, the gift of time in a bottle usually costs a bit more than cheap, bland, processed imitators. The deep deliciousness of global pantry products reflects hard-earned skills and, often, requires better ingredients. But many of these products are used in small amounts and will last on shelves or in the fridge or freezer for months. Many often come in small and light packages, so they ship economically, especially if you have a free shipping program or if you gang up several items in a single order, which also cuts down on environmental waste.

How We Embarked on Our Global Pantry Adventure

Way back in the '80s, as a greenhorn writer backpacking in Asia, Scott had lunch with a member of the Thai royal family in a tiny seaside village outside Bangkok. Mom Rajawongse Thanadsri Svasti was the most famous food critic in the nation of gourmands that is Thailand, a former pop singer and soap opera actor of national acclaim. He had grown up in palaces, eaten the royal cuisine, but championed the roots of his country's food, with little notion of class. The point of the visit to the fishing village was an exquisite lunch, but first, the prince announced, there would be a tasting of fish sauces made by local artisans.

What Scott supposed about straight-from-the-bottle fish sauce then was what a prairie-born child might suppose: *ick, fishy.* Prince Thanadsri smacked his lips with each spoonful of amber liquid and discussed with the beaming producers the nuances of production and style that yielded different-tasting sauces made a few hundred meters from one another. Stink was there, of course, in the same way that Roquefort or aged prime beef has the pong of enzymatic transformation, but also sweetness and caramel-savoriness and a lot more: profound qualities that we now know today by the word *umami.*

In Mississippi, about the same time, Ann was growing up, daughter of a Korean mother who had come to the United States with her husband, an American soldier, in the 1960s. Ann adored boiled peanuts and bulgogi, fried catfish and gimbap, gas-station potato logs and gojuchang-spiced ribs. Later she would win a James Beard award for her account in *Cooking Light* magazine of the complicated, sometimes heartbreaking entanglements of her heritage. The article's title, "Mississippi Chinese Lady Goes Home to Korea," conveys the confusions that came with growing up in an area where ignorant kids called her "some kind of Chinese." To be obviously foreign to most Southerners, yet not Korean enough to many Koreans, created a dual otherness that mixed-race children know well. (As her husband, Patrick, would tell her many years later, "Ann, you are a Hyundai. You might be born and made in America, but you are a Korean product.") Yet the Deep South, with some of America's oldest and greatest and most entangled cooking traditions, has always been, and always will be, her beloved home. It was the place where the joy of eating dialectically—Deep South, Far East—was understood.

This global/local mash-up heritage is the source of Ann's inspired recipe for smoky pimento kim cheese on page 30. The succulent flavor-bomb mixture is flecked with funky kimchi (a food now sold in her local Publix grocery store in Ann's home, Birmingham, Alabama). The pimento is

smoked because, well, *because.* The mass of sharp Cheddar goodness is given unctuous unity by the king of American mayos, Duke's. The result is a quintessential American treat with global ambitions. Why not scoop it up with the big krupuk—shrimp crackers—that Scott fell for at the age of 10 in Java? The recipe suggests you do, and we outline the fun job of frying those crunchy crackers on page 49.

About the year that Ann was born, Scott moved from Saskatoon, Saskatchewan, to Surakarta, Java, when his father, a doctor, took a job with CARE to teach in local hospitals. Back home, "spicy" food had contained quantities of chile barely detectable by laboratory equipment. At a meal at a Chinese restaurant in Jakarta, the universe was revealed to be a much richer, much more wonderful creation (and more painful, when a tiny green chile eaten whole seemed hotter than the sun). Soon, the family was eating Chinese frog's legs in black bean sauce, Sumatran fiery beef rendang, and Balinese stewed duck. Over seven and a half years of living in Indonesia and, later, Afghanistan, food-obsessed travel was the family's recreation, most of it in less-than-fancy restaurants, often from food stalls and roadside shacks and the kitchens of kind hosts.

In 2009, Scott and Ann met in Birmingham as food magazine editors at *Cooking Light,* where Ann directed a test kitchen that had developed thousands of recipes, many her own. The magazine had a huge audience, and its goal was to steer the concept of healthy American cooking away from outdated low-fat rules and into the wide world of global flavors and dishes where meat often played a supporting rather than starring role. It was a time of fun and ferment. The Korean-American Southerner introduced the ex-Canadian to field peas, scuppernongs, properly fried catfish, Benton's bacon, and the finer points of bourbon-fueled porch-sit storytelling—and to the milky Korean rice beer called makgeolli and the chewy rice cakes called tteokbokki. Scott shared peanutty Indonesian sauces, kecap manis–robed satays, salty palm sugar ice cream, and the great

Canadian tradition of the butter tart, which, he maintains—heretically in the South, but with some converts in Ann's family—is superior to any pecan pie (the butter tart recipe on page 277 is enhanced with Southern sorghum syrup, a beloved pantry star, more complex and tangy than the dark corn syrup usually used in the frozen north).

The roots of the recipes in this book, in the end, reflect the Heinz 57 cultural mash-up history of the authors. Our approach is social, casual, and communal. That's why you'll find lots of finger foods and snacks, grilled things, and cheaper cuts of meat. The recipes are mostly lively fusions. The main idea is relaxed cooking with big flavors, in the happy-family, good-friends-eating-together way, tapping into the endless joys of global flavor creativity. This is—with all those loyal pantry helpers invited to the party—our idea of fun.

So Whose Flavors Are These, Anyway?

To cook from the global pantry* is to taste the umami of human history, an infinitely tangled and often bloody story. Imagine a brilliantly colored map,

animating movement of global foods. Bright arrows shoot this way and that, representing flavor vectors that moved across time, space, and cultures.

On this flavor-vector map, sea and land trade routes—Asia to the Mediterranean, China to Rome, across North Africa, across pre-Columbian Central America—radiate as superhighways. The ruts and wakes are deep, broad, ancient. Carbon dating of Phoenician clay bottles suggests the spice trade from Southeast Asia to Europe dates back 3,000 years. Evidence of the storage of fermented foods stretches back at least 9,000 years. Foods that could survive a journey over land or water did, aided by all the

tricks of pantry preservation, following the migration of peoples as well as the returning-home paths of plundering armies.

The origin story of any given flavor vector is not always clear. Similar treats popped up half a world away. Consider fish sauce—oceanic umami in a jar—a quintessential flavor-alchemy powerhouse used in many of our recipes. The Romans adored fermented fish sauce, as did the Greeks before them. In Latin it was called garum. It flowed into Rome and out to all points of the Empire. Containers were often branded. Competition raged. Roman fish sauce barrels have been found in Germany and England. A factory discovered in what is now Morocco could produce hundreds of thousands of gallons of the stuff per year.

Meanwhile, in Southeast Asia, probably in the area now called Vietnam, fish sauce also appeared, precisely when is unknown, possibly adapted from the ancient fermentation skills of the nearby Chinese, possibly locally invented, possibly hauled as garum from Rome. Wherever it began, Asian fish sauce streamed outward to become a staple of pantries all over Southeast Asia, and related products are used in Japan, Korea, and China today. Now, Asian fish sauce is profusely manufactured, while garum, though still made in small quantities in Italy, is more or less a historical footnote.

The energy of the great flavor vectors was uncontainable. Even as Japan closed to the outside world for centuries, for example, one trading arrangement remained, centered around a tiny island, with the Dutch. It was Dutch ships, likely, that took soy sauce to England in the 17th century and to New Amsterdam in the 18th. Similar ships hauled Indonesian treasures back to Europe from the islands the Dutch brutally colonized; today, Dutch companies still make very good Indonesian sambals, and the Indonesian rice table meal is probably the best meal to be had in the Netherlands.

As for American cooking—and here, again, we mean *all the cooking* that happens in the country—it's a long tale of flavors from the tasty margins

---

* Remembering, first, that the American pantry has deep roots in plants and foods of the Indigenous peoples, including iconic foods like maple syrup, blueberries, wild rice, pecans, sarsaparilla, cranberries, and on and on. Such foods fueled early explorers and colonizers, shared by Indigenous peoples and often stolen from them. Pemmican was the original American energy bar, and the word is Cree.

fighting their way into the blander, dominant middle. To see how this worked, consider the story of soy sauce. The soybean brew—fermented agricultural umami in a bottle—is millennia old and among the most popular of global pantry ingredients. In recent years, it has outsold both barbecue sauces and hot sauces in the United States. Its path from "exotic" curiosity to immigrant symbol of identity to ubiquitous seasoning in Main Street Chinese restaurants to, today, dipping sauce in $300-a-meal omakase sushi temples traces the pain and triumphs of several cultures—Chinese, Japanese, and, later, Korean—whose people helped build the country but were repeatedly barred entry by laws and discrimination, and sometimes criminally interred even when they were citizens.

In 1918, a Japanese immigrant named Shinzo Ohki started the Oriental Show-You Company of Detroit. Show-You was a play on the Japanese word for soy sauce, shoyu, but Ohki was clearly bent on capitalizing on the first breakout dish of Asian cuisine in White America: chop suey. We have an undated copy of a 24-page Oriental Show-You recipe booklet, an early example of what is now called content marketing (today, Ohki would surely be on Instagram). It begins with a recipe for "Japanese Chop-Suey (Sukiyaki)"—served on toast if you didn't have rice—and proceeds through various chop sueys to an egg foo yung, a chow mein, and other noodle dishes, and then sprinkles in Spanish rice, meatloaf, and baked beans. Was this appropriation, pandering, or canny outreach? No, it was cooking in the context of small-business survival. It has long been the strategy of pantry-product hawkers to avoid what one Tabasco strategist told us years ago was the horror of "high household penetration and low usage." Imagine the challenges Ohki faced in 1918. Sell the stuff to anyone who will have it, and hope it doesn't languish on the pantry shelf, that's the ticket.

What is believed to be the first English-language Chinese cookbook in the United States was published in 1911 in Detroit a few years before the Show-You Company began: *Chinese Cookery in the Home*

Kitchen, by Jessie Louise Nolton, published by the Chino-American Publishing Company. Nolton pointed readers to the local availability of exciting new foods for their pantries, including what she called Chinese Seasoning Sauce—"a rather salty sauce with a meaty flavor"—surely soy sauce. *Get thee to Chinatown*, was the message: "The special ingredients used in the preparation of the Chinese dishes can be procured from the Chinese merchants and as these merchants are found in almost every city of any size in America, it is not a difficult matter to make the necessary purchases before beginning to experiment with the recipes."

Still, *American cooking*—and this time we mean the food of the bland dominant middle, celebrated in the "women's magazines"—rarely involved this sort of flavor outreach. You can call up the 1918 edition of the landmark *Boston Cooking School Cook Book* online, search its 650-plus pages, and find scant mention of "Chinese" or "Japanese" or "soy sauce" or "chop suey." No mention of barbecue (already a huge deal in the South and the North, claimed by whites but mostly the product of hundreds of years of kitchen ingenuity by Black people), and very limited use of "Mexican." Curry powder and cayenne had crept into the pantry, and there are a couple of gumbos, but cooking was stolidly European—more likely jellied than spiced—and even then, not much Italian or Greek. (This is not to condescend to the cooks of the past, whose pies and roasts and preserves could be sublime, it's just to say that the Main Street pantry was not much awake to the wider ferment in American cooking culture, whether the Creole or Gullah excitement in the South or the Portuguese deliciousness in New England.)

Then came the rise of the factories, like a culinary Skynet from the future. By the 1950s, if one trusts the ads (which one doesn't, really), Americans wanted to

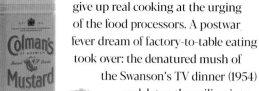

give up real cooking at the urging of the food processors. A postwar fever dream of factory-to-table eating took over: the denatured mush of the Swanson's TV dinner (1954) and, later, the sailing into port of that seafaring geezer, Cap'n Crunch, and his sugary brethren. *This*, it seemed, would be the efficient future of American cuisine. The Main Street pantry, if most recipes from the 1950s and early 1960s magazines and cookbooks are an indicator, was quite bare of the interesting foods that were bursting out of the pork stores of Little Italy or the shops of Chinatown.

Yet the global pantry would prove irresistible. The Second World War had tweaked the palates of the more adventurous returning soldiers. Asian flavors crept into tiki-bar restaurants such as Trader Vic's. As the '60s progressed, with global jet travel booming, American tourists invaded Europe, then Asia, India, and beyond. Waves of hippies made their stoned way from London to Kathmandu overland. They returned, palates enlightened. A new interest in natural foods arose at home, exploring fermentation and other ancient pantry-food practices. Most important, legal barriers fell and fantastic waves of immigrants came to the US, bringing their foods and foodways and opening shops and restaurants, food trucks and market stands. The great comingling of flavors could begin.

All this caused the American foodie revolution. It began, roughly, in the 1970s, although foreshadowed by Julia Child a decade earlier, and continues to accelerate and change the supermarkets and even the food processing industry today. There was a booming interest in so-called ethnic restaurants, an efflorescence of cookbooks and cooking shows, an explosion of farmers markets, and an astonishing rise of—by now—two generations of artisan-food makers. The revolution spread from the coasts to the middle. There was, too, the rise of chef culture (and then the recent reassessment of male-dominated, heroic chef culture), and a deeper sorting out of whose food traditions are actually responsible for all this bounty. Recently, on Instagram and TikTok, the revolution has been socialized.

All this, taken together, joyously, with the widest embrace, is what we mean by global pantry cooking. The way we think of it, each act of Global Pantryism keeps some thread of food culture alive and evolving—even as a great crisis, global warming, threatens agriculture around the world. The mantra of Global Pantryism is *learn, buy, cook, eat, repeat.* Blessed are the food makers. We love nothing more than to wander the aisles of H Mart, the farmers markets of Birmingham, the fine import stores of Brooklyn or Seattle, or the backroads of Vermont or New Mexico, where small farm-based artisans are tucked away: There's always something new, which usually turns out to be very old. To paraphrase Walt Whitman, American cooking is large. It contains multitudes. It only falls to each of us to stock the pantry well.

A Brief Note About How Our Recipes Work

First of all, they *do* work. We cross-tested each other's recipes to make sure the steps are clear, times are accurate, and flavors are as they're supposed to be. The importance of cross-testing was something we learned back in our magazine days. We would picture a cook in Akron or San Mateo putting their reputation on the line by cooking our version of chicken curry for family and friends. Their success at the table was something we took personally.

We know that even adventurous cooks will not have experience with every ingredient, method, and mash-up approach, so the recipe format is methodical, making its flavor "argument" in a headnote, providing shopping and cooking tips, then correlating the ingredients and steps in as logical a way as possible.

When the Yagisawa Shouten soy sauce factory was destroyed in the 2011 Japanese tsunami, the owners feared 200 years of family tradition had been lost. But a small amount of the "moromi"—the mold-injected rice mash that, like a sourdough starter, is used to perpetuate the fermentation indefinitely— was discovered unharmed. With crowdfunding, the factory was rebuilt.

Global Pantry Products Used in This Book

These are the globally made, and usually locally sold, short-cut flavor builders that you'll find in our recipes and that make so much difference in everyday cooking. This list—and the recipes for our own pantry favorites—is only a taste of the discoveries available. Every visit to good food shops yields new treasures. We like to support specialty stores in the community—Indian, Mexican, Arabic, French, Japanese, and on and on—where owners are often eager to advise about brands, flavor, and quality. When looking online, Amazon is the logical first choice, because it's a fantastic virtual global pantry in its own right, but specialty importers and makers, dedicated to national or regional foods or to ingredients such as spices, should be searched, too. The web is an aggregator of passionate specialists, and it's there that we found the best sumac and Tellicherry peppercorns, the best collection of Indonesian sambals, and of course the home page of Benton's country ham and bacon. Note that, in addition to the list here, you'll find additional products in this book under the Try This! heading.

Anchovies
Wee fish fillets cured in olive oil

Ocean umami, melt-away texture

Preserved fish are prized globally for their flavor-boost powers. Our recipes use anchovies that are filleted, cured, salted, and packed with olive oil. These are not the often more expensive—and fiddly—anchovies sold from large tins of salt. Sadly, anchovy populations are under enormous pressure because they are essential food for other fish and for birds. Very few fisheries rate as sustainable (and the "wild-caught" claim on labels is meaningless), though Argentina and Peru are working toward sustainability. Our solution is to use these fish judiciously, for maximum effect, and to buy from brands, such as King Oscar, that seem to be striving to improve.

Shopping Intel: The King Oscar brand is available in many supermarkets. Anchovy paste, in a tube, is an acceptable substitute in dishes in which you intend to entirely dissolve the fish.

Recipes: Slow tomato toasts, p. 41 • Chicken Marbella update, p. 134 • Spicy breadcrumb pasta, p. 224 • Pizza-ladière, p. 228

Other Uses: Finely chop and mash into good olive oil for a crudité dip, or make a simple vinaigrette for baked leeks or sautéed fennel. Drape on pizza and flatbreads.

Storage: Store tins in cool places. Once a tin is open, transfer the fish to a tight jar with their oil and store in the fridge, where they will keep for months.

Andouille Sausage
Louisiana's iconic sausage

Meaty, smoky, spicy

Andouille has French roots, of course, but the most famous andouille town in Louisiana, LaPlace, is in an area known as the German Coast, and Louisiana butchers of German descent see German DNA in their recipes. Where traditional French andouille is a coarse mixture of intestinal bits, Louisianan andouille is meatier. The heavily smoked sausage combines pork shoulder with pepper, chile, garlic, and sometimes a range of other herbs and spices. The result is spicy and dense, often with bits of fat visible, which lends smoky goodness to gumbos and such. Do *not* confuse with funky French andouille.

Shopping Intel: Of the national brands widely sold, Aidells is quite good. Venerable andouille makers like Jacob's in LaPlace (cajunsausage.com) will ship.

Recipes: Shrimp boil hush puppies, p. 46 • Smoked gouda grits, p. 131

Other Uses: Good andouille flavors any soup or stew it swims in, and marries well with beans, tomatoes, rice, chicken, and seafood, whether added in slices or diced with onions, garlic, and celery to get foundational flavors under way.

Storage: In fridge for a week unopened, in freezer for months.

Banyuls Vinegar
Long-aged French vinegar
Grapey, tart, ethereal

This vinegar is made from the grenache-based sweet wine of the same name in a southeast region of France, near Spain. Seek bottles with four, five, or even six years of barrel aging. Unlike industrial-production wine vinegars, Banyuls is deeply grapey though bone dry, with a haunting, persistent, piercing, sun-roasted fruity-nutty quality on the tongue and an aroma that you just have to experience.

Shopping Intel: Sold in some French or European specialty-food stores, but Amazon and other online sources are a good alternative. Pricey (up to $20 for a bottle), but powerfully worth every drop.

Recipes: Roasted cauliflower salad, p. 62 • Cherry-beet salad, p. 63 • Cantaloupe halloumi salad, p. 66 • All the Tomato Goodness, p. 70 • Pork and pineapple, p. 115 • Pork tenderloin, p. 118 • Leeks with pine nut sauce, p. 242 • Potato and leek salad, p. 254 • Custardy sweet potatoes, p. 255 • No-churn strawberry ice cream pie, p. 286

Other Uses: Pretty much any savory dish that will be elevated by a touch of acidic, nutty zing.

Storage: Months or longer in the pantry.

Benton's Bacon
Tennessee's old-timey bacon
Smoky, salty, piggy, powerful

Benton's is so smoky that a single slice can flavor a pot of sauce or soup or stew. We were privileged more than once to tour Allan Benton's modest cinderblock operation in the Tennessee Smoky Mountains, where rows of hams hang for nine months or more in dim rooms that have a sublime reek. This is, as Allan told us once, holler-born food of hillbilly heritage, based on family recipes for the long curing of pork in hot places.

Shopping Intel: We buy direct from bentonscountryham.com. Buy four or even eight packs (great gifts for foodie friends, or go halfsies with a neighbor) to bring the cost, including shipping, into reasonable territory.

Recipes: Hasseltots, p. 37 • Chicken soup with wontons, p. 85 • Tomato galette, p. 119 • Smoky bacon ketchup, p. 208 • Panko pain perdu, p. 234 • Potato and leek salad, p. 254

Other Uses: Although we deploy Benton's for its magnificent flavoring power in stews, soups, and tomato sauces, it's incredible when fried up for a bacon-and-eggs debauch. A half slice on a burger is great. Sprinkle bits into caramelized onions for an onion-feta pizza.

Storage: In the freezer for ages; an open pack will last for a week or longer in the fridge.

Black Walnuts
America's finest foraged nut
Earthy, tannic, crunchy

The eastern American black walnut tree drops nuts whose husks contain a black substance known to stain the mouths of squirrels who "scatter hoard" their treasures for winter dining. These are among the very best of all the nuts, with the familiar tannic edge and oily, tender crunch, plus an earthier flavor that you must taste. Black walnuts are rarely orchard-grown; they're hand-harvested by folks who have trees on their property or who forage in the woods. The Hammons company is at the center of keeping this sustainable industry alive.

Shopping Intel: Fairly easy to find in the nut section of good supermarkets. As with all nuts, larger quantities are far cheaper—buy online, toast (see page 26), and freeze.

Recipes: Baked Brie with honey, p. 36 • Multigrain pancakes, p. 185 • Chicken salad sandwiches, p. 199 • Coconut banana pudding, p. 279

Other Uses: Salads, banana breads, ice cream sundaes, muffins, cookies—any dish that would benefit from an earthy nut.

Storage: In an airtight container, with no light, they'll keep for a few weeks in the fridge, much longer in the freezer.

Calabrian Chiles
Italian heat in a jar
Fruity, bright, hot, supple

You'll taste a distinct, fruity flavor—as if a tomato and a serrano had a love child—and persistent though not devastating heat. Often sold chopped and jarred with olive oil (the sort used in this book), they don't have the raw quality of fresh chiles and don't need reconstituting like dried. They're supple and delicious out of the jar when thinly smeared on salami-and-cheese sandwiches, and maintain their bright flavor in, say, a tomato relish or simple oil-and-garlic pasta sauce. They have a Scoville heat rating somewhere in the zone of Tabasco sauce.

Shopping Intel: Look in the condiment section of better supermarkets and Whole Foods and in specialty food stores. Easily found online.

Recipes: Quick hummus, p. 33 • Brie with honey, p. 36 • Spicy breadcrumb pasta, p. 224

Other Uses: Try in any sauce, relish, or topping (for pizzas or focaccia) that benefits from heat. They play well with lemon, capers, anchovies, and the full range of Mediterranean flavors.

Storage: Unopened jars keep indefinitely in the pantry. Once open, they'll last for weeks in the fridge, but can eventually turn moldy; one option is to freeze half for later use.

Capers
Mediterranean sunshine flavor bombs
Earthy, "green," salty

Capers are the dried buds of the caper bush and taste like Mediterranean sunshine in a jar, if the sun were green and salty. They're the quintessential high-flavor pantry product, worth buying in big volume: super versatile, keeps for ages.

Capers are sorted in several sizes, but the wee "nonpareil" ones are the most common in the United States. They come packed in salt or vinegar, but we like the salted variety—more rustic, less pickly—which do need a rinsing and brief soaking to get the sodium-attack down.

Shopping Intel: In the pickle and condiment sections of most supermarkets, but pricey. Hunt for larger, cheaper quantities in specialty stores or online. We buy 28-ounce jars online for a third of the supermarket cost per ounce.

Recipes: Slow tomato toasts, p. 41 • Ravioli with very slow tomatoes, p. 214 • Spicy breadcrumb pasta, p. 224

Other Uses: Capers brighten almost any savory dish that has a Mediterranean flavor profile. We fry them in a bit of olive oil until crisp, for both the oil and the crunchy bits (see p. 41).

Storage: A jar of salted capers will keep for months on the shelf.

Chili Crisp
Chinese-style spoonable heat
Crunchy, roasty, spicy

The recent darling of American chile heads comes in many guises and from many places: China, of course, where Lao Gan Ma (Old Godmother brand) was launched in the late '90s, but also Japan and many small producers around the United States. Common to all is the primacy of crunch as much as fire. Dried things—chiles, sweet red peppers, onion, and garlic—are immersed in oil, along with, sometimes, sugar, sesame, black beans, soybeans, and more. Heat levels vary. (Nerdy spelling note: Although we typically spell the word "chile" with an -e when referring to hot peppers, Asian product names tend to use the -i spelling for the same.)

Shopping Intel: Many specialty stores carry chili crisp. Small fancy producers charge multiples of the $3 to $4 cost of Lao Gan Ma at Chinese or Asian food stores. Trader Joe's has its own inexpensive version, heavy on the onion. Lots of brands are available online.

Recipes: Chicken soup with wontons, p. 85 • Cabbage rolls with pork, p. 124 • Spicy chicken and waffles, p. 147 • Double-crispy eggplant, p. 175 • Mississippi potato logs, p. 256

Other Uses: Delicious spooned over grilled meat or shrimp. Lovely added to noodles as they stir-fry. Add to spicy marinades. Killer on fries or tater tots.

Storage: Keeps indefinitely in the fridge.

Chipotles in Adobo
Mexico's two-in-one pantry star
Hot, smoky-rich, tangy, saucy

Dried and smoked jalapeños are reconstituted in a mixture whose recipe has a Spanish origin, adobo. Mexican adobo usually contains onion, garlic, sugar, vinegar, paprika, and herbs such as bay leaves and oregano, plus salt and sugar. Think tangy, smoky, not-sweet barbecue sauce—quite hot—with a bonus clutch of supple whole smoky chiles in the mix.

Shopping Intel: Almost any Hispanic or Mexican section in a supermarket will have at least one variety. After tasting five brands, we loved La Morena for its smooth, smoky balanced adobo, not too hot, and its large, plump, succulent chipotles.

Recipes: Fast skillet chili, p. 91 • Birria-style sandwiches, p. 193 • Chipotle chili for hot dogs, p. 210

Other Uses: Puree for a ready-made thick sauce of considerable complexity and fire. Add to chilis, black beans, and barbecue sauces. Stir some of the adobo sauce into sour cream or Greek yogurt for a dip or taco topping. Chop and put in mashed Yukon gold or sweet potatoes.

Storage: In an unopened can, for years. After opening, a week or so in the fridge. Can chop or puree leftovers and freeze in ice cube trays for longer storage.

Coconut Milk and Cream
Plant-based curry and dessert essential
Creamy, rich, coconutty, mouth-filling

For richness, in savory and sweet dishes, nothing is as handy in the global pantry as a can of coconut milk. But shopper beware: Quality varies dramatically, both in taste and fat content. We've opened some cheaper cans and tossed the contents after tasting off flavors or additives or encountering a strange texture. Pay a bit more, and note the brands you prefer.

There are several reasons for this variability. It's surely true that production quality varies in the many countries involved in the booming coconut industry (just as there has been widespread fraud and adulteration in olive oil production for decades).

Manufacturing standards allow for plenty of leeway, in terms of fat and solids content. Most producers add stabilizers such as guar gum to smooth texture and reduce the separation of the fat and solids from the coconut water. Those stabilizers don't mean bad flavor, necessarily, but fewer additives are preferred, and if you find a brand that lists only coconut and water on the label, try it. Warming a can in hot water for a few minutes will make it easy to mix the solids by shaking.

Coconut milk is 10 percent fat, while the cream, used for richer dishes, has twice as much. (Make sure you don't accidentally buy cream of coconut, the sweet syrupy stuff used for piña coladas.) We tend to ignore less flavorful light coconut milk: You're paying for thickeners and water. Note that you can also find coconut milk powder in Asian stores and online: It's useful, in a pinch, when you run out of cans, in both savory and sweet recipes. There's also sweetened condensed coconut milk, a nondairy version of the milky version, that is powerfully coconutty. We use it in our no-churn ice cream with peaches and miso caramel, on p. 283.

Shopping Intel: Most supermarkets, as well as Whole Foods and Trader Joe's, carry both coconut milk and the richer coconut cream, and there are many house and organic brands. You'll find sweetened condensed coconut milk either near the evaporated milk or in the Asian foods section. In Asian food stores, you can find a huge selection, including tiny cans for smaller portions.

Recipes: Our wedge salad, p. 60 • Fish curry, p. 156 • Chile shrimp and coconut grits, p. 165 • Pan-seared scallops, p. 167 • Singapore-ish Succotash, p. 246 • Green beans in coconut gravy, p. 249 • Coconut banana pudding, p. 279 • Peach sundaes with coconut ice cream, p. 283

Other Uses: They are legion, in savory and curry-flavored sauces, stews, soups. Treat coconut milk and cream gently on the stove; they do not want to be boiled hard, lest the fat separate (unless making a dish like beef rendang).

And of course coconut milk is not a direct substitute for dairy cream, since it adds a boatload of coconut flavor. The one trick in cold dishes, such as ice creams, is making sure the coconut fat is thoroughly emulsified or blended; unlike heavy cream, it can resolve into fatty bits if you fail to gently warm and emulsify it before adding to other ingredients.

Storage: Stable for months or years in unopened cans. Once opened, store leftovers well sealed in the fridge and use within a week or two. We freeze leftovers, sealing 1-cup quantities in freezer bags.

Curry Leaves
Essential flavor of subcontinental cooking
Aromatic, herbal, peppery

Curry leaves add a unique, uncomparable "green" and faintly peppery foundational flavor during the crucial early stages of spice blending and tempering in many curries. They're also sometimes added later on, as a garnish. They are particularly popular in Southern Indian and Sri Lankan cuisine (and in Indian-influenced Southeast Asian cooking). They have nothing to do with curry powder.

Shopping Intel: Look in the fridge of any good Indian grocery store. They're delicate, so buy a day or so before use. (We have found dried versions pointless for our purposes.)

Recipes: Fish curry, p. 156 • Shakshuka with Indian flavors, p. 180 • Crispy-Crusty Roast Potatoes, p. 253

Other Uses: We toss curry leaves into the rice cooker with the rice and water, then fish them out before serving the rice, now gently infused with their leafy goodness. They add an intriguing note to a spicy chicken soup or fish stew. Delicious in tomato-based sauces and soups.

Storage: A few days in the fridge, longer in the freezer, where they will retain some of their flavor in a pinch.

Fish Sauce and Shrimp Paste
Ocean umami from fermented sea creatures
Savory, salty, fishy, strong

Fish sauce is made from small saltwater or freshwater fish that are salted and left to ferment in earthen vessels, wood barrels, or concrete tanks in the tropical heat for a year, sometimes two years or longer. The translucent amber-to-dark-maple-colored result, nuac mam in Vietnam and nam pla in Thailand, is one of the world's great umami engines (it's made and used in other East Asian countries, too, from Laos to the Philippines to Korea to China, where it goes by other names). The undeniable fishiness is a feature, not a bug, part of a vibrant and persistent salty-nutty-caramel sort of sea essence. Fish sauce is the basis of dipping and flavoring sauces you'll see at the table in Vietnamese and Thai restaurants, often mixed with garlic, chile, lime, and herbs. It's also widely used in salads, soups, marinated and grilled dishes, on and on. Think of it as the foundational sea-soul of these cuisines, used inland as well as on the coasts.

Quality varies and can be clearly tasted above the sea aromas. In recent years, Asian stores have made room for higher-end brands such as Red Boat, Megachef, and Son, which are worth seeking out. On some of the better sauces you'll see a rating, such as 30°N, indicating the nitrogen level, reflecting the amount of fish protein. Higher N counts generally mean more intense flavor and aroma: Red Boat's 40°N first-press sauce, for example, is notably more intense and concentrated than their second-press 31°N version. One interesting addition is sugar, reflecting regional tastes. It's found in Megachef's Thai sauce, which has a 30°N rating and is noticeably sweet, and in the very good Squid brand, also from Thailand; it's absent in Red Boat's sauces, which are from Vietnam.

Shrimp paste, meanwhile, called belacan in Malaysia, terasi in Indonesia, kapi in Thailand, and by other names in many countries in the region, is a dense solid made from fermented shrimp. It's a foundational ingredient in sambals and various dishes, fried with spices and garlic and onion into a fragrant flavor base to which chiles, seafood, or vegetables are added.

Shopping Intel: Because a bottle will last ages (recipes usually call for a teaspoon to a tablespoon), it's worth buying a top-rated brand—as much as $15. The popularity of Thai food has pushed fish sauce into the international aisles of better supermarkets, but of course you'll find a much wider variety—and lower prices—in a good Asian supermarket, including our favorite brands, named above, which may cost three or four times as much as a cheap sauce does. It's worth it.

Recipes: Shrimp cocktail, p. 45 • BBQ short ribs, p. 102 • Cabbage rolls with pork, p. 124 • Chewy rice cakes, p. 128 • Crabby fried rice, p. 161 • Chile shrimp and coconut grits, p. 165 • Indonesian-style fried noodles, p. 223 • Singapore-ish Succotash, p. 246 • Green beans in coconut gravy, p. 249

Other Uses: Because of its ocean-umami power, fish sauce is great lightly brushed onto grilled seafood and beef (see page 98), and of course in many Thai and Vietnamese dishes including green papaya and green mango salads. You wouldn't put it into a very subtle chowder, but it adds zing to, say, a cioppino-style seafood soup or a gumbo, especially if you don't have good fish stock for those dishes. Go easy, though— you can always add more.

Storage: Keeps indefinitely in the pantry after opening, but watch for finicky pop-up lids that stay popped up and lead to evaporation.

Furikake
Bits of sea and seeds for sprinkling
Savory, seedy, earthy, herbal, sweet

To address a national dietary calcium deficiency in Japan in the early 20th century, a pharmacist named Suekichi Yoshimaru created a nutritional supplement from ground-up dried fish bones (calcium— but also umami), crumbled seaweed, sesame seeds, and poppy seeds. The mixture was called Gohan no Tomo ("Friend of Rice"). It was a hit. Today, there are many blends, consisting of dried fish and chopped or crumbled nori (seaweed) mixed with things like toasted sesame seeds, chiles, dried egg, shiso, wasabi, yuzu, or umeboshi (salted pickled plums).

Shopping Intel: You'll find the widest variety of furikake options at Japanese grocery stores or large Asian supermarkets. We've seen it in the Asian foods sections of chain supermarkets, too, and at Trader Joe's.

Recipes: Sesame wokcorn, p. 53 • Our wedge salad, p. 60 • Avocado toast, p. 211

Other Uses: Sprinkle on anything that could use a crunchy-savory lift: eggs, noodles, stir-fried or roasted vegetables, hummus, French fries or tater tots, creamy soups, even a seafood pizza.

Storage: Tightly sealed, will last for months in the pantry.

Ghee
The other great cooking fat
Beefy, milky, rich, aromatic

Butter is heated, separating and lightly cooking the milk solids, yielding a flavor that many call "nutty" or "grassy" but the best ghee to us tastes profoundly of the cow, the way that pecorino cheese tastes of the sheep. With the solids removed, ghee tolerates higher heat than butter. Its flavor infuses curries and anything else it's used in. Some varieties are made from cultured cream and have a tangy aspect.

Shopping Intel: Several small-production American makers sell through health-food stores and Whole Foods, but good ghee is ubiquitous—and usually less expensive—in Indian supermarkets. It's also sold in Middle Eastern stores. Avoid so-called vegetable ghee, which is basically margarine.

Recipes: Hasseltots, p. 37 • Strip steak, p. 106 • Lamb kebabs, p. 107 • Creamy curry with paneer, p. 173 • Shakshuka with Indian flavors, p. 180 • Roasted squash, p. 251 • Crispy-Crusty Roast Potatoes, p. 253

Other Uses: Any time you're browning beef or other foods that would benefit from a beefy flavor, you can use ghee. It's lovely brushed on hot chapatis and other Indian breads and stirred into basmati rice.

Storage: Shelf-stable in the pantry after opening.

Gochujang
Essential Korean chile paste
Hot, roasted, complex, funky, sweet

Thick, glossy, and deep red, gochujang is a powerhouse of spicy, salty, fermented flavors, rounded out with a little sweetness. It's made from fermented soybeans, gochugaru (Korean ground red pepper), salt, and sticky rice. It's essential in Korean cooking, starring in Ann's beloved street food treat tteokbokki (chewy rice cakes in a spicy-sweet sauce) and landing on Korean barbecue tables as an integral part of ssamjang (the spicy, salty sauce served with the meat).

Shopping Intel: Look for the iconic red tubs, not the squeezable, thinner, vinegary gochujang-flavored sauces. Sold in Asian markets or Korean-focused stores like H Mart. One brand we like is Chung Jung One.

Recipes: Korean-spiced chicken wings, p. 42 • Beef bulgogi sloppy joes, p. 196 • Korean Fire Chicken Pizza, p. 231

Other Uses: Work into a marinade for meat (especially grilled pork), adding a little rice vinegar, honey, and miso. Mix with oil and toss with potatoes before roasting. Stir a spoonful into a meaty ragu or a marinara sauce for a kick of spice.

Storage: Once opened, gochujang keeps in the fridge, well sealed with a layer of plastic wrap under the lid, for ages.

Harissa
Seductive spice paste of the Maghreb
Complex, deep, hot, sweet

A beloved, fiery, fragrant, tinged-with-sweetness condiment/ingredient found on tables along the Mediterranean coast of North Africa, including Tunisia (which claims it as essential to its culinary heritage), Algeria, Morocco, and Libya, and beyond to Israel and other countries. It's typically made from roasted sweet peppers, hot chiles, garlic, spices, lemon or vinegar, and olive oil. Smoked paprika can be used, and saffron, and even rose petals. Heat ranges dramatically, from mild to hot.

Shopping Intel: Better supermarkets may offer a harissa or two in the condiment or pickles section, and fancy food stores go deeper. Middle Eastern food shops almost certainly carry several brands. Online, the selection is vast.

Recipes: Spice-Market Tomato Soup, p. 76 • Vegan tofu bowl, p. 170

Other Uses: We love to just dip crackers or breadsticks in the stuff, or crudités. Add to a burger or a pulled-pork or meatloaf sandwich. Stir into tomato sauces. Marries well with roasted vegetables. Gives hummus a little kick.

Storage: We store it in the fridge after opening for maximum freshness.

Kecap Manis
Glorious soy-sauce syrup of Indonesia
Syrupy, sweet, savory, intense

The sweet and dark flavor notes of many Indonesian dishes, including mie goreng (fried noodles) and sate babi (pork satay) come via this beloved soy sauce, which is thickened with gobs of palm sugar. Kecap manis pours like molasses and has a deeply savory quality.

Shopping Intel: Large Asian food stores often carry it, but be aware "sweet soy sauce" is made in other countries as well—you want the Indonesian stuff. In the last few years, the ABC brand has been joined on the US shelves by Bango and the harder-to-find, delicious Wayang. All are good, but ABC has the most additives on its ingredient label. Sold online.

Recipes: Homemade peanut sauce, p. 18 • Sticky rice cakes with tuna, p. 56 • BBQ short ribs, p. 102 • Pork satay, p. 112 • Hainan-style chicken and rice, p. 141 • Kecap Manis Onions, p. 210 • Indonesian-style fried noodles, p. 223

Other Uses: Mix with garlic and/or ginger and brush onto grilled ribs, beef, or wings. Add to a homemade BBQ sauce.

Storage: On a shaded pantry shelf, well sealed, it keeps for ages.

Kimchi
Korea's exalted national pickles
Thick, spicy, sour, crunchy

"Koreans cannot live without kimchi," Ann was told on a visit to Seoul, and it was *always* in her mother's Mississippi kitchen. Most familiar in the West is baechu kimchi, a sour-spicy-crunchy mass of fermented napa cabbage seasoned with Korean ground red pepper, garlic, scallions, and, often, shrimp or oysters. But there are hundreds of versions. Spice and sourness levels vary widely. This is a live food, sometimes fizzing with fermentation in its container. It dances on the tongue and lends its jazz to anything it touches.

Shopping Intel: Many small US companies are making kimchi, but quality varies. Weak versions taste more like sauerkraut. We find the best— the funkiest, sourest, spiciest, garlicky-est—in the refrigerated section of Asian markets, some of it made in-house.

Recipes: Smoky pimento kim cheese, p. 30 • Kimchi Coleslaw, p. 209

Other Uses: Chop some up and add to fried rice, vegetable- or grain-based fritters, quesadillas, grilled cheese sandwiches, or noodle dishes. Try as a topping for tacos, nachos, rice bowls, and instant ramen.

Storage: Keeps in the fridge for a couple of months, still fermenting and turning more sour.

Korean Toasted Sesame Oil

Powerful expression of nutty essence

Roasty-toasty, silky, tannic

One's first taste of the best Korean toasted sesame oil is a big revelation of flavor and texture. The best, most roasty-toasty Korean oils attack with rich "high notes" in the nose; a silky, supple feel in the mouth (with a light cut from tannins); and a clear, persistent nutty flavor unlike any other. It's a bedrock ingredient in Korean cooking, and also used in Chinese, Japanese, and other cuisines.

Shopping Intel: Avoid inexpensive industrial oils; good sesame oil will cost $10 or more for a small bottle or can. Look for dark-hued oil, extracted from carefully roasted seeds—not the clear, light un-toasted variety that sells for much less (the words roasted or toasted may not be on the label, though). The oil will be the color of light maple syrup. Brands we like include Chung Jung One Premium, Otoggi Premium Roasted (made in China—but many Korean oils are made with imported seed), and Beksul. H Mart and similar stores are good sources, or look online.

Recipes: Korean-spiced chicken wings, p. 42 • Sesame wokcorn, p. 53 • Spinach-grapefruit salad, p. 73 • Chicken soup with wontons, p. 85 • BBQ short ribs, p. 102 • Cabbage rolls with pork, p. 124 • Chewy rice cakes, p. 128 • Hainan-style chicken and rice, p. 141 • Stovetop-smoked salmon, p. 154 • Bulgogi sloppy joes, p. 196 • Kimchi Coleslaw, p. 209 • Cold sesame noodles, p. 218 • Korean Fire Chicken Pizza, p. 231

Other Uses: Add to stir-fries of all sorts, gingery vinaigrettes in the Japanese style, spicy dipping sauces for dumplings and noodles, and to ice creams or cookies that want a bit of extra nutty oomph.

Storage: Will keep for many weeks in a cool, dark place, even longer in the fridge.

Lemongrass

Stalks of citruslike power

Fragrant, lemony, herbal

Another superb pantry ingredient—actually, freezer ingredient, if you follow our method—adding brilliant flavor to Thai, Vietnamese, and many other Asian cuisines. It's not sour, more about citrus aromatics and oils, with a lovely quality all its own. Because lemongrass is so fibrous, our favorite approach is to make a pile of fragrant snow from frozen stalks, using a Microplane. When you need bigger chunks, a frozen stalk zapped in the microwave for 30 seconds will be easier to cut than the fresh version.

Shopping Intel: Often in the produce sections of good supermarkets, but bountiful in Asian food stores, where you can buy scads at a good price, then trim, wash, and freeze.

Recipes: Homemade peanut sauce, p. 18 • Pork satay, p. 112 • Chile shrimp and coconut grits, p. 165 • Green beans in coconut gravy, p. 249

Other Uses: Use our "snow" method and grate right into soups as they cook, or pound a length of stalk, put in soup or curry, then remove before serving. Infuse gin or vodka overnight with the snow, then strain out, for cocktails.

Storage: In the fridge for a week or more, in the freezer, well sealed, for months.

Makrut Lime Leaves

Potent, floral punch

Limey, jungly, very fragrant

The powerful, alluring citrus fragrance of makrut lime leaves will be familiar from Thai and other Southeast Asian dishes. Look for frozen leaves in Asian markets. Leftover leaves can infuse gin or vodka for cocktails (pound and add to the hooch, then fish out after a few days), and in spicy soups and curries. If you don't find leaves but are lucky to spot the limes in a produce section (we find them at Whole Foods about once a year), buy a dozen and freeze. The frozen peel, finely Microplane-grated directly into food, has similar aromatic qualities to the leaves, and the limes will keep frozen for months.

Shopping Intel: Sold refrigerated or frozen in Thai food stores and pan-Asian stores such as H Mart.

Recipes: Homemade peanut sauce, p. 18

Other Uses: Muddle into your next mojito, gin and tonic, or glass of iced tea. Cook whole in soups or sauces to add citrus essence, then fish out. Chop super-finely (almost to the consistency of ground pepper) and add to vinaigrettes, ice creams, cupcake batter, or even whipped cream.

Storage: Will keep for a few days in the fridge, for weeks or longer in the freezer.

Marmite
Britain's umami cult goop
Meaty, salty, yeasty

A sticky, salty, dark brown paste, by-product of the beer-brewing process that UK-born folk enjoy on toast and crumpets but that we use in cooking for its umami-amplifying power. Marmite shares some flavor qualities with the browned bits that form in the drippings of a roast or a pan of searing meats. It is therefore good in meaty things like stews and gravies. Having the consistency of road tar, Marmite needs to be dissolved in something hot—water or some of the developing gravy in a pan—before being added to a whole dish.

Shopping Intel: Marmite has found a toehold in some supermarkets, on the condiment, baking, or international foods shelves, but if you can't find it there, it's sold online.

Recipes: "Diner-style" French Onion Soup, p. 81 • One-pot pork chili, p. 93 • Veggie burger, p. 177 • Umami mayo, p. 179

Other Uses: Dissolve a spoonful in oniony gravies and beef stews and black bean soups for meaty oomph. Wow your kids by melting some into browned butter and tossing noodles in the mix.

Storage: On the shelf, probably forever.

Marsala
Fortified essence of sun-baked Sicilian grapes
Grapey, tangy, roasty, bitter

Marsala wine, little enjoyed in America and sometimes marketed in its cheapest, sweetest incarnations, is part of a category of fortified—i.e., alcohol-spiked—red wines which, in their best guises, are superb: deeply flavored from grapes grown on sun-roasted Mediterranean landscapes, aged in barrels for caramel-like citrusy-fruity richness. Marsala comes from Sicily. There are several quality designations, reflecting time in the barrel. We use two-year-aged Superiore.

Shopping Intel: Good wine stores usually carry a bottle or two on the same shelves that hold sherry, madeira, and port; just make sure it's Italian (there are American imitators), of Superiore designation, and dry (secco). It should be about $15 a bottle.

Recipes: "Diner-style" French Onion Soup, p. 81 • Beef stew, p. 95 • Tiny pasta cooked like risotto, p. 219 • Rigatoni with onion gravy, p. 225

Other Uses: Enriches gravies for beef, pork, or strong game. Similarly good in oniony or meaty sauces. Good over ice to reward the cook in the hot kitchen.

Storage: In a cool, dry place for weeks or months.

The Many Masalas
Subcontinental spice magic
Aromatic, pungent, herbal, spicy, essential

There was a time when Indian recipes for American kitchens called for such small amounts of generic curry powder as to be almost homeopathic. In the ancient cooking of the subcontinent, hundreds of vivid spice blends, or masalas, traditionally hand-ground, are used. Today you'll find a profusion of recipe- and region-specific masalas in Indian food stores. Our hybrid approach is often to buy a commercial masala and then do a little more work for a lot more flavor—adding, say, fresh curry leaves, or hand-ground cumin and coriander seeds, or cloves or asafetida, or toasted mustard seeds, depending on the curry. We find that masala powders are generally superior to jarred masala pastes, which can be quite acidic.

Shopping Intel: Look in Indian stores for masalas in small boxes that contain an ounce or two, from brands like MDH, Everest, Shan, Swad, and more. Finding masalas on the web is also easy.

Recipes: Chicken and rice, p. 143 • Fish curry, p. 156 • Creamy curry with paneer, p. 173 • Shakshuka with Indian spices, p. 180 • Kebab-dogs, p. 194 • Roasted squash, p. 251

Other Uses: Lovely on roasted vegetables (try roasting with ghee), in ginger and garlic marinades for grilled meats, and in deviled eggs.

Storage: These keep for weeks in well-sealed containers, but the flavors do fade with time.

Mexican Chorizo
Sausage for heat and depth
Meaty, earthy, tangy, aromatic

A soft, fresh, lightly cured sausage—not to be confused with the dried Spanish variety—usually made from ground pork and pork fat, though other meats may be used. We love the balance of roasty, medium heat—from toasted, dried chiles such as pasilla and ancho—with a distinct tang from vinegar and earthy notes from cumin, oregano, and other herbs, plus garlic. Usually sold as a loose mass that easily breaks into tasty small bits when fried and poked in the pan, the rendered fat a lovely vermilion from the peppers.

Shopping Intel: Most good supermarkets sell chorizo, but watch for very cheap tubes whose ingredient list features lips and glands and other discards. Meat counters and good butchers may also make house versions. If you visit a large Mexican or Latin American supermarket, you should hit pay dirt at the butcher counter.

Recipes: Fast skillet chili, p. 91 • Chicken with chorizo relish, p. 140 • Chorizo burgers with fixin's, p. 190 • "Pizza" in the style of a tlayuda, p. 239

Other Uses: Work into your favorite meatloaf or meatball mixture. Fry for tacos or papas con chorizo, in which the rendered fat and meat enlivens precooked potatoes and onions.

Storage: Keeps a day or two in the fridge; otherwise, freeze for weeks.

Mirin
Soulful cooking wine of Japan

Sweet, rich, syrupy, savory

A backbone Japanese ingredient, winey and sweet but with savory undertones. Like sake, it's brewed from rice and koji—a mold-rice culture that converts the starch into sugars. The good stuff has an almost sherry-like savor amid a flavor all its own. There are cheap imitations, but you'll love the deep nuance of the real stuff, usually with about 7 percent alcohol.

Shopping Intel: Japanese and Asian-food stores, of course, but mirin is increasingly available in the Asian or international aisles of supermarkets. Avoid a cheap product called Aji-Mirin, which means "tastes like Mirin," industrially produced, with glucose or corn syrup, versus the carefully brewed "hon" or genuine mirin—the ingredient label will tell you which you're buying. Amazon and online outlets also sell it.

Recipes: Quick ramen, p. 88 • Stovetop-Smoked Salmon, p. 154

Other Uses: Mirin is used in teriyaki sauce and works nicely in dipping sauces for tempura or other fried things, mixed with soy, ginger, and sometimes lime or yuzu. It will add body to a gravy or a stew and can be brushed on fish or seafood or chicken while they're grilling.

Storage: In the pantry until opened, then in the fridge, where it keeps for months.

Miso
Fermented Japanese soy paste

Salty, toasty, savory, intense

This thick soy-based paste is one of the most profound things in the global pantry. It's as complex as a beautifully aged Parmesan and comes in varieties that range from mild to robust, sweetish to very salty, pale beige through yellow to dark red or chocolate brown. There are said to be more than 1,000 varieties in Japan. Soybeans are steamed, fermented with koji (a mold grown on rice and other grains known as the "national fungus") and then aged, giving miso some of the same flavors as a proper soy sauce. The longer the aging, generally, the deeper the color and the flavor.

Eat a pea-size bit of saikyo sweet white miso, among the mildest misos, straight from the tub. It bursts with nutty-caramel umami, almost like that of an off-dry sherry or vintage Bual madeira. Eat a bit of dark organic brown rice miso and you'll taste roasted grains or coffee in its sharp, almost vinegary tang and pebbly texture. There are misos infused with dashi—the dried-fish and kelp essences used in Japanese soup stocks—for a shortcut route to making miso soup, and misos made from barley koji rather than rice koji. You'll see reduced-salt versions, too.

Shopping Intel: Natural-food stores often carry miso, as do, increasingly, good supermarkets. But Japanese stores and supermarkets like H Mart are likely to have the widest assortment, in the refrigerated section. There are plenty of misos made by small American companies, but we recommend a visit to a Japanese or Asian food store to buy a couple of tubs (or pouches)—perhaps a milder white (also known as shiro) or yellow, and a saltier, more intense red version. Also available online, but it ships as a refrigerated product.

Recipes: "Diner Style" French Onion Soup, p. 81 • Quick ramen, p. 88 • Hamburger steaks, p. 105 • Stovetop-Smoked Salmon, p. 154 • Shrimp scampi pasta, p. 227 • Peach sundaes with coconut ice cream, p. 283

Other Uses: Miso will become your go-to secret to inject umami into soups, stews, sauces, meatloaf and burgers, vinaigrettes, marinades, and as part of a glaze to brush onto grilling meats and veg. Try stirring with a wee bit of hot water until a thick slurry forms, then blend. You can also mash it in with a spatula. Delicate and complex, miso retains its flavor best when added later in the cooking cycle, and not boiled.

Storage: Properly airtight in the refrigerator, miso will keep for many weeks or longer. We find some of the tubs tend to lose their seal, so consider transferring to a jar with a tight lid.

Oyster Sauce
Asia's instant umami-booster

Velvety, sweetish, briny, savory

The flavors of oyster sauce are familiar to anyone who has eaten stir-fried vegetable and seafood dishes in Chinese-American restaurants. It's a glossy star in Cantonese and Hong Kong cooking. For many brands, expensive boiled-oyster stock is stretched with gums, preservatives, starches, coloring, and more. But hunt and ye shall find a few less-processed brands that add oceanic umami without the assertive sea power of fish sauce or shrimp paste.

Shopping Intel: There's usually an oyster sauce in chain supermarkets, but it may not be the best stuff. Try a large Asian food market. Labels should list oysters first; otherwise, claims of "premium" quality are dubious. Two favorite brands are Lee Kum Kee Premium Oyster Sauce and Megachef, from Thailand, which is clean, intense, and tangy.

Recipes: Chuck roast with root vegetables, p. 101 • Meatloaf, p. 104 • Cabbage rolls with pork, p. 124 • Chewy rice cakes, p. 128 • Turkey meatballs, p. 149 • Rigatoni with onion gravy, p. 225 • Roasted asparagus, p. 245

Other Uses: Add to meaty gravies, sauces, and glazes, and of course to stir-fry sauces and noodles. When meats are headed for the slow cooker, add a glug.

Storage: It will keep in the fridge for weeks after opening.

Palm Sugar
Intense, richly flavored
Deeply caramel, crumbly, tangy

Many Southeast Asian palm tree sugars are pale in color and mild in taste, but gula jawa, from Indonesia, is chocolate-dark and has an almost briny, profound caramel intensity that is simply remarkable. It's critical in many Indonesian dishes, both savory and sweet.

Shopping Intel: Look in a good Asian-food store like H Mart, where it will sit with many other types of sugar. It's sold in cylinders and blocks, variously called palm sugar, coconut sugar, gula jawa, gula merah, or even—in one case—"Island Ambrosial Nectar Palm Sugar." Key factors: It should be very dark brown and made in Indonesia. If you have no local store, Amazon sells several varieties.

Recipes: Homemade sambal, p. 21 • Green beans in coconut gravy, p. 249 • Almond butter and palm sugar cookies, p. 266

Other Uses: Stir small chunks into half-thawed vanilla ice cream and refreeze. Microplane onto oatmeal or grits, melt to make a powerful syrup, sprinkle into cookie dough, or use in place of brown sugar for a streusel.

Storage: Once opened, gula jawa will quickly turn from its moist, almost crumbly texture to sugary stone. To avoid that, triple wrap with plastic and store in a tight jar, where it will keep for ages. If it does harden, make a syrup on the stove with water.

Panko Breadcrumbs
Breadcrumbs, elevated
Crunchy, sturdy

Panko, the crunch factor in Japanese fried delicacies such as tonkatsu (pork cutlets) and ebi furai (fat prawns in a sublime coating), is made by shooting an electric current through bread dough as it bakes, then drying and shredding the result. The magic lies in the big, almost crystalline form of each crumb, far from the sawdusty stuff sold in cardboard canisters. Panko has mild bready flavor until fried or toasted, when it turns nutty. Its crunch persists on pretty much anything it's used to bread and fry.

Shopping Intel: Panko is sold in most supermarkets, on the international foods or breadcrumb shelves, but the coarser varieties we favor are more common in Asian food supermarkets or online. Most packages have little windows so you can check the crumbs.

Recipes: Meatloaf, p. 104 • Hamburger steaks, p. 105 • Super Croque!, p. 201 • The Ebi Filet-O, p. 203 • One-pot mac and cheese, p. 220 • Spicy breadcrumb pasta, p. 224 • Panko pain perdu, p. 234

Other Uses: Wherever breadcrumbs are indicated. Our toasted version (recipe here) is lovely on all manner of salads, and we've been known to sprinkle on soups and stews just before serving.

Storage: Panko will keep for ages in the pantry.

Toasty Garlic Breadcrumbs
ACTIVE TIME: 10 minutes
TOTAL TIME: 10 minutes
MAKES ABOUT 3 CUPS

Panko becomes a toasty, garlicky treat by browning in a dry pan, then further cooking with garlic, olive oil, and salt. These rich crumbs, star of Emmy's Big Bowl of Pasta with Breadcrumbs (page 224), will keep in a tight, opaque canister for several weeks in the pantry and in the freezer for months. Sprinkle liberally on salads, soups and stews, pastas, roasted veg, and gratins.

3 tablespoons extra-virgin olive oil

¾ teaspoon kosher salt

3 cloves garlic, grated on a Microplane

1 box (8 ounces) panko breadcrumbs (about 3 cups)

1 Have the olive oil, salt, and garlic portioned out beside your stove. Put a sheet pan on your counter and have an oven mitt handy. Heat a large cast-iron or other heavy skillet—the wider the better—over medium heat for 1 minute. Add the panko and salt to the pan. Use a silicone spatula to stir the panko as soon as you see hints of browning around the edges of the pan. The goal is to constantly turn over and migrate the crumbs until they are a uniform pale-brown color without burning—a process that takes about 4 minutes, depending on heat and pan.

2 When the crumbs are pale brown, make a crumb ring around the edge of the pan and pour the oil into the empty center, then add the garlic and immediately begin to mash the oil and garlic into the crumbs using the spatula, pushing everything around as you do. When everything is a nice and toasty nut brown and fragrant, about 1 minute, remove the crumbs to the sheet pan and spread out to cool.

Peanut Butter Powder

All the nut, less of the fat, no goo

Peanutty, toasty

Peanut butter powder, also called peanut powder and sometimes powdered peanut butter, has a flour-like consistency and intense, roasted-peanut flavor. It mixes well into dry and wet ingredients in cases where peanut butter can be stubborn and even seize up. But make sure to buy a version that contains no sugar or other additions—sometimes hard to find, but available online, and we like the PB Fit brand's version of the no-sugar powder.

Shopping Intel: Peanut butter powder has crept into supermarkets, sometimes sold alongside the regular peanut butter, honeys, and jams. As noted, it's in health food and food-supplement stores, and widely sold online.

Recipes: Homemade peanut sauce, at right • Oaty McOatface!, p. 187 • Cold sesame noodles, p. 218

Other Uses: When you want to import peanut flavor into ice creams, icings, muffins, smoothies, stews or soups, sauces, and even marinades without adding bulk or oil, this does the trick.

Storage: Because of its low-fat content, it will keep in the pantry or cupboard after opening, away from light, for at least 3 months (the manufacturer of PB Fit claims 4 to 6).

Our Best Shortcut to Homemade Peanut Sauce

ACTIVE TIME: 6 minutes
TOTAL TIME: 6 minutes
MAKES 1 CUP POWDER (8 servings)

This recipe is a joyful dance through the Southeast Asian section of the global pantry, and *so* worth making for satay (see page 112) or Gado-Gado (page 69) or as a dip for the big-crunch Indonesian shrimp chips called krupuk (see page 51). We avoid the usual peanut butter shortcut in favor of unsweetened peanut butter powder; it's less goopy to work with and produces a better final texture. Make a double batch and store the mixture in the freezer for weeks or even months—just add hot water, kecap manis, and soy sauce as specified below when you want to make some sauce.

1 piece (4 inches trimmed) lemongrass, fresh or frozen (see Note)

3 tablespoons palm sugar, finely crumbled, or dark brown sugar

2 teaspoons garlic powder

1 teaspoon onion powder

½ teaspoon kosher salt

2 makrut lime leaves or zest of 1 lime

1 small green or red chile (stemmed)

⅔ cup unsweetened peanut butter powder

2 tablespoons kecap manis

½ teaspoon tamari or soy sauce

1 Cut the lemongrass into ¼-inch rings. Combine the sugar, garlic powder, onion powder, salt, lime leaves, and chile in a small bowl. Put the mixture in a mini food processor with the lemongrass and process on high for 30 seconds or until you have an even powder. Transfer to a jar or ziplock freezer bag, stir in the peanut butter powder, and store in the freezer (it will keep for at least a month).

2 To make the peanut sauce, put ½ cup of powder mixture in a small bowl and add 2 tablespoons hot water, the kecap manis, and the soy sauce. Stir until thick like applesauce; add a little more water if necessary. Use immediately or cover with plastic wrap until ready to use. (Note that as it sits, it can seize up. Simply add a bit of hot water, drops at a time, to return to form just before serving.)

NOTE: If using frozen lemongrass, zap it for 30 seconds on High in the microwave to soften before cutting.

Peanut Oil

The best is a revelation

Super nutty, golden brown

Not the bland refined stuff, but expeller-pressed oil that has full-on peanut aroma, color, and flavors that persist in cooked food (don't use as a substitute for a neutral oil such as canola unless you want that peanut intensity). Peanut oil is popular in Indian, Southeast Asian, and Chinese cooking. Once you taste the best, you'll want a bottle in the pantry for any dish that benefits from its savory nuttiness. Pricier than the industrial stuff, but infinitely better.

Shopping Intel: In Asian and Indian food stores, look for bottles that specify the expeller method, and for oil that has a darker hue, such as Longevity Peanut brand from China. We loved oil from the Daana brand, produced by a group of organic farms in India worth supporting (you can find their oil online). Specialty oil producers in the United States, such as La Tourangelle, also deliver big peanut payoff.

Recipes: Pork satay, p. 112 • Hainan-style chicken and rice, p. 141 • Crabby fried rice, p. 161 • Singapore-ish Succotash, p. 246 • Green beans in coconut gravy, p. 249

Other Uses: We don't use it in many vinaigrettes; we do put it in quick-pickled side salads, such as one with cucumber, chiles, garlic, and lime juice. Add to marinades for grilled meats. A couple of teaspoons added to long-grain rice before cooking lends a lovely note.

Storage: As with any good oil, tuck into a cool, dark place in the pantry, or in the fridge, where it will keep for weeks or longer.

Piment d'Espelette
France's best pepper
Piquant, fruity, complex

Piment d'Espelette is in that class of chiles that combine modest heat with fruity-raisiny flavors. Aleppo chiles from Syria and Turkey are in that zone, as are Turkish marash chiles, though a bit hotter. Piment d'Espelette comes from the Basque region of southwest France—where it has its own official designation, like grapes do, and flavors the rustic cooking of that region.

Shopping Intel: Rare in supermarkets. A good spice shop should carry it, and there are plenty of Basque-sourced bottles online.

Recipes: Pork tenderloin, p. 118 • Chicken with chorizo relish, p. 140

Other Uses: The relatively modulated heat makes piment d'Espelette especially good for sprinkling on scrambled and deviled eggs, as well as in soups, grilled meats, even salads and fruit—anything where you want a bit of fruity-spicy lift. Useful in rubs for fish or poultry.

Storage: Keeps in a tightly sealed jar for months in the pantry or spice drawer.

Pine Nuts
Pricey nuggets, absolutely worth it
Seductive, sapid, nutty, mild

A premium, rich nut, with its own mouth-filling flavor. Pine nuts must be fished out of rugged cones at harvest, hence the high cost. Many are foraged; cultivated trees can take decades to yield. Pine nuts are essential to pesto, but we love them in nut-butter–style sauces and on baked treats, where their toothsome texture and lovely flavor stand out. Small amounts go far. We toast them (see guide on page 26), which deepens their flavor.

Shopping Intel: In tiny jars, prices are silly—up to $80 a pound! Look online (also, sometimes, Costco) for larger bags—about $30 per pound as we write this. Buy raw, then carefully—oh so carefully—toast according to Ann's method on page 26. Seal well and put in the freezer.

Recipes: Quick hummus, p. 33 • Roasted cauliflower salad, p. 62 • Lamb kebabs, p. 107 • Spicy breadcrumb pasta, p. 224 • Lamb flatbreads, p. 237 • Leeks with pine nut sauce, p. 242 • Pine nut ice cream, p. 284

Other Uses: A handful enhances any lightly dressed green salad beautifully. Sprinkle on oatmeal for a treat. Lovely with caramel sauce on an ice cream sundae.

Storage: In the freezer, for several weeks or months.

Preserved Lemon
Morocco's most glorious pickle
Supple, salty, lemony, deep

This is one of our favorite flavor boosters in the global pantry, and unequivocally worth making yourself (see the recipe on the next page). Preserved lemons are used in many North African and Middle Eastern cuisines but are absolutely central to Moroccan cooking. Both the peel and the flesh are gorgeous after the 1-month fermentation.

Shopping Intel: In a pinch, jarred versions can be found in fancy foods stores and of course in Middle Eastern and North African food shops. We've tried several and found they have a cooked-citrus quality that detracts from the pure lemony bliss of the homemade stuff.

Recipes: Quick hummus, p. 33 • Chicken Marbella update, p. 134 • Slow-roasted salmon, p. 152 • Chicken salad sandwiches, p. 199 • Potato and leek salad, p. 254 • No-churn lemon ice cream, p. 285

Other Uses: In cream cheese spreads, tahini-enriched vinaigrettes, spicy tomato soups and stews, on flatbreads with spices, with eggplant or stewed lamb, even in icings for lemon muffins. By the way, the syrupy brine is also delicious.

Storage: Sealed in jars before opening, for months in a cool, dark place. After opening, in the fridge for many weeks.

Brilliant Preserved Lemons

ACTIVE TIME: 20 minutes
TOTAL TIME: 30 days
MAKES 1 QUART

Few kitchen tasks produce more flavor power than this one. Lemons, fermented and preserved in their own juice and salt, are one of the indispensable simple gems of our pantry, adding citrus zing to stews, vinaigrettes, even ice cream. After 30 days in their salty-juicy bath, the peel turns luscious and supple. The flavor somehow seems even more lemony than fresh lemons. Look for lemons that are heavy for their size but squeezable, indicating lots of juice. Here, thick skins are fine, since you eat the whole fruit, but the lemons should still feel hefty for their size.

We studied a lot of recipes for this traditional Moroccan preserve, and settled on the simplest one of all, adapted here from a formula by the great San Francisco chef Mourad Lahlou.

Once opened, a jar will keep in the fridge for weeks or even months.

6 large, or 7 or 8 medium, plump lemons	1 cup freshly squeezed lemon juice (from about 5 lemons)
¾ cup kosher salt	

1 In a large pot of boiling water, boil a 1-quart jar, lid, and seal, completely submerged, for 10 minutes. Remove the jar with tongs and set it on the counter, leaving the lid and seal in the hot water.

2 Wash and dry the lemons, and cut lengthwise into quarters, but not all the way through—leave an inch or so at one end so that each lemon opens like a flower but holds together. (Don't bother seeding them now—you can do that when you use the lemons.) Stuff some of the salt more or less evenly into each lemon and stuff the lemons into the jar, pressing down to pack them in. The last lemons may be cut all the way through and separated into quarters to fit. Add any remaining salt, then pour the lemon juice into the jar so that it reaches the top. Close the lid tightly and place the jar on a shelf in a cool, dark place.

3 Flip the jar once a day every day for 10 days (one day on its lid, the next on its bottom). After that, leave the jar upright for 20 more days. Voilà, preserved lemons!

Reminder!
The jars really do need to be flipped once daily for 10 days to fully dissolve and mix the salt, so set a reminder on your watch, phone, or computer—it's unfailingly easy to forget if you don't. Or place the jars beside the sink in your bathroom!

Ras El Hanout
King of the North African spice blends
Aromatic, complex, floral, intense

There is no definitive formula for this enticing Moroccan spice blend, whose name refers to best-in-shop ingredients. It's also featured in Tunisian and Algerian cooking. It generally contains a heady blend of aromatics such as mace, ginger, allspice, cardamom, and cloves, along with regionally favored spices or herbs. It's not hot, in our experience, but it is floral and intense.

Shopping Intel: Versions can be found in most supermarkets, but look for jars or tins with lots of top-shelf ingredients—they'll usually cost more, but deliver far more bang. Two brands we like online are from Villa Jerada (villajerada.com), from Seattle, magically complex, and from TheSpiceHouse.com.

Recipes: Roasted cauliflower salad, p. 62 • Chicken salad sandwiches, p. 199 • Lamb flatbreads, p. 237

Other Uses: Lovely as a rub for lamb, chicken or other meat destined for skewering and grilling, or roasted with vegetables. It takes stews, flatbreads, and even pizzas in a North African direction. Blend it into meatloaf or meatballs for a similar flavor edge.

Storage: In airtight jars it will retain its power in spice drawers or pantry for months, but like all spices will eventually grow tired.

Roasted Hazelnut Oil
Essence of an excellent nut
Ethereal, toasty, silky, and supple

Proper nut and seed oils are a lovely class of fats, containing flavors as distinct as that of oil from olives. They have some of the tannic "cut" and bitterness of nuts and a softer, lighter mouthfeel than one gets from industrial corn or canola. "Proper" here means the nuts are carefully roasted to amplify flavor, then traditionally crushed—expressed is the term—to expel the oil.

Shopping Intel: A small French firm with a plant in California near western nut orchards dominates in the United States: La Tourangelle. Their various oils are very good. If you want to compare, there are a few other brands of small-batch hazelnut oil, including high-end LeBlanc from France and a few from natural-food companies.

Recipes: Cherry-beet salad, p. 63 • Hazelnutty Pasta Aglio e Olio, p. 217

Other Uses: The slightly bitter nuttiness of hazelnut oil dances well with flavorful and crunchy greens like frisée, escarole, chicory, radicchio, and endive in simple salads. This is a beautiful finishing oil, drizzled just at serving time over roasted vegetables, fish, or some pastas, or stirred, at the last moment, into sauces that need a nutty effect.

Storage: To avoid it going stale or rancid, store in the fridge after opening. It will keep there for many weeks.

The Many Sambals

Essential spice pastes of Southeast Asia

Variously rich, hot, sweet, salty, toasty, oceanic

Sambals are spicy condiments, often relish-thick, some cooked, some raw. They're often said to be Indonesian in origin (IndoFoodStore.com, an importer to the United States, says there are more than 300 sambals in Indonesia alone), but are essential to many meals in Malaysia, Singapore, and well beyond. There are sweet soy versions for satays, unripe mango ones for grilled seafood, tomato-enriched ones for fried chicken, green-chile sambals used in the marvelous Batak food of northern Sumatra, and on and on. They're used as foundational ingredients in dishes such as sambal-fried shrimp.

The ubiquitous sambal on US shelves is sambal oelek, made by Huy Fong Foods (the LA rooster-label company behind the Sriracha craze). Though hot and useful, it's rather generic and sharp, mostly chile and vinegar. We often add at least palm sugar to it in cooking, or use it to build a more complex sambal for the table by adding garlic, palm sugar, herbs, and spices. We suggest that serious heat-heads seek out a range of sambals. One gorgeous version is Javanese sambal badjak, often rich, sweet, and less hot than many other sambals.

Shopping Intel: Found in most supermarkets in the international section. Beyond that, a trip to H Mart or another Asian supermarket should be on the agenda. Online, Indofood.com is one source, and Amazon sells several sambals, including some good ones from Conimex, a Dutch company that feeds the Netherlandish enduring love of Indonesian food, an artifact of that country's long and brutal colonial occupation. Note that the many curry pastes for preparing Southeast Asian dishes, often sold in single-use packets in Asian supermarkets, are not the same as sambals.

Recipes: Shrimp cocktail, p. 45 • Gado-gado salad, p. 69 • Pork satay, p. 112 • Hainan-style chicken and rice, p. 141 • Spicy chicken and waffles, p. 147 • Chile shrimp and coconut grits, p. 165 • Cold sesame noodles, p. 218 • Indonesian-style fried noodles, p. 223 • Singapore-ish Succotash, p. 246

Other Uses: Depends on the sambal, of course, but many are an excellent condiment for any meal that tilts in a Southeast Asian direction. Add to barbecue sauces and marinades for meat, poultry, and seafood. Put a dollop on a vegan or vegetarian rice bowl with tempeh.

Storage: In the jar, for weeks or months after opening, though we usually keep our sambals in the fridge.

The Best Sambal Is Your Own Sambal

ACTIVE TIME: 25 minutes
TOTAL TIME: 25 minutes
MAKES ABOUT 2 CUPS

Javanese sambal was Scott's first lesson in the joys of culinary heat as a kid, and the first one that completely seduced him was a sambal tomat served beside a marvelous scrawny fried ayam kampung, or village chicken, outside the city of Solo. The sauce was hot but not too hot, sweet, thick, mysteriously rich (from fried shallot and shrimp paste, it turned out), and a perfect accompaniment to white rice, cucumber pickle, shrimp chips, and the world-class crispy bird, which was fried in coconut oil after being boiled in stock to make the tough creature tender.

½ pound Fresno chiles

1 cup Very Slow Tomatoes (page 25), or 1½ cups seeded and drained canned San Marzano tomatoes plus 1 tablespoon double-concentrated tomato paste

2 teaspoons palm sugar or dark brown sugar (4 teaspoons if you used canned tomatoes)

1 teaspoon kosher salt

4 large cloves garlic, coarsely chopped

4 large shallots (about 8 ounces), coarsely chopped

4 tablespoons peanut oil or a neutral oil like canola

1 teaspoon shrimp paste (see page 11)

1 Stem the chiles, cut in half lengthwise, and remove the pithy bit near the fat end. Remove most or all of the seeds, too, depending on the heat level you like. Coarsely chop the chiles.

2 Combine the chiles, tomatoes, sugar, salt, garlic, and shallots in a food processor; process until you have a mixture that resembles a sweet relish.

3 Turn on the stove vent fan and open the windows (you can also do this over a gas grill flame outside). Heat the oil in a nonstick or cast-iron skillet over medium heat for 2 minutes, then add the shrimp paste, breaking the paste with a wooden spoon until it dissolves and slightly colors (but does not burn), about 1 minute. Add the sambal mixture and fry, stirring frequently, until it bubbles and ripens in the pan (don't let it burn). It should not be watery. This will take about 7 minutes (canned tomatoes may take longer, up to 12 minutes). Remove from the heat to a storage container. When cool, put in the fridge where it will keep for at least 2 weeks.

Less Irritating

Vent the Fumes. If you've ever cooked with hot chiles, you know that the stovetop's heat will send up pungent fumes that can trigger a choking fit. This recipe uses a half-pound of chiles, so turning your vent on high is especially useful here.

Smoked Paprika
A world of complexity
Peppers, heat, smoke

Paprika is divided into eight grades in its world capital, Hungary, reflecting a discernment rivaling that of the other great chile-parsing country, Mexico. Hungarian paprika ranges from the sweet "special quality" stuff, tasting of dried, sweet, fruity peppers, through "pungent exquisite delicate" to "erös," a light brown gunpowder of highest heat. Smoking is more common in Spain, where paprika is called pimenton and is used in chorizo and paella and many other dishes, but not unknown in Hungary—and any grade of paprika may be smoked.

Shopping Intel: Most supermarkets carry a smoked paprika now, but the web carries far more, with specialists like The Spice House and The Spice Lab standing out for quality.

Recipes: Nacho-ish Wokcorn, p. 54 • Fast skillet chili, p. 91 • Pork tenderloin, p. 118 • Coca-Cola chicken, p. 137 • Veggie burger, p. 177

Other Uses: Adds smoky goodness to dishes containing tomato, sausage, potato, onion, rice, eggs, mussels, and on and on. A beautiful addition to grilling rubs, too. Add to ketchup for a nice burger boost.

Storage: Keep well sealed and in a dark, cool place. It stores for months.

Sorghum
The most interesting syrup in America
Tangy, bright, deep, savory, sweet

Sorghum syrup—from the cooked-down juice of a high-sugar-content grass that looks like sugarcane—is like barrel-strength whiskey compared with corn syrup's boring light beer character. It has a brighter tang and a deeper, more rounded and complex flavor than molasses. It was a dominant sweetener in the 19th century, and not just in the South; by 1860, Iowa alone was producing 3 million gallons. But it's a pain to make, and today there are probably fewer than a million gallons produced nationally, mostly by small, artisan producers, many in the South.

Shopping Intel: You may see it in better supermarkets and specialty food stores, but many several small producers sell online, directly or through big aggregators like Amazon and Walmart.

Recipes: Custardy sweet potatoes, p. 255 • Ultimate cornbread, p. 259 • Butter tarts, p. 277

Other Uses: Peerless topping for buttered biscuits or grits, also good on oatmeal, and a great substitute in molasses cookies or gingerbread. Adds rich notes to a homemade barbecue sauce.

Storage: In pantry, keeps for ages.

Soy Sauce
The greatest brew of all
Salty, malty, savory, rich, concentrated

The ancient origin of soy sauce is not perfectly understood, but the Chinese were making qu—the fermentation medium used in soy sauce, miso, and grain-based brews—in 300 BCE, and surely far earlier. Soy sauce was introduced to Korea around the 7th century and Japan in the 13th century. It became a global pantry candidate early: The Dutch brought soy sauce to New York in 1750, most likely from Japan.

Proper soy sauce (jiàngyóu in Chinese, shoyu in Japanese) is a slow concoction of soy, wheat, plus qu (in China) or koji (in Japan), though other grains may be used. The rise of fast industrial chemical fermentation dates back a century, but the pokier, natural fermentation process yields deeper, richer flavors, and most additives don't add anything for the eater. Look for labels that mention natural and traditional brewing methods, or, in Chinese products, "superior" or organic versions.

There are two main styles, light and dark. To our palates, the former often has, to use a musical analogy, more treble notes, while the darker has more bass—along with sweetness in some bottles from added sugar. But the designations can be confusing: There are marked differences between, say, a superior dark Chinese sauce from Pearl River Bridge (which has a delicious molasses-y attack on the nose and tongue, considerable viscosity, and an almost black color that lends its hue to "red" braised dishes) and a Japanese

Yamasan Koikuchi (dark) shoyu, which is coffee-colored, thin, intensely toasty, and has a lively winey-wheaty nose. Lighter Chinese sauces complement delicate vegetables and stir-fried seafood, while darker ones embolden rich braises and stews. Dark Japanese soy sauce is the dominant version used in Japan, including for dips and sushi—but is often comparable to a light-style Chinese soy sauce.

Beyond that, there are scads of variations: mostly wheat-free tamari from Japan (look for "gluten free" on the label if that's an issue, because some tamaris aren't quite free of gluten); low-sodium; mushroom-infused; and small-batch brews from Japan and China that have been aged a year, 500 days, and even 1,000 days.

Shopping Intel: We recommend sampling several soy sauces from Japan, China, and Korea—light and dark varieties—and settling on favorites. It's worth having several in your pantry. Our Chinese favorites include Pearl River Bridge (both their Superior Light and Superior Dark), common in Chinese and pan-Asian supermarkets. Pearl River's Premium Deluxe Light is delicious and very slightly sweet. From Japan, Yamasan is delicious, as well as Takesan Kishibori Shoyu, lovely and intense, which is aged for a year in cedar barrels; both will likely require an online order unless you have a very good Japanese food store nearby. In the tamari line, widely available San-J offers a gluten-free variety, also from Japan. Korea also has several small-batch producers. For small-production Japanese soy sauces and other specialty pantry products, thejapanesepantry.com is a good source.

Recipes: Homemade peanut sauce, p. 18 • Shrimp cocktail, p. 45 • Chicken soup with wontons, p. 85 • Quick ramen, p. 88 • Pork satay, p. 112 • Stovetop-smoked salmon, p. 154 • Crabby fried rice, p. 161 • Chile shrimp and coconut grits, p. 165 • Bulgogi sloppy joes, p. 196 • Cold sesame noodles, p. 218 • Indonesian-style fried noodles, p. 223

Other Uses: Soy sauce is an umami powerhouse in stews, sauces, soups, marinades, and dips; when using it, reduce or eliminate added salt as it packs a big sodium punch.

Storage: Soy sauce is shelf-stable for months after opening if kept in a cool, dark place, though we keep the more pricey, long-aged stuff in the fridge for better flavor protection.

Sriracha
Thailand's most famous hot sauce
Hot, sweet, vivid, garlicky

The American version of a Thai sauce of somewhat obscure origin is like a sambal riff on ketchup, and we suspect it's that smooth sweetness that made sriracha such a US craze in the 2010s, ubiquitous now in the familiar rooster-festooned, green-topped squeeze bottle designed by California's Huy Fong Foods. It's not a complex sauce, but nicely balances the heat with salt and vinegar as well as sugar, along with a hint of garlic.

Shopping Intel: We still favor the rooster brand, found in most supermarkets, although there are small-batch choices, usually more expensive. (Even Tabasco has gotten into the game.) If you find Sriraja Panich from Thailand, it's worth trying.

Recipes: BBQ short ribs, p. 102 • Meatloaf, p. 104 • Bulgogi sloppy joes, p. 196

Other Uses: A fine hot dog topping. Any spicy tomato-based glaze can benefit. A few drops mixed into melted butter make a tasty finish for grilled corn on the cob. Drizzle on a rice-and-veggie bowl, and on pan-fried tofu.

Storage: We keep it in the fridge after opening, where it will last for months.

Stone-Ground Grits
Southern staple from dried corn
Chewy, corny, creamy, comforting

The triumphant revival of Southern cooking brought true grits back to the American table—not the bleached, mushy instant stuff but the stone-ground grits that fueled Southern lives for centuries, dating indeed to the cooking of indigenous peoples. We like our grits (whether white, yellow, blue, or from other heirloom varieties) coarsely ground, full-flavored, and fairly chewy, a nice mix of bumpy bits and creamy integration.

Shopping Intel: Proper grits have crept into supermarkets, with mills like Anson being instrumental. You'll find them also in natural-food stores. To support the smaller mills, order bags and boxes online (just Google "stone-ground grits mills"). Amazon sells a few varieties.

Recipes: Smoked gouda grits, p. 131 • Chile shrimp and coconut grits, p. 165 • Ultimate cornbread, p. 259

Other Uses: Try grits the purists' way—cooked with water and salt and served in a bowl with a pat of butter. Also use them any way that you would use polenta or mashed potatoes: as a bed for a meaty ragù, pot roast, or saucy braise.

Storage: Store as you would any grain, in a cool, dry place, tightly sealed against mice and bugs.

Sumac
Crushed red berries of the Mediterranean
Lemony, astringent, earthy, herbal

Sumac has a tart flavor reminiscent of lemon—plus complex notes of a fruity chile (but no heat), some astringency, and a hint of earthy mustiness, in a good way. Use dates at least to the Roman Empire, where it was a popular provider of tang before the arrival of lemons. It's a key ingredient in za'atar blends. It lends a beautiful red color to dishes on which it's sprinkled. It's also rich in antioxidants.

Shopping Intel: Easy to find in Mediterranean, Turkish, and Middle Eastern markets, as well as gourmet food stores. Online, The Spice House ships free in low-weight flat packs.

Recipes: Quick hummus, p. 33 • Cantaloupe halloumi salad, p. 66

Other Uses: Reach for sumac when you want a lemony hit of flavor in dry form—for a spice rub for beef, lamb, or chicken; a tangy topper for focaccia, pita chips, or other bread. Delicious sprinkled on rice or roasted vegetables, or as a finishing touch to grain or veggie salads.

Storage: Keeps in the pantry for several months.

Tabasco Sauce

More than 150 years in, still the American hot-sauce gold standard

Hot, bright, vinegary, pungent

The elixir developed on a small salt dome island called Avery in Iberia Parish in Louisiana in the mid-19th century endures not only as an iconic American pantry product but as one of the best hot sauces. We like Tabasco's unabashed but not overwhelming heat, and its vinegar punch bound up with a pungent sourness that comes from long oak-cask fermentation. Tabasco is still made from descendants of the "founder peppers" used in 1868. A friend who wrote the authoritative history of Tabasco says it's "the oldest continuously running family business in US history."

Shopping Intel: Available in virtually every supermarket. There are many Tabasco variations now, but we like the original best.

Recipes: Shrimp boil hush puppies, p. 46 • Smoked chicken sandwich, p. 198

Other Uses: Tabasco's strong character shows its full effects as a finishing drizzle, added late in a recipe or stirred into a sauce. It can't be beat on a fried-fish sandwich or shrimp po' boy.

Storage: We store in the fridge to slow its tendency to continue fermenting.

Tahini

Pure spoonable sesame goodness in a Middle Eastern essential

Unctuous, bitter, rich, nutty, toasty

Tahini has the sensual, tongue-seizing, catch-in-the-throat quality of peanut butter, and brings creamy body to anything it's added to. It's a bit tannic and bitter, in a good way, rich, and "broader" in aroma and flavor than sesame oil. Proper tahini contains only seeds (often hulled for a paler look and milder flavor), but care with grinding and quality of seeds means that the best stuff is markedly more delightful. We first grasped this at a women-owned shop in New York called Seed + Mill, whose tahini is made from Ethiopian seeds. Israel is one source of much tahini in the United States; Lebanon is another.

Shopping Intel: In most supermarkets, but you'll find a broader selection at Middle Eastern or Israeli food stores. Online, there are scads of choices.

Recipes: Quick hummus, p. 33 • Quick ramen, p. 88 • Choco-tahini ice cream bars, p. 291

Other Uses: With a bit of oil, preserved lemon, herbs, and vinegar, it makes a rich vinaigrette. Adds nutty body to soups. Superb drizzled on ice cream. Thin with warm water if it gets too thick.

Storage: Shelf-stable in a cool pantry after opening for many weeks.

Tajín

Mexico's ubiquitous chile-lime sprinkle

Citric, salty, hot, toasty

Made of chile, lime, and salt, tajín was introduced in Mexico by a Jalisco company in 1985, then spread to the United States in 1993 and later globally. By 2019, the company was making more than 22 million pounds of the stuff annually. It answers the Mexican taste for jazzifying not only savory foods but also fruit and candies and other sweets such as paletas. Nothing artisanal here, but it sure is tasty and handy. It's rather mild, heat-wise, more distinctive for the bracing tang from powdered lime and citric acid. The company makes several varieties, but we stick to the first—now called Clásico.

Shopping Intel: More and more common in supermarkets (look in the Hispanic or international shelves) and of course in almost every Mexican food store.

Recipes: You-Fry-'Em Crackers, p. 49 • Savory corn pancakes, p. 182 • Mango meringue pie, p. 275

Other Uses: Tajín adds zing to pineapple, mango, even peaches, and to sorbets with a similar flavor profile. Also good on cucumbers, corn, avocado. We've doused it on a creamy slaw. We like it on the rim of a mezcal margarita. Try on popcorn, as a spice rub for chicken, or as a perky stir-in for taco meat.

Storage: Keeps for ages in the pantry.

Turmeric

Golden powder beloved in India, trendy in America

Sunny, earthy, elusive

Turmeric lends its subtle but persistent peppery-earthy flavor and spectacular golden-orange color to curries, and is found in many garam masala blends. It's a powerful antioxidant and has been used in traditional Indian Ayurvedic and East Asian medicine for about 4,000 years.

Shopping Intel: Turmeric powder is in any spice aisle, but cheaper in Indian stores. The fuller-flavored fresh root, resembling small orange fingers of ginger, is sometimes found in the produce section of large supermarkets but more reliably in Asian and Indian markets.

Recipes: Lamb kebabs, p. 107 • Fish curry, p. 156 • Fried catfish and chowchow, p. 159 • One-pot mac and cheese, p. 220 • Lemon bundt cake, p. 270

Other Uses: In coconut-milk soups, sauces, and curries. Stir a teaspoon of ground turmeric into the water for your next pot of rice or whole grains, or into oil for vegetables (especially cauliflower) you're going to roast with spices.

Storage: Store dried turmeric in a tightly closed jar for months. Keep fresh turmeric in a plastic produce bag in the fridge for a week or two, or freeze it for several months and grate frozen as we do with ginger.

Very Slow Tomatoes

ACTIVE TIME: 25 minutes
TOTAL TIME: 5½ to 6½ hours
MAKES 5 TO 6 PACKED CUPS

Meaty Roma tomatoes, used in many Italian sauces, are often pink and hard in the off-season, with the texture of packing peanuts. But five or six hours in a low oven concentrates their virtues amazingly, resulting in succulent, intense, tangy flavor bombs that we use in several recipes in this book and, chopped or blitzed, to brighten tomato sauces, soups and savory dips. We like to do a really big batch and then tuck 1-cup quantities away in the freezer in ziplock freezer bags.

Cooking spray

10 pounds Roma tomatoes

3 tablespoons extra-virgin olive oil

¾ teaspoon kosher salt

1 Preheat the oven to 250°F. If you have two racks, place both toward the middle of the oven. If you have three racks, keep them equidistant from each other and the top and bottom of the oven.

2 Line three rimmed sheet pans (or two sheet pans and two smaller pans, such as cake pans, that you can tuck beside the sheets in a two-rack oven) with aluminum foil and spray the foil with cooking spray.

3 Cut the stem tips off the tomatoes with a serrated knife, then cut each tomato in half lengthwise. Over the sink or a sheet pan, scoop the seeds and juice out of each half with your thumbs. This can be a squirty business.

4 If the tomatoes are large, cut the halves in half again, then divide sections equally on your pans. Pour 1 tablespoon olive oil over each batch, jostle the tomatoes so they're covered with oil, then turn them so they are all skin side down. Sprinkle each batch with ¼ teaspoon salt (just a bit—you don't want to oversalt) and put the pans in the oven.

5 Slow-roast until the tomatoes are slightly dry to the touch, a little shriveled, but still moist, 5 or more hours, checking once per hour. Shuffle and rotate the pans if the cooking is uneven, tossing or stirring the tomatoes with tongs. (The time can vary—even with rotating, we've had batches take anywhere from 5½ to 6½ hours in the same oven.)

6 Let the tomatoes cool, then portion for use or freezing. They'll keep in a ziplock bag in the fridge for a week or more, but the freezer is best for longer.

Shopping Intel

Select Uniform Fruit. Pick the reddest Roma-variety fruit of similar size and firmness from the bin, but don't bother with expensive hothouse tomatoes. Look for sales—we've seen them for less than $1 a pound—and then do a big weekend batch.

Worcestershire Sauce
Famous old English elixir, still yummy
Tangy, bright, aromatic, savory

Worcestershire was a sensation in 19th-century England. The Lea and Perrins recipe evokes England's colonial reach: Tamarind and cloves are prominent, along with other spices and the umami of anchovies. L&P became standard issue on steamship dining tables, where the chow no doubt became more ripe as the voyage lengthened. There are popular accounts of it on American westward-ho wagon trains. It's tangy, aromatic, and savory, a dance of sweet and sour. Worcestershire sauce is particularly beloved in Japan, where it forms the backbone of a thick sauce for tonkatsu—deep-fried pork cutlets.

Shopping Intel: Although there are supermarket house brands and small-batch artisanal versions, we've never tasted any as good as Lea and Perrins, available in any supermarket. Even better is the longer-aged UK version, available online. Japanese versions, such as Bulldog, are also good.

Recipes: Meatloaf, p. 104 • Coca-Cola chicken, p. 137 • Smoked chicken sandwich, p. 198

Other Uses: In marinades or sauces for beef, in tomato-based sauces (marinara, sloppy Joe mix), and in vinaigrettes.

Storage: Keep well sealed and in a dark, cool place. It stores for months.

Yuzu
Japan's most delicious citrus
Brilliant, fragrant, fragile, lemon-limey

Yuzu is a bumpy-skinned, sour East Asian citrus prized for its powerfully perfumed zest and distinctive but scant tart juice. If you see the fresh fruit, stash a bunch for months in the freezer for zest. Yuzu flavors several pantry products: yuzu kosho, a paste of salt and hot chiles; yuzu ponzu, a mirin-soy dipping sauce; and little bottles of "pure" salted yuzu juice that tastes cooked but still packs yuzu zing for sauces or drinks.

Shopping Intel: In pan-Asian and Japanese food supermarkets. Yuzu ponzu is also found on the international shelves of better supermarkets.

Recipes: Pan-seared scallops, p. 167 • Shrimp rolls, p. 202 • The Ebi Filet-O, p. 203

Other Uses: Yuzu ponzu adds zing to dipping sauces for gyoza and other dumplings (add garlic, ginger, chile, a bit of sugar), and the same mixture can be brushed on seafood or chicken as it grills. Yuzu kosho paste brings intense green-pepper flavor and tingling heat to sauces and even in Bloody Marys, and a dab is lovely with fish and rice.

Storage: Yuzu is fragile, so we store products in the fridge after opening.

Za'atar
The taste of Arabian mountain herbs
Wild, herbal, stemmy, earthy

Think of a walk in fragrant high arid mountains rather than through a bustling spice market. Think of those qualities in a dish. That's za'atar at work. The name refers to both a Middle Eastern herb *Origanum syriacum* and an herb mix made from it, often with added sesame, salt, and sumac. The plant is relatively rare, though, so some big-brand za'atar mixes don't even list it on their ingredient labels.

Shopping Intel: You'll find za'atar blends in good spice stores, some supermarkets, and online. We love a version made by Tyme Foods in Virgina. The mixture should look somewhat coarse and fluffy rather than powdery.

Recipes: Quick hummus, p. 33
• Tahini-Za'atar Wokcorn, p. 54
• Spice-market tomato soup, p. 76

Other Uses: In meat rubs or marinades, especially for lamb or chicken. Also in meatballs, burgers (especially lamb burgers), stews, soups, and sausage dishes in which the oregano-thyme flavor profile works. It's delicious on flatbreads. Try it in a stuffing along with sage.

Storage: Shelf-stable in a cool pantry for many months after opening.

A Brief Guide to Making the Toastiest Nuts

Proper toasting turns bland raw nuts into a luxurious pantry ingredient that we use to add deep flavor to salads and to sauces like the pine-nut mixture on roasted asparagus, page 245. They enhance any sundae, and produce a wonderful, nutty ice cream using the hack on page 284. The key to maximum flavor is slow, gentle cooking that gets the nuts toasted all the way to their cores, which also produces a delightful, snappy texture.

A Few Tips

· Toast up a large batch that you can freeze for later use.

· Use a heavy, sturdy sheet pan lined with parchment paper. See our recommendations on page 297.

· Roast all nuts at 300°F. Do not be tempted to roast at a higher temperature for a shorter amount of time; you run the risk of burning.

· Don't even think about *not* setting a timer. We've learned that lesson the hard way.

· Toast in a regular oven, not a toaster oven, and stir the nuts occasionally as they roast.

· Always check for doneness a few minutes early in case your oven runs hot. We tend to check several times during cooking.

· Once toasted, remove the nuts to a plate; if they stay on the pan, they might burn. Cool nuts to room temperature, and transfer to a ziplock freezer bag. Freeze for up to a year.

Roast All of These Nuts at 300°F for the Time Specified Below:

Almonds, whole
22 to 25 minutes

Almonds, sliced or slivered
7 to 9 minutes

Black walnuts, chopped
20 to 22 minutes

Cashews, whole
25 to 28 minutes

Hazelnuts, whole
24 to 26 minutes
(cool a few minutes and rub off skins)

Pecans, whole
22 to 25 minutes

Pine nuts, whole
15 to 18 minutes

Walnuts, whole
22 to 25 minutes

Anchovies • Yuzu • Black Walnuts • Wondra • Sumac • Calabrian Chiles • Sorghu
Millet • Tabasco Sauce • Coconut Milk • Roasted Hazelnut Oil • Curry Leaves • F
Sauce • Shrimp Paste • Worcestershire Sauce • Furikake • Sriracha • Saffron • Bany
Vinegar • Gochujang • Harissa • Marmite • Kecap Manis • Chili Crisp • Freeze-Dr
Strawberries • Tajín • Kimchi • Korean Toasted Sesame Oil • Dulce de Leche • S
Sauce • Lemongrass • Whole Wheat Pastry Flour • Pomegranate Molasses • Mexic
Chocolate • Smoked Paprika • Chipotles in Adobo • Shichimi Togarashi • Makrut Li
Leaves • Crema Mexicana • The Many Masalas • Capers • Mexican Chorizo • Miri
Oyster Sauce • Panko Breadcrumbs • Ras El Hanout • Andouille Sausage • Marsa
The Many Sambals • Benton's Bacon • Miso • Stone-Ground Grits • Tahini • Ghee • Pa
Sugar • Ají Amarillo Paste • Thai Curry Paste • Mustard Powder • Turmeric • Cultu
Butter • Kashmiri Mirch • Dried Porcini Mushrooms • Sweetened Condensed Mi
Anchovies • Yuzu • Black Walnuts • Wondra • Sumac • Calabrian Chiles • Sorghu
Millet • Tabasco Sauce • Coconut Milk • Roasted Hazelnut Oil • Curry Leaves • F
Sauce • Shrimp Paste • Worcestershire Sauce • Furikake • Sriracha • Saffron • Bany
Vinegar • Gochujang • Harissa • Marmite • Kecap Manis • Chili Crisp • Freeze-Dr
Strawberries • Tajín • Kimchi • Korean Toasted Sesame Oil • Dulce de Leche • S
Sauce • Lemongrass • Whole Wheat Pastry Flour • Pomegranate Molasses • Mexic
Chocolate • Smoked Paprika • Chipotles in Adobo • Shichimi Togarashi • Makrut Li
Leaves • Crema Mexicana • The Many Masalas • Capers • Mexican Chorizo • Miri
Oyster Sauce • Panko Breadcrumbs • Ras El Hanout • Andouille Sausage • Marsa
The Many Sambals • Benton's Bacon • Miso • Stone-Ground Grits • Tahini • Ghee • Pa
Sugar • Ají Amarillo Paste • Thai Curry Paste • Mustard Powder • Turmeric • Cultu
Butter • Kashmiri Mirch • Dried Porcini Mushrooms • Sweetened Condensed Mi
Anchovies • Yuzu • Black Walnuts • Wondra • Sumac • Calabrian Chiles • Sorghu
Millet • Tabasco Sauce • Coconut Milk • Roasted Hazelnut Oil • Curry Leaves • F
Sauce • Shrimp Paste • Worcestershire Sauce • Furikake • Sriracha • Saffron • Bany
Vinegar • Gochujang • Harissa • Marmite • Kecap Manis • Chili Crisp • Freeze-Dr
Strawberries • Tajín • Kimchi • Korean Toasted Sesame Oil • Dulce de Leche • S
Sauce • Lemongrass • Whole Wheat Pastry Flour • Pomegranate Molasses • Mexic
Chocolate • Smoked Paprika • Chipotles in Adobo • Shichimi Togarashi • Makrut Li
Leaves • Crema Mexicana • The Many Masalas • Capers • Mexican Chorizo • Miri
Oyster Sauce • Panko Breadcrumbs • Ras El Hanout • Andouille Sausage • Marsa
The Many Sambals • Benton's Bacon • Miso • Stone-Ground Grits • Tahini • Ghee • Pa
Sugar • Ají Amarillo Paste • Thai Curry Paste • Mustard Powder • Turmeric • Cultu
Butter • Kashmiri Mirch • Dried Porcini Mushrooms • Sweetened Condensed Mil

Wow-a-Crowd Snacks and Apps

Shortcut

Store-Bought Convenience.
You can shave off a few minutes
by using half of a jarred roasted
red pepper instead of starting
with a fresh one. Just be sure
to rinse it and pat it dry before
smoking it.

Avoid This Mistake

Do It Yourself. One crucial
detail: Be sure to buy a block
of cheese and shred it yourself
because preshredded cheese,
with additives, will never get
as creamy.

Ann's Smoky Pimento Kim Cheese

ACTIVE TIME: 15 minutes
TOTAL TIME: 30 minutes
SERVES 8

Every Southern cook Ann knows
has her or his own special way of
doing pimento cheese (God forbid
being caught serving a store-bought
version). Like the cook who created
it, this version is part Korean and part
Southern—blending funky chopped
kimchi into a cheesy mixture bound
with the king of all mayos, Duke's, and
given a deep whiff of stovetop smoke.
Yes, this cheesy blend has a few more
steps than regular pimento cheese,
but there's really nothing complicated.
People go nuts for it. Some swear it
contains meat, which it doesn't.

½ small red bell pepper

¼ cup apple or hickory wood chips
(no need to soak)

¼ medium yellow onion

8 ounces sharp Cheddar cheese
(in a block)

½ cup mayonnaise (preferably Duke's, or
our Umami Mayo on page 179)

¼ cup finely chopped drained kimchi

2 tablespoons chopped fresh chives or
scallion greens

½ teaspoon freshly ground black pepper

¼ teaspoon kosher salt (optional)

Crudités, crackers, pork rinds, or
Indonesian krupuk (shrimp crackers,
page 51), for serving

1 Preheat the broiler to high with a rack
in the top position. Line a sheet pan with
aluminum foil. Stem and seed the bell
pepper half and place it, skin side up, on the
sheet pan; flatten as much as possible with
your hand. Broil until blackened, 8 to 10
minutes. Remove from the oven and fold the
foil around the bell pepper to seal tightly; let
stand for 10 minutes. Unwrap the foil; peel
and discard the skin from the bell pepper.

2 Turn an 8-inch square or 11 × 7-inch
aluminum foil pan upside down over a
cutting board. (Photos of this technique
are on p. 155.) Pierce 6 to 10 holes on one
side of the pan, near the edge, using a knife.
Turn the pan right side up. Arrange the
dry wood chips over the holes in the pan.
Arrange the peeled bell pepper on the other
side of the pan. Cover the pan tightly with
foil. Turn on the overhead fan. Arrange the
pan over a gas or electric burner so that the
holes will come in contact with the heat.
Turn the burner on high; let burn until
smoke begins to seep out from the foil,
10 to 30 seconds. Reduce the heat to
medium-low, and smoke for 4 minutes.
Remove the pan from the heat, and carefully
uncover it. You can spritz the wood chips
with water to stop them from burning.
Remove the bell pepper pieces to a cutting
board and finely chop.

**Setting Up Your
Stovetop Smoker**
The smoker described in
Step 2 of this recipe is easy
to use; see the full set of
photos on page 155. The
smoker can be saved and
deployed for other recipes,
such as Stovetop Smoked
Salmon with Miso Sauce
(page 154) and Superfast
Smoked Chicken Sandwich
with Alabama White Sauce
(page 198).

3 Peel the onion and lay out some paper towels. Grate the onion onto the paper towels using the large holes on a box grater. (No need to squeeze the onion dry; the paper towels are there to absorb some of the pungent liquid.) Place the grated onion in a medium bowl. Shred the cheese on the large holes of a box grater and add to the bowl with the onion. Add the mayonnaise, kimchi, chives, black pepper, and the smoked bell pepper; stir well to combine. Taste for seasoning; add salt, if desired. Store in the refrigerator for up to 2 weeks.

4 Serve with your favorite crudités, crackers, pork rinds, or Indonesian krupuk.

After placing wood chips atop the small holes punched in the pan, seal the pan and set the holes over a burner. See more process photos on page 155.

The Creamiest Quick Hummus
with Four Toppings

ACTIVE TIME: 10 minutes (for the hummus; toppings vary)
TOTAL TIME: 10 minutes
MAKES 1½ CUPS

There are approximately 1 trillion varieties of hummus in supermarket coolers. Why make your own? Because store-bought versions usually skimp on the expensive ingredient that makes for a really creamy, seductive result: tahini. We don't. A full half cup of pure sesame-paste power ensures the swoopiest, dreamiest texture and richest, nuttiest flavor. We use canned chickpeas (aka garbanzo beans) for speed and deploy a blender for sublime smoothness. This simple hummus is divided among four bowls, with flavorful additions in the middle.

---

1 can (15 ounces) unsalted chickpeas

1½ teaspoons baking soda

½ cup tahini

3 tablespoons extra-virgin olive oil, plus extra for drizzling

¾ teaspoon kosher salt

1 clove garlic, minced

Toppings of your choice (optional; see Four Toppings and More Ideas on page 35)

Warm, soft pitas or naan and/or crudités, for serving

1 Pour the chickpeas and the liquid from the can into a small saucepan; stir in the baking soda. Bring to a simmer over medium heat, and cook, stirring occasionally, for 3 minutes. The mixture may foam over, so keep an eye on it. Drain well in a colander, working the skin bits out under streaming cold water; discard as many skin bits as you can collect.

2 Put the drained chickpeas, ¼ cup water, the tahini, olive oil, salt, and garlic in a blender and begin to blend on high speed. The mixture will likely cling up the sides and require you to push it down with a spatula. You may need to add more water as well, a bit at a time, up to another ¼ cup. The hummus will begin to emulsify and spin and integrate. Continue to blend until the mixture is very smooth and creamy.

3 To serve, use a silicone spatula or the back of a spoon to schmear the hummus around the edges and bottoms of 4 shallow bowls (about the size of shallow cereal or soup bowls). Place a healthy dollop of your toppings (if using) on each schmear. Drizzle a bit of olive oil in an artistic pattern. Serve with pita or naan and/or crudités. Untopped hummus will keep in an airtight container in the refrigerator for up to 5 days. Toppings can hold separately in the fridge for 1 to 2 days.

Global Pantry Ingredients

Calabrian Chiles, *p. 9*
Pine Nuts, *p. 19*
Preserved Lemon, *p. 19*
Sumac, *p. 23*
Tahini, *p. 24*
Very Slow Tomatoes, *p. 25*
Za'atar, *p. 26*

Texture Tips

Chickpea Hack. Homemade hummus usually starts with dried chickpeas, but rehydrating them is time-consuming. Canned chickpeas are fast but often have slightly fibrous skins. We use a little baking soda (also used in the dried-chickpea process) to soften or dissolve the skins.

Oil, Even Water, Works. You want the final texture to be seductively smooth rather than grainy. If the hummus gets over-thick while blending, add olive oil or even water (seriously, it emulsifies like oil!) until the hummus has the texture almost of buttercream. Be sure to use a blender; a food processor will not get you as smoothly to your destination.

Four Toppings and More Ideas

The range of flavors that jazz up hummus is vast—salty, savory, nutty, acidic, herby, spicy, garlicky. At Alon Shaya's Israeli restaurant, Safta, in Denver, for example, we have swooned over spicy lamb ragù, curried cauliflower and onions, mushrooms with spiced butter, and lots more. A few of our suggestions follow, but think of this hummus as your canvas—explore your pantry and fridge for treats with which to paint it using contrasts in acid, texture, sweetness and salt.

We like to serve hummus with pita bread, of course, but also with our za'atar-enriched naan soldiers (see recipe, page 76). Or you can take a platter in a veggie direction with carrots, celery, blanched sugar snap peas, multicolored cauliflower florets, endive leaves, or halved baby zucchini.

Za'atar and Your Best Olive Oil

Smooth hummus with the back of a spoon, then drizzle with oil and sprinkle on the za'atar. Or try it with flaked salt and smoked paprika.

Pine Nuts and Very Slow Tomatoes

Chop up a tablespoon or two of our Very Slow Tomatoes (page 25), add some smoked paprika if you like, place at the center of the hummus, and top with a generous tablespoon of toasted pine nuts (see page 26). If you don't have the tomatoes, a tomato jam or chopped sun-dried tomatoes in oil will work.

Castelvetrano Olives and Preserved Lemon

Chop a tablespoon of Preserved Lemon (page 19) and 8 or so pitted Castelvetrano olives (kalamatas will also work, or any other delicious olive) into a fine mixture and place at the center of the bowl.

Calabrian Chiles, Scallions, Sumac, and Feta

Finely chop the green and white parts of a scallion and mix that, plus 1 teaspoon of chopped Calabrian chiles (page 9) in oil and ½ teaspoon ground sumac, into a tablespoon or two of crumbled feta. Place the mix at the center of the hummus.

Sumac brings lemony lift in sprinkle form.

Global Pantry Ingredients

Black Walnuts, *p. 9*
Calabrian Chiles, *p. 9*

Prep Tip

Not Too Much Off the Top. We cut some of the edible, bloomy top off the Brie wheel for easier scooping. Be careful, though, to leave at least a half-inch rim of rind so the wheel retains some structure and doesn't slump to a puddle in the oven. And be sure the cheese is sufficiently chilled—it's easier to remove the rind from a cold wheel.

Shopping Intel

Buy a Bargain Brie. Since you're baking and topping this cheese with bold flavors, use an inexpensive grocery store option.

Throwback Baked Brie
with Spicy Honey Upgrade

ACTIVE TIME: 6 minutes
TOTAL TIME: 21 minutes
SERVES 6

For the life of us, we can't figure out why baked Brie fell out of style. Uncool among purists, sure, but it's gooey, mild, rich, creamy, and always the hit of the party. We update it here with a Calabrian chile–infused topping that gives a gentle kick to the honeyed sweetness, and the unique earthy crunch of the black walnuts is the final touch.

---

1 round (8 ounces) Brie cheese, chilled

¼ cup honey

¼ cup chopped dried tart cherries

2 teaspoons chopped Calabrian chiles

1 teaspoon fresh thyme leaves

¼ teaspoon kosher salt

¼ cup chopped toasted black walnuts

Crackers and apple slices, for serving

1 Preheat the oven to 350°F with a rack positioned in the center.

2 Working with the cold cheese, cut out a circle from the top rind, leaving a ½-inch border; peel off and discard the circle from the middle of the rind. Place the cheese in a round gratin dish or on an ovenproof plate. Bake until gooey, about 15 minutes.

3 Meanwhile, combine the honey, cherries, chiles, thyme, and salt in a small saucepan. Cook over medium-low heat until warmed, stirring occasionally, 2 to 3 minutes. Remove the pan from the heat and stir in the walnuts.

4 Spoon the honey mixture over the baked cheese in the dish. Serve warm with crackers and apple slices.

Ghee-Basted Hasseltots
with Various Delightful Toppings

ACTIVE TIME: 19 minutes
TOTAL TIME: 1 hour 10 minutes
SERVES 8

Hasselback potatoes stormed the internet many years ago, with their accordioned, crispy thin edges and fluffy baked-potato interiors. We like them as adorable appetizers made with baby or small potatoes, which we call hasseltots or hasselteens, depending on size. Ghee elevates things with its lovely beefy musk, even though it's vegetarian. The warm potatoes are then topped in luxurious fashion with crème fraîche and caviar, or with humbler flavor bursts from yogurt and chutney—several ideas follow on page 38. These are best served warm, but they're still damn good at room temperature.

24 Honey Gold or baby Dutch yellow potatoes (about 1¼ pounds), or 16 small golden potatoes (1¼ pounds)

3 tablespoons ghee, melted (butter or extra-virgin olive oil works if you don't have ghee)

½ teaspoon kosher salt

Toppings of your choice (see page 38)

1 Preheat the oven to 425°F with a rack in the center. Line a sheet pan with aluminum foil or parchment paper.

2 Place 1 potato on a cutting board; arrange a chopstick or butter knife on either side of the potato. Starting at one end, carefully slice through the potato at ⅒- to ⅛-inch intervals, cutting most of the way through (see Prep Pointer). Repeat the process with the remaining potatoes.

3 Arrange the potatoes on the prepared baking sheet. Brush 1 tablespoon ghee over the potatoes; bake for 20 minutes. Brush another 1 tablespoon ghee over the potatoes, and sprinkle with ¼ teaspoon salt; continue to bake until some of the slices begin to fan open, 10 minutes. Brush the remaining 1 tablespoon ghee over the potatoes, and sprinkle with the remaining ¼ teaspoon salt; bake until tender when pierced with a knife, about 10 minutes (40 minutes total bake time).

4 Remove the pan from the oven. Cool the potatoes slightly, 5 minutes. Top the potatoes with one of the toppings that follow, or a combination.

Global Pantry Ingredients

Benton's Bacon, *p. 9*
Ghee, *p. 12*
Smoked Paprika, *p. 22*

Prep Pointer
Give Yourself Guard Rails. Hasselback slicing is another of those careful but simple jobs best done at a meditative pace. It's easy to accidentally cut all the way through the wee potatoes, so we arrange a chopstick at the base of the potato on either side, like railway ties, which stop the knife blade from cutting to the cutting-board surface. You still need to be careful at the ends, but in the middle of the tuber the rails keep things on track.

Shopping Intel
Sustainable Caviar. Wild sturgeon populations have been devastated globally, so only buy farmed sturgeon eggs from certified producers such as Tsar Nicoulai, a US-based company. Great Lakes wild whitefish roe harvest is also monitored, and we like those small, yellow, inexpensive pearls on our tots.

The Toppings

Crème Fraîche and Caviar

¼ cup crème fraîche

2 teaspoons thinly sliced chives

1 jar (2 ounces) sustainably sourced American sturgeon or golden whitefish caviar

Add to each potato, in this order: ½ teaspoon crème fraîche, a few chive pieces, and a scant ¼ teaspoon caviar.

Smoky Ketchup and Scallions

¼ cup ketchup

½ teaspoon smoked paprika

2 scallions, finely chopped

Thoroughly mix the ketchup and paprika in a small bowl and dab ½ teaspoon on each potato; top liberally with the scallions.

Sour Cream and Bacon

2 pieces of Benton's bacon or other smoky, thick bacon

¼ cup sour cream

1 Cut the bacon into 24 triangular pieces. Place on a microwave-safe plate, cover with paper towels, and microwave on High until crisp, 2 to 3 minutes. Put triangles on paper towels to drain.

2 Dab ½ teaspoon sour cream on each potato and top each with 1 bacon shard.

Yogurt and Spicy Chutney

¼ cup plain Greek yogurt

¼ cup hot mango chutney or other sweet chutney, such as Patak's

Dab each potato with ½ teaspoon yogurt and top each with ½ teaspoon chutney.

Smoked paprika adds heat and woodfire aroma to the tater ketchup.

Very Slow Tomato Toasts
with Fried Capers and Anchovies

ACTIVE TIME: 20 minutes
TOTAL TIME: 30 minutes (with a 10-minute cool-off of the bread)
SERVES 5 AS AN APPETIZER—OR 3-ISH FOR LUNCH

We love the classic bread-and-tomato combination, epitomized by the fresh, simple pan con tomate found in the best tapas and pintxos restaurants in Barcelona and San Sebastián. But a peak summer tomato crop is a must for that. This version deploys our Very Slow Tomatoes for year-round pan con tomate–ish pleasure. The bright flavor is more concentrated and sweet, but there's a salty counterpoint from the anchovies and the crunchy, wild-mountain-plant-tasting fried capers.

---

1 cup lightly packed Very Slow Tomatoes (page 25)

1 large clove garlic, pressed or grated

1 cup extra-virgin olive oil

¼ cup salt-cured capers (½ cup if you want to make the ravioli [page 214] the next day), rinsed well, drained, and patted dry with paper towels

1 long baguette or ciabatta loaf

3 anchovies in oil, halved lengthwise (double the quantity for anchovy lovers)

1 Place the tomatoes and garlic on a cutting board and chop with a sharp knife, drawing the mixture into a pile repeatedly and chopping until you have a coarse, integrated mixture. Drizzle with 1 tablespoon oil and toss to combine.

2 Arrange the oven rack 6 inches below the broiler. Preheat the broiler to low.

3 Pour some of the oil into your smallest saucepan to a depth of ⅓ to ½ inch. Turn the burner to medium and, using a thermometer, heat the oil to 350°F. Carefully add the capers to the oil. Fry until browned but not blackened, 2½ to 3 minutes, then use a slotted spoon to remove the capers to a paper towel. They will be feathery-crispy in texture.

4 Cut the baguette or ciabatta in half lengthwise so you have 2 long halves, then cut each half into 5 equal pieces, yielding 10. Arrange the bread pieces on a sheet pan and brush each piece to its edges liberally with the remaining olive oil. Place the bread under the broiler and broil, watching like a hawk. The goal is not completely toasted bread that will be dry and crunchy but rather bread that is a bit charred about the edges and brown on top but still chewy within. After 1½ minutes, you may need to rotate the pan if the bread is cooking unevenly. In our testing, the total cook time was about 2 minutes 15 seconds, but this will vary.

5 Remove the bread from the oven, let it cool for 5 to 10 minutes, then spread the tomato mixture across each slice. On 5 pieces, sprinkle about 10 capers each; on the other 5, place an anchovy slice diagonally (or 2 in an X for anchovy lovers).

Global Pantry Ingredients

Anchovies, *p. 8*
Capers, *p.10*
Very Slow Tomatoes, *p. 25*

Shopping Intel
Supermarket Bread Is Fine. You don't need a seven-dollar artisanal loaf here. A dense-ish ciabatta or baguette of the sort baked in some supermarkets works just fine—a chewy bread with a bit of heft.

Kitchen Efficiency
Save That Oil! The oil used to fry the capers takes on a subtle caper-y flavor. Save in the fridge and make our Ravioli with Very Slow Tomatoes, Crispy Capers, and Caper Oil (page 214, double the caper quantity used here to have some for the pasta), or use the oil in a vinaigrette.

Texture Tip
Keep the Crunch. If the capers are fried long enough—until thoroughly crunchy but not burnt—they maintain their texture for a long time (we like to use them the next day in salad or on a vegetable such as steamed asparagus). But if they soften up, put them in a small bowl and zap them for a minute in the microwave on High.

Kitchen Science

Baking Powder Trick Made Even Simpler. Adding baking powder to improve oven crisping was a technique that swept the interwebs after J. Kenji López-Alt detailed the pH and peptide-bond effects that, as a bona fide scientist, he said were involved. We tried it and were converted. That was years ago. Here, we reduce the cleanup mess by eliminating the usual wire roasting rack, letting the wings crisp in their own fat on parchment paper.

Shopping Intel

Best Chicken to Buy. Cheap chicken wings are processed with water and additives, bloating them. For max crispness, pay a bit more for air-chilled chicken (often promoted as all-natural, but check the label to verify there's no added water). A drier bird bakes better. We usually buy ours at Whole Foods, either the store brand or the Bell and Evans brand.

A Heap of Honey-Glazed, Gochujang-Spiced
Baked Chicken Wings

ACTIVE TIME: 10 minutes
TOTAL TIME: 55 minutes
SERVES 8

There's optimal crunch in these glossy-shiny-sticky wings, despite being baked, and a deep, spicy kick from gochujang, the essential Korean sweet-and-rich chili paste that's one of our global pantry staples. Here we give you a range for gochujang and honey quantities, but don't change the ratio. As an appetizer, these wings will serve a small crowd. As a main, count on them serving no more than four people.

2½ pounds air-chilled chicken wings, separated into drumettes and flats (about 28 pieces)

1½ teaspoons kosher salt

1½ teaspoons baking powder

1 teaspoon ground ginger

3 to 4 tablespoons gochujang

3 to 4 tablespoons honey

1 tablespoon Korean toasted sesame oil

1 tablespoon rice vinegar

2 tablespoons thinly sliced scallion greens, for topping

1 teaspoon toasted sesame seeds, for topping

1 Preheat the oven to 450°F with a rack in the center. Line a large sheet pan with parchment paper.

2 Pat the wings as dry as you can get them with paper towels and place in a large bowl. Combine the salt, baking powder, and ground ginger in a small bowl; sprinkle over the wings and toss well to coat. Arrange the wings on the prepared pan, fattier side down. Bake until just barely starting to brown, 25 minutes. (Wash out the bowl at this point; you'll need it later.)

3 Remove the pan from the oven and turn the wings over. Bake until browned and crisp, 22 to 25 more minutes.

4 Meanwhile, combine the gochujang, honey, oil, and vinegar in a small saucepan. Bring to a boil over medium heat; cook until slightly syrupy, 3 to 5 minutes. If it gets too thick, add a bit of water. When the wings are done, place them in the large bowl. Drizzle the sauce over the wings and toss well to coat; serve hot or at room temperature. Sprinkle with the scallions and sesame seeds before serving.

Pan-Seared Shrimp Cocktail

with Kicky Sambal-Citrus Sauce

ACTIVE TIME: 17 minutes
TOTAL TIME: 50 minutes
SERVES 4

These jump from the platter whenever we serve them. Quick-brined shrimp get a gorgeous seared edge in hot butter, gaining sweet umami and snappy texture with no rubbery overcooked-ness. Supermarket cocktail sauce is made lively with our simple, aromatic citrus sambal, which you prepare while the shrimp briefly marinate.

16 large, shell-on American-caught shrimp (1 pound, 16 count)

1 teaspoon sugar or agave syrup

1 teaspoon fish sauce

1 teaspoon soy sauce

2 tablespoons cold unsalted butter, thinly sliced

Kicky Sambal-Citrus Sauce (recipe follows)

1 If the shrimp have heads, pull them off. With kitchen scissors, insert the point of the scissor blade deeply into the center of the fat end of the shrimp and cut the shell all the way along its back, exposing the vein. Pull the shell and legs off (keep the tail on, if desired). Remove the vein by wiping with a paper towel.

2 Place the shrimp in a large ziplock bag. Add the sugar, fish sauce, and soy sauce, and work the mixture until the shrimp are evenly coated. Marinate in the refrigerator for 20 minutes.

3 Heat a skillet large enough to accommodate the 16 shrimp over medium-high heat for 2 minutes, then add the butter slices. As soon as the butter has melted, add the shrimp, keeping a bit of separation between them. It's fine to do this in two batches for maximum sear, and important if your pan is small. Cook until the shrimp begin to brown around the edges, about 1½ minutes, then flip and cook until lightly seared, another 1½ minutes. Remove from the pan to a plate and put in the fridge for 20 minutes to cool. Serve with the Kicky Sambal-Citrus Sauce.

Kicky Sambal-Citrus Sauce

⅓ cup store-bought cocktail sauce

⅓ cup The Best Sambal Is Your Own Sambal (page 21)

Zest of 1 lime

Juice of ½ lime

Combine all ingredients and chill. The sauce will keep in an airtight container in the refrigerator for up to 5 days.

Sambal Substitute: If you don't have our homemade sambal sauce—though you should!—use ⅔ cup cocktail sauce, 1 teaspoon store-bought sambal oelek, and 1 teaspoon sugar (plus the lime zest and juice).

Global Pantry Ingredients

Fish Sauce, *p. 11*
Sambal, *p. 21*
Soy Sauce, *p. 22*

Quick Technique

Shell Off, Vein Out in a Snap. Fat shrimp have dark veins, basically intestines, so you want them out. The scissor method described in Step 1 splits the shell so you can pull it off while cutting a furrow that exposes the vein for easy removal. Once you get the knack, you'll clean 16 shrimp in less than 5 minutes.

Texture Tip

Don't Skip the Sugar Brine. We first saw this speedy idea online, from *America's Test Kitchen*, and it's brilliant: A brief bath in a sugary brine causes the shrimp to brown in the pan more quickly (the sugar caramelizes in seconds), *before* they overcook.

Foolproof Frying

Don't Fear the Frying.
The only trick about deep-frying is keeping the oil in the temperature sweet spot of 365°F to 370°F. Any hotter, and the hush puppies will get too brown on the outside before the inside (including the raw shrimp) cooks through. Any cooler, the hush puppies will absorb too much fat and become soggy, oily, sadness incarnate.

Fry a Bit Longer, a Bit Darker.
After moving to the South, Scott noted that your average Mississippi fry-station jockey could turn out better fried catfish than most Michelin chefs in NYC. The secret was cooking until the batter is darker than the paler northern standard—never burnt, but the color of dark maple syrup. This yields maximum caramelization and crunch.

Quick Substitution

Stand-ins for Buttermilk.
Buttermilk can be hard to find in some parts of the country. Swap in whole-milk kefir (increasingly available in mainstream supermarkets) or whisk together whole Greek yogurt with enough water to reach a consistency similar to heavy cream—try ½ cup plus 1 tablespoon yogurt with 3 tablespoons water to get the ¾ cup you need for this recipe.

Shrimp Boil Hush Puppies
with Tabasco Aioli

ACTIVE TIME: 30 minutes
TOTAL TIME: 30 minutes
SERVES 6

This idea came from Ann's husband, Patrick, who wondered, as a good Southerner would, how to use leftover corn, sausage, and other ingredients from a traditional shrimp boil feast. The goodies are folded into a cornbread-ish hush puppy batter and fried until deeply browned and very crisp on the outside. Proper frying, easily done, leaves them chunky and moist and full of chewy bits within. Tabasco lends its unique Louisiana-fermented tang to the dipping sauce. Double the quantities (except the frying oil) for a larger group, and fry in stages. These puppies are at their absolute best right out of the fryer, but if you don't want to fry in your party frock, they will hold up pretty well for about an hour in a warm (250°F) oven. Place them on a wire rack set inside a sheet pan to allow air to circulate.

FOR THE HUSH PUPPIES

1 cup (5 ounces) medium-grind yellow cornmeal (such as Bob's Red Mill)

⅓ cup (1½ ounces) all-purpose flour

1 teaspoon baking powder

½ teaspoon kosher salt

¼ teaspoon baking soda

¾ cup whole buttermilk

1 large egg, lightly beaten

¼ medium yellow onion

½ cup fresh corn kernels

¼ cup chopped scallions

4 ounces peeled and deveined medium or large shrimp, chopped

3 ounces andouille sausage, chopped

4 cups canola oil

FOR THE AIOLI

½ cup mayonnaise

1 tablespoon whole-grain mustard or Dijon mustard

1 tablespoon Tabasco sauce

¾ teaspoon sweet paprika

1 tablespoon finely chopped scallions

1 small clove garlic, grated on a Microplane grater

1 To prepare the hush puppies, whisk together the cornmeal, flour, baking powder, salt, and baking soda in a medium bowl. Add the buttermilk and egg and stir until well combined. Grate the onion on the large holes of a box grater. Stir the onion, corn, scallions, shrimp, and sausage into the batter. Let the batter stand at room temperature for 10 to 15 minutes (however long it takes your oil to heat up).

2 Pour the oil into a Dutch oven. Heat the oil to 365°F over medium-high heat.

3 To prepare the aioli, while the oil heats and the batter stands, stir together the mayonnaise, mustard, Tabasco, and paprika in a small bowl until well combined. Stir in the scallions and garlic; set aside.

4 Arrange a platter lined with paper towels by the stove. Carefully drop the batter by 2-tablespoon mounds (a 2-tablespoon cookie scoop works perfectly for this) into the hot oil to form 9 hush puppies. Adjust the heat to maintain a temperature between 360°F and 370°F. Fry until the hush puppies are deeply browned and crisp, 3 to 4 minutes, turning a few times with a long-handled slotted spoon. (Watch out for any corn kernels that stick out of the batter and are exposed directly to the oil; they can sputter or pop.) Scoop out the hush puppies and drain on the paper towels. Repeat the process with the remaining batter. Serve the hush puppies with the aioli.

Note: You can save the oil for another deep-frying adventure down the road. Allow it to cool to room temp, and strain it through a fine-mesh sieve into a clean container. Store the oil in a cool, dark place. The shelf life varies and depends on all kinds of factors (how hot you heated the oil, what you cooked in it, etc.); just give the oil a sniff before you go to use it. If it has gone rancid, you'll know.

Khichiya, Krupuk, and Chicharrones de Harina

These You-Fry-'Em Crackers Are the Best Crackers

Crackers are a global phenom, and each of the ones here is among the world's best, yielding great cocktail-friendly platforms for dips, sauces, salsas, chutneys, and more, enlivening any party. Kids adore them, too. Yes, you can buy premade versions, but the foodie angels will weep. It's time to get serious about a little deep-frying.

What krupuk from Java, khichiya papad from India, and chicharrones de harina from Mexico have in common is the remarkable transformative effect of hot oil on pieces of dried starch (made of rice, tapioca, or wheat flour, plus binders and flavorings) that look like plastic before cooking. Those pieces quickly expand to several times their original size, forming puffy, porous networks of crunchy goodness.

Two cups of neutral oil such as canola or corn in a wok, a cast-iron frying pan, or a sturdy stainless-steel pot are most of what you need to start a fun production line. Tips on tools and techniques for safe and successful frying are on page 52. We recommend making double or triple batches once you get an assembly line going.

Khichiya Papad

Khichiya papad, made from rice flour, taste similar to Indian pappadams—those shatteringly thin fried cracker-breads made of lentil flour or other pulses, dotted with spices like cumin or black pepper. However, they fry up into big, fabulously crunchy, bubble-blistered crackers (they can double in size). They are sold in Indian food stores and online, where they come in various sizes, sometimes with added spices such as cumin. Our favorite so far is the chile-garlic flavor.

Fry Notes: Frying takes about 20 seconds. They puff and writhe while cooking. After a few seconds of that, push them down with tongs in the center to yield a flat-ish result, and fish out before they brown, then drain on paper towels.

Suggested Accompaniments: Delicious with a spicy mango or other sweet chutney as a snack or app, and with any curry as a side, such as our fish curry (see page 156) and vegetarian curry (see page 173). Also tasty with the shakshuka with Indian spices (see page 180).

Krupuk

Shrimp- and seafood-flavored crackers, made with tapioca or other starch, are common all over South Asia and in parts of China, but the Indonesian shrimp variety, called krupuk (sometimes kerupuk) udang, are the gold standard: thicker, crunchier, more shrimpy, more savory. They generally come in two pre-fry sizes, the small being not much bigger than a quarter, puffing up to 3 or 4 inches across, and the large being the size of a child's palm and puffing to the dimensions of a small dinner plate. The Indonesian aisle in stores like H Mart usually has krupuk udang. One reliable brand is Komodo. Store staff may send you to the snack section, where prefried shrimp crackers dwell, but you want the uncooked kind, product of Indonesia. Also available online. Unfried, they keep forever in the pantry.

Fry Notes: The larger krupuk writhe and curl and uncurl and sometimes arch out of the oil. Let this happen for a few seconds until the cracker begins to uncurl, then use a spider or tongs to get them as flat as possible. Flip once and press down. As soon as they show signs of light browning about the edges, about 20 seconds, fish them out to drain on paper towels.

Suggested Accompaniments: Fantastic with peanut sauce (see page 18) but equally delicious with Ann's Smoky Pimento Kim Cheese (page 30). Serve with a meal of rice and pork satay (see page 112) and/or the Indonesian coconut milk green beans on page 249.

Chicharrones de Harina

We adore the rich, fried pork-belly snacks called chicharrones, popular in Mexico and many Latin American countries, but cooking them is best left to specialists (big Latin-food stores with butcher shops often fry them in-house). Chicharrones de harina are another story, made of flat, dry wheat dough that is shaped into small rectangles or wagon wheels, the latter being more fun (you can find both at stores that sell Mexican or Latin foods, or online). Raw, they are an odd, rusty orange color. Fried, they turn pale beige. They're bland on their own but supremely crisp, begging for a spicy dip.

Fry Notes: You can cook several at once, using a spider or slotted spoon to fish them from the oil. They puff in about 15 seconds. Fish them out when all signs of the dense orange parts are gone, before they brown Drain on paper towels..

Suggested Accompaniments: Sprinkle with Tajín, the spice of lime and chiles (page 24), and serve with your favorite salsa spiked with lime juice, or an avocado dip.

Tips for a Successful Cracker-Fry

EQUIPMENT: An instant-read thermometer such as a Thermapen, metal-tipped long tongs, slotted spoon or Chinese "spider," sheet pan, and copious paper towels

THE FRY STATION: Position a sheet pan covered with a layer of paper towels near the stove—but not so near they can catch fire from the burner. Turn the vent fan (if you have one) on high. Have tongs, crackers, thermometer, and more paper towels at hand. Make sure the tongs are completely dry—any water in the oil will spatter. Banish all pets and small kids from the room.

THE FRYING: The method is the same for all varieties, with a few notes for each. Raw crackers are gently lowered into 360°F oil—one at a time if they are big, a few at a time if small—and begin their 15- to 20-second metamorphosis. Do a test cracker to get a feel for the process. Check the oil temperature after every batch or two and adjust.

Two cups of oil usually take 4 to 5 minutes over high heat to reach 360°F. When the sheet pan is covered with crackers, add another layer of paper towels, gently pressing the paper onto the cooked crackers to dab some oil. Repeat until all crackers are cooked. Let the oil cool on the back of the stove.

STORING THE CRACKERS: They're irresistible on the day of the fry but will remain crisp for several days in an airtight plastic ziplock bag or other sealed container.

Hard-as-plastic shrimp crackers magically expand to many times their size in hot oil.

5 Flavors of Super-Crunchy Wokcorn

Ann tested seven ways to make plain popcorn for a website, gauging for easy, fluffy-crunchy results and fewest old maids. This method of popping in a wok is now our go-to for movie night. The concavity of the pan urges kernels to the hottest place as you agitate the batch. The wok's handle and (if your wok is carbon steel) overall lightness make easy work of shaking. If you don't have a very wide lid, you can use an upside-down colander to cover the pan. These butter-free popcorns are either vegan or easily made so with suggested ingredient substitutes.

The Basic Super-Crunchy Wokcorn Recipe

ACTIVE TIME: 10 minutes
TOTAL TIME: 10 minutes
SERVES 4

---

1 teaspoon kosher salt

2 tablespoons liquid (refined) coconut oil

½ cup popcorn kernels

1 Place the salt in a mortar and grind to a fine powder (akin to powdered sugar) with the pestle.

2 Combine the salt, oil, and 2 popcorn kernels (these are your test kernels) in the bottom of a wok. Cover and heat over medium heat, shaking the wok occasionally, until you hear the test kernels pop. Add the remaining kernels and cover the wok.

3 Cook over medium heat, shaking the pan frequently, until the new kernels start to pop. Then reduce the heat to medium-low and cook, shaking the pan constantly, until the popping subsides. Transfer immediately to large bowls or a sheet pan.

Sesame Kettle Wokcorn with Furikake

ACTIVE TIME: 30 minutes
(if popcorn is already made)
TOTAL TIME: 30 minutes
SERVES 4

This is crunchy kettle corn with a Japanese twist from a sprinkling of furikake, made from sesame, nori, sugar, salt, and seasonings. Irresistible. Use a vegan butter substitute and vegan furikake blend to make it vegan.

Cooking spray

½ cup packed light brown sugar

½ cup light corn syrup

2 tablespoons butter or vegan butter substitute

2 tablespoons Korean toasted sesame oil

12 cups (1 full recipe) Basic Super-Crunchy Wokcorn

¼ cup furikake

1 Preheat the oven to 350°F with a rack in the center. Line a large sheet pan with aluminum foil; coat the foil with cooking spray.

Global Pantry Ingredients

Ají Amarillo Paste, see Try This!, p. 54

Freeze-Dried Strawberries, see Try This!, p. 55

Furikake, p. 12

Ghee, p. 12

Korean Toasted Sesame Oil, p. 14

Smoked Paprika, p. 22

Tahini, p. 24

Za'atar, p. 26

Key Technique

The Best Salt Trick Ever. Simply place a little kosher salt in a mortar and pestle and grind it to a fine powder. It takes only a dozen turns or so of the pestle, and the powder disperses perfectly when added at the beginning of the wok-cooking.

Flavor Booster

Buttery Without Butter. We pop with refined, clear liquid coconut oil, which has a neutral flavor that comes across as intensely buttery in the finished popcorn. Refined solid oil works, too—but don't use the unrefined variety, which tastes very coconutty.

Try This!

Ají Amarillo Paste. This bright yellow puree is made from an ancient chile of Peruvian cuisine. It's a bit salty but not vinegary, with a unique, high-toned aroma and almost roasted-pepper taste. We like the Inca's Food and Costa Peruana brands, most easily found online. If you ever see the frozen peppers in a specialty store, buy a bag for a unique chile flavor in soups, stews, or dips, such as our butternut bisque on page 79.

2 Combine the sugar, corn syrup, and butter or butter substitute in a small, heavy saucepan. Bring to a boil over medium heat; boil 3 minutes, stirring occasionally. Remove the pan from the heat and let stand until the mixture is no longer boiling; stir in the sesame oil.

3 Place the Wokcorn in a large bowl. Pour the hot syrup mixture over the Wokcorn; toss well to coat. Spread the mixture onto the prepared sheet pan; sprinkle evenly with the furikake. Bake at 350°F until crisp, 10 to 15 minutes, stirring every 5 minutes. Cool completely before serving. (It will get crispier as it cools.)

Tahini-Za'atar Wokcorn

ACTIVE TIME: 5 minutes
(if popcorn is already made)
TOTAL TIME: 5 minutes
SERVES 4

Ann tried this on a lark and was amazed how irresistible it is: spicy and nutty with a hint of sweetness.

---

2 tablespoons extra-virgin olive oil

2 tablespoons tahini

1½ teaspoons agave nectar

12 cups (1 full recipe) Basic Super-Crunchy Wokcorn (page 53)

2 tablespoons za'atar

1 Whisk together the oil, tahini, and agave nectar in a small, heavy saucepan. Bring to a boil over medium heat. Reduce the heat to medium-low and cook 3 minutes, whisking frequently.

2 Place the Wokcorn in a large bowl. Drizzle with the tahini mixture and toss well to coat. Sprinkle with the za'atar and toss well to coat.

Nacho-ish Wokcorn

ACTIVE TIME: 3 minutes
(if popcorn is already made)
TOTAL TIME: 3 minutes
SERVES 4

If the pantry-grab-bag ingredient list raises an eyebrow, the popcorn brings universal smiles: It's spicy and aromatic and savory and even a bit cheesy because of the nutritional yeast.

¼ cup ghee

2 teaspoons ají amarillo paste (see Try This!)

¼ cup nutritional yeast

1 teaspoon ground cumin

¾ teaspoon smoked paprika

¾ teaspoon garlic powder

12 cups (1 full recipe) Basic Super-Crunchy Wokcorn (page 53)

1 Place the ghee in a small microwave-safe bowl. Microwave on High until melted, 20 to 30 seconds. Whisk in the ají amarillo paste.

2 Combine the nutritional yeast, cumin, smoked paprika, and garlic powder in a small bowl. Place the Wokcorn in a large bowl. Drizzle with the ghee mixture and toss well to coat. Sprinkle with the nutritional yeast mixture and toss well to coat.

White Chocolate–Strawberry Wokcorn

ACTIVE TIME: 6 minutes
(if popcorn is already made)
TOTAL TIME: 16 minutes
SERVES 6

The freeze-dried berry powder, one of our favorite global pantry products of modern food technology, adds a clean, fruity note that deftly balances the white-chocolate sweetness in this rich treat. At which point the Szechuan peppers rocket it into another dimension. We've served small amounts as a sweet snack before dessert at dinner parties.

---

1 teaspoon Szechuan peppercorns or pink peppercorns (optional)

¾ ounce freeze-dried strawberries (see Try This!)

11 ounces white chocolate chips

1 tablespoon liquid (refined) coconut oil

12 cups (1 full recipe) Basic Super-Crunchy Wokcorn (page 53)

1 If using the peppercorns, place them in a small skillet. Heat over medium heat until toasted, about 1 minute, shaking the pan constantly. Place the peppercorns and strawberries in a mini food processor; process until ground.

2 Place the chocolate chips in a medium microwave-safe bowl; drizzle with the coconut oil. Microwave on High for 1½ minutes, stirring every 20 seconds, until the chocolate is melted and smooth.

3 Place the Wokcorn in a large bowl. Drizzle with the chocolate mixture and toss well to coat. Sprinkle with the strawberry mixture; toss well to coat. Spread the popcorn on a sheet pan lined with parchment paper. Chill until set, about 10 minutes.

Try This!
Freeze-Dried Strawberries. In freeze-drying, water turns directly into gas with no icy-slushy phase, leaving bits of super concentrated, uncooked, sugar-free flavor in a delicately crunchy form— ideal for icings, batters, and frozen desserts. Most major stores, including Target, Walmart, and Whole Foods, carry freeze-dried fruit in 1- or 2-ounce bags, the latter sufficient for two batches of the cupcakes on page 272. Leftover berries should be stored in a tight jar.

Freeze-drying boosts berry flavor with no water.

Shopping Intel
The Myth of "Sushi-Grade" Tuna.
This term is not regulated by the
USDA or FDA, so look instead for
a beautiful piece of sustainable
tuna from an impeccable fish
seller. The best stuff for raw eating
is also sold frozen, but needs to be
thawed for 24 hours in the fridge.
Check seafoodwatch.org for the
latest word on responsible fishing.
Yellowfin and bigeye tuna (both
sometimes called ahi) from certain
parts of the Pacific are generally
regarded as the most sustainable.

Try This!
Thai Curry Pastes. These, which
come in red, green, and yellow
varieties, only hint at the
complexity and pungency of the
hand-pounded and fried pastes
they imitate—which can contain
lemongrass, galangal, makrut
lime leaves, cilantro leaves and
roots, basil, mint, chiles, shallots,
and much more—but are useful in
recipes like this. Look for brands
with long ingredient lists.

Key to the Crisp
Rice Flour vs. Cornstarch.
Rice flour produces the lightest,
crispiest texture; cornstarch
creates a heartier crust. Look for
rice flour (not glutinous/sweet
rice flour) at Asian markets. It has
a texture similar to powdered
sugar; the rice flour sold by
natural-food companies can be
gritty.

Sticky-Rice Crunch Cakes
with Thai-Curry Tuna Topping

ACTIVE TIME: 25 minutes
TOTAL TIME: 25 minutes
MAKES 8 PIECES

These will produce wide-eyed glee at
your table or appetizer buffet. They
are Ann's version of a classic appetizer
popularized by sushi restaurants, but
easy and fun to make at home. There
are all sorts of shortcuts: precooked
sticky rice; jarred Thai curry paste, with
its complex herby-chile flavor; and
a sweet-salty finish from a drizzle of
kecap manis. The rice cakes will keep
their crunchy overcoats just fine in a
low oven if you want to double or even
triple this recipe.

---

6 ounces raw tuna for sushi, such as bigeye
  or yellowfin

2 tablespoons chopped scallions

1½ tablespoons mayonnaise

1½ teaspoons Thai red curry paste

¼ teaspoon kosher salt

2 cups precooked sticky or short-grain rice
  (see Note)

⅓ cup rice flour or cornstarch

6 tablespoons canola oil

8 thin jalapeño slices

1½ tablespoons kecap manis

1 Thinly slice the tuna, and then go over
it with your knife, back and forth, until
finely chopped. Mix together the scallions,
mayonnaise, curry paste, and salt in a
medium bowl. Add the tuna and stir well.
Refrigerate until ready to serve.

2 If you haven't warmed your rice briefly
(see the note below), do so now. Moisten
your hands and a ¼-cup measuring cup.
Scoop the warmed rice by ¼ cupfuls and
shape into thin round or oval patties each
2 to 2½ inches in diameter. Place the rice
flour or cornstarch on a saucer. Lightly
dredge both sides of each rice cake in the
flour or cornstarch; set on a plate.

3 Heat a large nonstick skillet over medium
heat. Add 3 tablespoons of oil to the pan
and swirl to coat. Add the rice cakes; cook
until crisped on the bottom, 3 to 5 minutes
(they won't really brown). Remove the cakes
to a plate. Add the remaining 3 tablespoons
oil to the pan and swirl to coat. Return the
rice cakes to the skillet, uncooked side down;
cook until crisped on the bottom, 3 to 5
minutes.

4 Arrange the rice cakes on a platter. Top
evenly with the tuna mixture. Top each with
1 jalapeño slice; drizzle with kecap manis.

Note: To streamline prep, precooked sticky
rice or short-grain rice can save time. You'll
find it with the Asian foods at many large
supermarkets (the Annie Chun's brand is
widely available). To warm before using, heat
for only half the time on the label. It doesn't
have to be hot, just supple.

Anchovies • Yuzu • Black Walnuts • Wondra • Sumac • Calabrian Chiles • Sorghu
Millet • Tabasco Sauce • Coconut Milk • Roasted Hazelnut Oil • Curry Leaves •
Sauce • Shrimp Paste • Worcestershire Sauce • Furikake • Sriracha • Saffron • Bany
Vinegar • Gochujang • Harissa • Marmite • Kecap Manis • Chili Crisp • Freeze-Di
Strawberries • Tajín • Kimchi • Korean Toasted Sesame Oil • Dulce de Leche •
Sauce • Lemongrass • Whole Wheat Pastry Flour • Pomegranate Molasses • Mexi
Chocolate • Smoked Paprika • Chipotles in Adobo • Shichimi Togarashi • Makrut Li
Leaves • Crema Mexicana • The Many Masalas • Capers • Mexican Chorizo • Mir
Oyster Sauce • Panko Breadcrumbs • Ras El Hanout • Andouille Sausage • Marsa
The Many Sambals • Benton's Bacon • Miso • Stone-Ground Grits • Tahini • Ghee • Pa
Sugar • Ají Amarillo Paste • Thai Curry Paste • Mustard Powder • Turmeric • Cultu
Butter • Kashmiri Mirch • Dried Porcini Mushrooms • Sweetened Condensed Mi
Anchovies • Yuzu • Black Walnuts • Wondra • Sumac • Calabrian Chiles • Sorghu
Millet • Tabasco Sauce • Coconut Milk • Roasted Hazelnut Oil • Curry Leaves •
Sauce • Shrimp Paste • Worcestershire Sauce • Furikake • Sriracha • Saffron • Bany
Vinegar • Gochujang • Harissa • Marmite • Kecap Manis • Chili Crisp • Freeze-Dr
Strawberries • Tajín • Kimchi • Korean Toasted Sesame Oil • Dulce de Leche •
Sauce • Lemongrass • Whole Wheat Pastry Flour • Pomegranate Molasses • Mexi
Chocolate • Smoked Paprika • Chipotles in Adobo • Shichimi Togarashi • Makrut Li
Leaves • Crema Mexicana • The Many Masalas • Capers • Mexican Chorizo • Mir
Oyster Sauce • Panko Breadcrumbs • Ras El Hanout • Andouille Sausage • Marsa
The Many Sambals • Benton's Bacon • Miso • Stone-Ground Grits • Tahini • Ghee • Pa
Sugar • Ají Amarillo Paste • Thai Curry Paste • Mustard Powder • Turmeric • Cultu
Butter • Kashmiri Mirch • Dried Porcini Mushrooms • Sweetened Condensed Mi
Anchovies • Yuzu • Black Walnuts • Wondra • Sumac • Calabrian Chiles • Sorghu
Millet • Tabasco Sauce • Coconut Milk • Roasted Hazelnut Oil • Curry Leaves •
Sauce • Shrimp Paste • Worcestershire Sauce • Furikake • Sriracha • Saffron • Bany
Vinegar • Gochujang • Harissa • Marmite • Kecap Manis • Chili Crisp • Freeze-Dr
Strawberries • Tajín • Kimchi • Korean Toasted Sesame Oil • Dulce de Leche •
Sauce • Lemongrass • Whole Wheat Pastry Flour • Pomegranate Molasses • Mexi
Chocolate • Smoked Paprika • Chipotles in Adobo • Shichimi Togarashi • Makrut Li
Leaves • Crema Mexicana • The Many Masalas • Capers • Mexican Chorizo • Mir
Oyster Sauce • Panko Breadcrumbs • Ras El Hanout • Andouille Sausage • Marsa
The Many Sambals • Benton's Bacon • Miso • Stone-Ground Grits • Tahini • Ghee • Pa
Sugar • Ají Amarillo Paste • Thai Curry Paste • Mustard Powder • Turmeric • Cultu
Butter • Kashmiri Mirch • Dried Porcini Mushrooms • Sweetened Condensed Milk

Crunchy, Vibrant Salads

Our Lighter Version of the
Splendid Wedge Salad / 60

Roasted Cauliflower Salad
with Quick-Pickled Raisins / 62

Cherry-Beet Salad
with Hazelnut Gremolata / 63

Pear-Arugula Salad
with Bitters Vinaigrette / 65

**Cantaloupe, Cucumber, and
Seared Halloumi Salad** / 66

Gado-Gado: An Indonesian
Classic Made Glorious with
Peanut Sauce / 69

All the Tomato Goodness / 70

A Very Lively Tomato Salad
with Chili Crisp Dressing / 72

**Spinach, Grapefruit,
and Avocado Salad** with
Sesame Vinaigrette / 73

Texture Tip

Don't Avoid the Iceberg.
No lettuce packs more crunch
than iceberg in its prime, and
its mild flavor highlights the
subtle, soothing quality of
the dressing.

Our Lighter Version of the
Splendid Wedge Salad

ACTIVE TIME: 7 minutes
TOTAL TIME: 37 minutes
SERVES 6

The classic wedge salad, heavy with creamy (and often blue-cheesy) dressing and crunchy bits of bacon, evokes fine, relaxing expense-account lunches at old-timey restaurants in San Francisco, New York, and Chicago, back when folks had such lunches. We ease up a bit by nixing the bacon and cheese and then add extra crunch and deep "green" flavors from bits of sesame and seaweed in the Japanese store-bought spice mix furikake. The dressing, basically a coconut-based ranch, gets body from coconut cream and is spiked with a blizzard of fresh chives—yet it's lighter overall. Make this the grand opener for a summer dinner or a main at lunch, with a glass of spritzy white wine (we like it with Spanish Txakoli or a lively West Coast sparkler from Oregon or the Sonoma coast).

FOR THE DRESSING

½ cup light sour cream

½ cup coconut cream

½ cup plus 2 tablespoons whole buttermilk

3 tablespoons finely chopped fresh chives

1 tablespoon freshly squeezed lemon juice

½ teaspoon kosher salt

½ teaspoon onion powder

½ teaspoon garlic powder

¼ teaspoon mustard powder

FOR THE SALAD

1 large, firm head of iceberg lettuce,
   cut into 6 wedges (leave the core as
   intact as possible)

2 tablespoons furikake

Freshly ground black pepper

1 Whisk together the dressing ingredients in a bowl and set aside for 30 minutes in the fridge for the flavors to incorporate (it will keep for up to 2 days).

2 When ready to serve, arrange the lettuce wedges on salad or dinner plates. Pour ¼ cup of the coconut ranch dressing over each serving, shower each wedge with 1 teaspoon of the furikake, and grind some fresh pepper on top.

Global Pantry Ingredients

Banyuls Vinegar, *p. 9*
Pine Nuts, *p. 19*
Ras El Hanout, *p. 20*

Flavor Technique

Increase the Surface Area.
If you halve or third the cauliflower florets with a knife, such that some pieces gain a flat surface, that will increase the contact with the hot pan and boost the browning.

Roasted Cauliflower Salad
with Quick-Pickled Raisins

ACTIVE TIME: 12 minutes
TOTAL TIME: 45 minutes
SERVES 4

Cauliflower roasted with ras el hanout spice mix and olive oil is fantastic when the florets have maximum caramelized edges for total roasty huzzah. Arugula adds a peppery bite, and microwave-pickled raisins sing some sweet-tart harmony, made beautiful by the ethereal background notes of Banyuls vinegar (if you want to make extra raisins, use them in any salad, on a grain bowl, or over soft chèvre spread on crostini). This is a great salad for any meal of grilled or roasted meat or poultry. If you don't have toasted pine nuts, see page 26 for timing, or use toasted pistachios, or eliminate. If there's no good arugula in the market, a mixture of radicchio or endive (for peppery effect) and baby spinach would make a nice substitute.

FOR THE QUICK-PICKLED RAISINS

½ cup golden raisins

1 tablespoon sugar

1 tablespoon Banyuls or a fine, aged sherry vinegar

¼ teaspoon kosher salt

½ teaspoon paprika

FOR THE CAULIFLOWER SALAD

1 small head cauliflower (1½ to 1¾ pounds)

4 tablespoons extra-virgin olive oil

1 tablespoon ras el hanout

¾ teaspoon kosher salt

1 medium onion, cut lengthwise into quarters and then thinly sliced crosswise

5 ounces arugula

2 teaspoons Banyuls or sherry vinegar

¼ cup toasted pine nuts (optional)

1 Preheat the oven to 425°F with a rack in the center.

2 Combine the raisins, ½ cup water, the sugar, vinegar, salt, and paprika in a small microwave-safe bowl. Microwave on High for 1 minute; set aside to cool.

3 Meanwhile, prep the cauliflower: Remove any green leaves and excess stems and pull the head apart. Pull and cut into small, evenly sized pieces (see Flavor Technique about surface area). Line a heavy sheet pan with aluminum foil and pour 2 tablespoons of oil onto the pan. Sprinkle the oil with the ras el hanout and the salt, mixing with your fingers. Add the cauliflower and onion and toss with your hands until evenly coated. Roast until the cauliflower is nicely browned—even charred a bit on the edges here and there—but not dried out or burnt, 25 to 30 minutes. Halfway through, stir the cauliflower on the pan with tongs. Remove the pan to a rack to cool for 15 minutes.

4 When the cauliflower is cool enough (warm is OK, but not hot), drain the raisins and discard the pickling liquid. In a large salad bowl or on a large platter, toss the arugula with the remaining 2 tablespoons oil and the vinegar; top with the cauliflower, onion, raisins, and pine nuts (if using).

Cherry-Beet Salad
with Hazelnut Gremolata

ACTIVE TIME: 30 minutes
TOTAL TIME: 36 minutes
SERVES 4

The unusual cherry-beet combo not only forms a lovely dark-ruby monochrome but is also a dreamy pile-on of earthy-sweet and juicy-tart flavors—for those who love beets, as we do. One of Ann's friends declared it the best thing she'd ever tasted, while the friend's teenage daughter, who dislikes beets, was a hilarious hard no. Vary the supporting cast of nuts and oils as you like—try pistachios and pistachio oil, or walnuts and walnut oil, but an oil with a toasty character is best. The beets and cherries are made for each other; we found that swapping in plums just didn't work.

1 pound small trimmed beets (about 6)

1 pound fresh sweet cherries

2 tablespoons roasted hazelnut oil

1½ tablespoons Banyuls vinegar

1 teaspoon Dijon mustard

1 teaspoon honey

½ teaspoon kosher salt

¼ teaspoon freshly ground black pepper

⅛ teaspoon ground cardamom

¼ cup chopped toasted, skinned hazelnuts

1 tablespoon finely chopped fresh mint

1½ teaspoons lemon zest

1 Cut off any "tails" from the beets, and trim any stems flush with the top of the beet. Pierce each beet once with the tip of a paring knife. Place the beets on a large sheet of microwave-safe parchment paper; fold and wrap the paper tightly around the beets. Microwave on High for 6 minutes or until the beets are tender. (If they're larger than what we used, they will take longer. Cook in 1-minute increments until they're tender.)

2 Cool the beets slightly, just until you can handle them. Trim off the stem ends to reveal the flesh, and rub off the skins. Cut the beets into thin wedges.

3 Remove the stems and pits from the cherries; cut the cherries in half. (Yep, a cherry pitter is a worthwhile investment.)

4 Combine the oil, vinegar, mustard, honey, salt, pepper, and cardamom in a small jar; seal and shake until well emulsified. Combine the beets and cherries in a large bowl. Drizzle with the vinaigrette; toss gently to coat (you can prep the salad up to this point and keep it in the fridge for up to 1 day).

5 Combine the hazelnuts, mint, and lemon zest in a small bowl; sprinkle over the salad just before serving.

Global Pantry Ingredients

Banyuls Vinegar, *p. 9*
Roasted Hazelnut Oil, *p. 20*

Key Technique
Faster "Roasting." Roasted beets take at least an hour. We use a simple microwave method to cut the process to just 6 minutes.

Avoid This Mistake
Prevent the Dreaded Stains. Both cherries and beets will stain everything in sight— your cutting board, your countertop, your hands—so take precautions. Use a dark cutting board, or line it with parchment paper, and wear inexpensive latex or vinyl gloves (they're a great thing to keep in the kitchen). And please, for heaven's sake, change out of that best white shirt.

Pear-Arugula Salad
with Bitters Vinaigrette

ACTIVE TIME: 13 minutes
TOTAL TIME: 13 minutes
SERVES 4

Ever since our friend Mark Bitterman—a bitters, salt, and chocolate genius who opened a delightful global pantry shop called The Meadow in Portland, Oregon, with branches in New York and Tokyo—mentioned using bitters in a vinaigrette, we've been obsessed. Here, a heavy splash of Angostura adds intense fruit-and-spice-basket aromas and, yes, some pleasing bitterness. Sweet pears and salty cheese—in this case, it has to be bona fide Parmigiano-Reggiano—do a flavor cha-cha-cha as it all comes together in perfect balance. We've deployed this vinaigrette with a mix of watercress (for peppery bite) and escarole (for crunch and balance) when arugula was poor, and that worked beautifully. Experiment with whatever distinctive green is freshest in the market or out of your garden.

3 tablespoons extra-virgin olive oil

2 tablespoons champagne vinegar

2 teaspoons Angostura bitters

1 teaspoon honey

1 teaspoon Dijon mustard

½ teaspoon kosher salt

¼ teaspoon freshly ground black pepper

5 ounces baby arugula

¼ cup slivered red onion

1 pear, thinly sliced

½ cup shaved Parmigiano-Reggiano cheese

1 Combine the oil, vinegar, bitters, honey, mustard, salt, and pepper in a small jar; close the lid and shake vigorously until emulsified. It will keep in the refrigerator for up to 5 days.

2 Combine the arugula, onion, and pear in a large bowl. Drizzle the dressing over the salad; toss gently to coat. Top with the cheese.

Global Pantry Ingredient

Angostura Bitters,
see Try This!

Try This!
Angostura Bitters. Good old Angostura bitters, on every respectable dad's drinks cart in the *Mad Men* era, endure today, even respected by the PhD mixologists of the cocktail renaissance. And they're essential in this recipe (don't use other bitters). They date to the 19th century and are made in Trinidad from citrus and cardamom and dozens of other warming, aromatic spice-box ingredients. They have a surprising sweetness to offset the bite—we've had a cocktail that was mostly made of Angostura (which is boozy), and it was delicious.

**Global Pantry
Ingredients**

Banyuls Vinegar, *p. 9*
Sumac, *p. 23*

Shopping Intel
Ripe and Ready Melon.
Fully ripe cantaloupe is key—
no rock-hard, flavorless fruit,
please. Smell the cantaloupe's
"belly button," where the stem
was, for a deeply fragrant,
musky aroma. Failing that, Ann
leaves a cantaloupe on her
kitchen counter until it almost
smells rotten; every time, it's
super juicy and sweet. Room
temperature melon yields the
best texture and flavor.

Avoid This Mistake
Sidestep Cheese Squeak.
The cucumber and cantaloupe
should be mixed with the
dressing before you begin
cooking the cheese. Plate the
salad as soon as the cheese
is done—and eat right away
while the cheese is warm and
soft. As it cools, halloumi
heads in a Goodyear direction,
squeaking like a tire on an
auto-showroom floor.

Cantaloupe, Cucumber, and Seared Halloumi Salad

ACTIVE TIME: 15 minutes
TOTAL TIME: 20 minutes
SERVES 4

In the heat of summer, a juicy, crunchy salad is all we want to eat. This one has two surprises that elevate it to special: lemony sumac, a Middle Eastern spice we love for its high-mountain-herb aromas and flavors, and halloumi, a Greek cheese, usually made from sheep and goat milk, that sautés to a unique, chewy texture.

2½ tablespoons extra-virgin olive oil

1 tablespoon Banyuls or sherry vinegar

¼ teaspoon kosher salt

¼ teaspoon freshly ground black pepper

1 small English cucumber

½ medium (5-pound) fully ripe cantaloupe

¼ cup fresh mint leaves

5 ounces halloumi cheese,
    cut lengthwise into ¼-inch-thick slices

2 teaspoons ground sumac
    (optional but recommended)

1 Whisk together 2 tablespoons oil, the vinegar, salt, and pepper in a large bowl. Cut the cucumber into very thin (about ⅛ inch) slices on a severe diagonal for oblong pieces; a mandoline works great for this. Add the cucumber to the bowl and toss to coat.

2 Scoop out and discard the seeds from the cantaloupe half. Cut the cantaloupe into 4 large wedges; slice off the rind and discard. Cut the wedges in half crosswise, then cut each half into slices lengthwise. Add the cantaloupe and mint to the bowl and toss gently to coat. Let the mixture stand for 5 minutes.

3 While the fruit stands, heat the remaining 1½ teaspoons oil in a large cast-iron or other heavy skillet over medium-high heat. Add the cheese to the hot pan; cook until seared and browned, about 2 minutes on each side.

4 Arrange the salad in a large, shallow bowl or a long platter. Top with the warm cheese and sprinkle with the sumac, if desired. Serve immediately.

Gado-Gado

An Indonesian Classic Made Glorious with Peanut Sauce

ACTIVE TIME: 35 minutes (if you've made our peanut sauce powder and pre-made the eggs)
TOTAL TIME: 35 minutes
SERVES 6

Gado-Gado is the iconic national salad of Indonesia, a country whose complex cuisine rivals that of India. Indonesia is often overlooked in the American excitement about Southeast Asian food, possibly because—although Indonesia is the fourth largest country in the world by population—its contributions to US immigration are a third that of Thailand and less than one tenth that of Vietnam. Serve with shrimp crackers (see page 51) for a hearty lunch, and with rice, pork satay (see page 112), and coconut milk green beans (see page 249) for a feast. You can cook the vegetables well ahead of serving and keep them at room temp.

¾ pound small, waxy potatoes (such as baby red or baby yellow potatoes)

Kosher salt

½ pound green beans, cut in half (about 2 cups)

3 cups thickly sliced green cabbage

1 cup Our Best Shortcut to Homemade Peanut Sauce powder (page 18) or 1 block (200 grams) peanut sauce mix (see Shopping Intel, right)

¼ to ⅓ cup hot water

1 small English cucumber, cut into ½-inch chunks

1 red bell pepper, thinly sliced

3 just-hard-boiled eggs, halved (optional)

½ cup fried onions or shallots

Sambal oelek, or The Best Sambal Is Your Own Sambal (page 21), for serving

1 Place the potatoes in a large pot (such as a Dutch oven), fill with water, and salt it generously. Bring the water to a boil over high heat and cook the potatoes until just approaching tender, 12 to 15 minutes after it comes to a boil. Remove the potatoes with a slotted spoon to a second large pot and cover with a lid or a plate to finish cooking. With the water still at a boil, add the green beans and cook until al dente, about 9 minutes. Remove the beans with a slotted spoon to a strainer, and run them under cold water until cooled to room temperature. With the water still at a boil, add the cabbage and cook until snappy but done, about 3 minutes. Drain in a strainer and run the cabbage under cold water until cooled to room temperature.

2 Put the peanut sauce powder in a medium bowl and slowly drizzle in the hot water, stirring until you have a sauce that is the consistency of thick gravy. If using a peanut sauce mix, crumble it into a medium bowl and do the same. Note that sauce will thicken over time; just drizzle in more hot water.

3 Assemble the salad. Cut the potatoes into quarters (or halves, if very small). On a large platter, arrange the potatoes and other vegetables and the eggs in separate clusters. Spoon the peanut sauce over (or serve it on the side if you prefer). Sprinkle the fried onions on top and serve with sambal on the side. If using sambal oelek, you can sweeten with a bit of sugar to taste.

Global Pantry Ingredients

Our Best Shortcut to Homemade Peanut Sauce, *p. 18*

Sambal, *p. 21*

It's Your Call

Improvise the Veg. Along with what you see here, blanched and cooled bean sprouts work well, as do snow peas, blanched and quartered baby bok choy, and even shredded carrots.

Shopping Intel

Fried Onions and Shallots. Crispy, slightly bitter fried onions and shallots are eaten and jarred in many East Asian countries and found in any good Asian food store. In a pinch, try the supermarket versions used on green bean casserole.

Peanut Sauce Mix. Jarred peanut sauces are disappointing, but there's big, authentic Indonesian flavor packed into little peanut-and-spice bricks made by the Rotary company; any of these will work: Bumbu Gado-Gado, Bumbo Sate, Bumbo Pecel, Bumbu Lotek. Crumble, dribble in a little warm water, and stir until you have a thick sauce. Available at big pan-Asian markets like H Mart and from the online vendor IndoFoodStore.com. Buy a bunch if you find them at a good price (less than $4 per block). Another brand we like is Karangsari.

Banyuls Vinegar, *p. 9*

Flavor Booster

450°F for Intense Flavor. Halved cherry or grape tomatoes are roasted at a high temperature for a short time, just until they collapse and give up some juice. This adds sweet harmony notes to the fresh heirlooms beneath them in the finished salad.

Cheesy Shortcut

Room Temp in a Flash. If your burrata is cold, you can warm it by placing it in a ziplock plastic bag, squeezing out the air, and putting the bag in a bowl of warm water as you proceed with the recipe. By the time you need it, it'll be at the perfect temperature for serving.

All the Tomato Goodness

ACTIVE TIME: 7 minutes
TOTAL TIME: 25 minutes
SERVES 4

One day in the tomato-resplendent South, Ann wondered how to amp up the sweet pleasure of summer toms even further. Her idea: Roast grape tomatoes and add them, still a bit warm, to slices of meaty heirloom beefsteaks. All done? No. The caprese genius of fresh mozzarella for milky counterpoint is here, too, pushed further by the use of oozy-creamy room-temperature burrata. This is a tomato salad turned up to 11 by the haunting tang of Banyuls vinegar.

---

1 pint multicolored cherry or grape
   tomatoes, halved

3 tablespoons extra-virgin olive oil

¾ teaspoon kosher salt

½ teaspoon freshly ground black pepper

2 pounds assorted heirloom beefsteak
   tomatoes, cut into ½-inch-thick slices

2 balls (4 ounces each) burrata cheese,
   at room temperature

2 teaspoons Banyuls or sherry vinegar

⅓ cup torn fresh basil

1 Preheat the oven to 450°F with a rack in the center. Line a small sheet pan with aluminum foil.

2 Combine the cherry or grape tomatoes, 1 tablespoon of oil, and ¼ teaspoon each of salt and pepper in a small bowl; toss well to coat. Arrange the tomato mixture in a single layer on the prepared pan (doesn't matter if they're cut side up or down; just let them lie how they want). Roast until wilted and juicy, about 10 minutes. Remove the pan from the oven, and stir the mixture. Let stand to cool a bit as you prepare the rest of the salad.

3 Arrange the heirloom tomatoes on a platter. Break each burrata ball in half (do this over the platter to catch any cream) and arrange on the platter. Sprinkle the sliced tomatoes and burrata evenly with the remaining ½ teaspoon salt and ¼ teaspoon pepper. Drizzle the remaining 2 tablespoons oil and the vinegar over the salad. Arrange the roasted tomatoes on the salad and drizzle their juices over all. Sprinkle with the basil.

Prep Tip

Taming of the Shallot. Raw shallots are sometimes sweet, sometimes aggressive. If yours fall in the latter camp, soak the slices in cold water for a few minutes, then drain and pat dry before adding to the salad.

A Very Lively Tomato Salad
with Chili Crisp Dressing

ACTIVE TIME: 10 minutes
TOTAL TIME: 10 minutes
SERVES 4

This salad, with a dead-simple two-ingredient dressing, is about as subtle as your crazy cousin's politics, so it's a great way to either snazz up a mild entrée (grilled fish or chicken) or to hold its own as a bold accompaniment to something more robust (seared steak). The chili crisp brings complex heat and crunch, and lime juice adds a fresh tropical burst of acid.

2 tablespoons chili crisp

2 tablespoons freshly squeezed lime juice

1 medium shallot (about 1 ounce), halved lengthwise and thinly sliced crosswise

1½ pounds multicolored grape and/or cherry tomatoes, halved lengthwise on the bias

½ cup torn Thai basil

Stir together the chili crisp, lime juice, and shallot in a medium bowl. Add the tomatoes and basil; toss gently to coat.

Chili crisp can become an eat-from-the-jar habit.

Spinach, Grapefruit, and Avocado Salad

with Sesame Vinaigrette

ACTIVE TIME: 10 minutes
TOTAL TIME: 10 minutes
SERVES 4

The profound toastiness of fine Korean sesame oil might not be the first ingredient that comes to mind for a salad anchored by juicy grapefruit, but the combination is absolutely alluring and delicious. Because the oil is so strong, we blend it with neutral-flavored canola to yield enough dressing to coat the greens without overwhelming. This is a simple, clean-flavored stunner.

---

1 package (5 ounces) fresh baby spinach

1 head (about 2 ounces) Belgian endive, thinly sliced crosswise

2 ruby red grapefruits

1 ripe avocado, pitted, peeled, and thinly sliced

1½ tablespoons canola oil

1½ tablespoons rice vinegar

1 tablespoon Korean toasted sesame oil

¼ teaspoon kosher salt

½ teaspoon gochugaru (coarsely ground Korean red pepper), piment d'Espelette, or Aleppo pepper

¼ teaspoon flaky sea salt

1 In a large bowl, combine the spinach and endive. Cut the top and bottom off each grapefruit so the fruit stands upright on your cutting board. Slide the knife down the sides of each grapefruit to remove the peel and pith; turn the fruit over and remove any remaining bits of peel and pith from the other side. Holding one grapefruit over the spinach mixture, cut between the membranes to extract the supremes (that is, sections of the fruit unadulterated by any bitter white pith). Repeat with the remaining grapefruit. Top the mixture with the avocado slices.

2 In a small jar, combine the canola oil, vinegar, sesame oil, and kosher salt. Shake vigorously until well combined and emulsified. Drizzle the dressing over the salad; toss gently to coat. Arrange the salad in a large bowl or on a platter; sprinkle with gochugaru and flaky sea salt.

Global Pantry Ingredients

Korean Toasted Sesame Oil, *p. 14*

Piment d'Espelette, *p. 19*

Shopping Intel

Grapefruit Options. Ruby red grapefruit are in their plump prime in winter through spring—sweeter and less acidic, brightening our salads with color and zing. If you can't find them, white grapefruit, which is often less sweet and maybe a bit more bitter, will work fine. We have found that some of the best ruby red grapefruit is sold by Costco.

Flavor Booster

Pick a Fruity Pepper. It seemed right and proper in a salad with Korean oil to use Korean ground red pepper (gochugaru) as the finishing flourish. But any fruity, not-too-hot ground chile will do, such as the suggested Piment d'Espelette or Aleppo.

Anchovies • Yuzu • Black Walnuts • Wondra • Sumac • Calabrian Chiles • Sorghu
Millet • Tabasco Sauce • Coconut Milk • Roasted Hazelnut Oil • Curry Leaves •
Sauce • Shrimp Paste • Worcestershire Sauce • Furikake • Sriracha • Saffron • Ban
Vinegar • Gochujang • Harissa • Marmite • Kecap Manis • Chili Crisp • Freeze-D
Strawberries • Tajín • Kimchi • Korean Toasted Sesame Oil • Dulce de Leche •
Sauce • Lemongrass • Whole Wheat Pastry Flour • Pomegranate Molasses • Mex
Chocolate • Smoked Paprika • Chipotles in Adobo • Shichimi Togarashi • Makrut L
Leaves • Crema Mexicana • The Many Masalas • Capers • Mexican Chorizo • Mir
Oyster Sauce • Panko Breadcrumbs • Ras El Hanout • Andouille Sausage • Marsa
The Many Sambals • Benton's Bacon • Miso • Stone-Ground Grits • Tahini • Ghee • P
Sugar • Ají Amarillo Paste • Thai Curry Paste • Mustard Powder • Turmeric • Cultu
Butter • Kashmiri Mirch • Dried Porcini Mushrooms • Sweetened Condensed M
Anchovies • Yuzu • Black Walnuts • Wondra • Sumac • Calabrian Chiles • Sorghu
Millet • Tabasco Sauce • Coconut Milk • Roasted Hazelnut Oil • Curry Leaves •
Sauce • Shrimp Paste • Worcestershire Sauce • Furikake • Sriracha • Saffron • Ban
Vinegar • Gochujang • Harissa • Marmite • Kecap Manis • Chili Crisp • Freeze-D
Strawberries • Tajín • Kimchi • Korean Toasted Sesame Oil • Dulce de Leche •
Sauce • Lemongrass • Whole Wheat Pastry Flour • Pomegranate Molasses • Mexi
Chocolate • Smoked Paprika • Chipotles in Adobo • Shichimi Togarashi • Makrut L
Leaves • Crema Mexicana • The Many Masalas • Capers • Mexican Chorizo • Mir
Oyster Sauce • Panko Breadcrumbs • Ras El Hanout • Andouille Sausage • Marsa
The Many Sambals • Benton's Bacon • Miso • Stone-Ground Grits • Tahini • Ghee • P
Sugar • Ají Amarillo Paste • Thai Curry Paste • Mustard Powder • Turmeric • Cultu
Butter • Kashmiri Mirch • Dried Porcini Mushrooms • Sweetened Condensed M
Anchovies • Yuzu • Black Walnuts • Wondra • Sumac • Calabrian Chiles • Sorghu
Millet • Tabasco Sauce • Coconut Milk • Roasted Hazelnut Oil • Curry Leaves •
Sauce • Shrimp Paste • Worcestershire Sauce • Furikake • Sriracha • Saffron • Ban
Vinegar • Gochujang • Harissa • Marmite • Kecap Manis • Chili Crisp • Freeze-D
Strawberries • Tajín • Kimchi • Korean Toasted Sesame Oil • Dulce de Leche •
Sauce • Lemongrass • Whole Wheat Pastry Flour • Pomegranate Molasses • Mexi
Chocolate • Smoked Paprika • Chipotles in Adobo • Shichimi Togarashi • Makrut L
Leaves • Crema Mexicana • The Many Masalas • Capers • Mexican Chorizo • Mir
Oyster Sauce • Panko Breadcrumbs • Ras El Hanout • Andouille Sausage • Marsa
The Many Sambals • Benton's Bacon • Miso • Stone-Ground Grits • Tahini • Ghee • P
Sugar • Ají Amarillo Paste • Thai Curry Paste • Mustard Powder • Turmeric • Cultu
Butter • Kashmiri Mirch • Dried Porcini Mushrooms • Sweetened Condensed Milk

Soups and Comfort Stews

Spice-Market Tomato Soup
with Naan Soldiers / 76

Punched-Up Butternut Bisque
with Microwave-Crisped
Prosciutto / 79

"Diner-Style" French Onion Soup:
An Easy and Almost One-Pot
Way / 81

Loads-of-Chicken–Flavored Soup
with Shrimpy Corn Wontons / 85

Brilliant Bowl of Ramen Pleasure
in Less Than an Hour / 88

Lightnin' Fast Weeknight
Skillet Chili / 91

One-Pot Green Chili with
Rich, Falling-Apart Pork / 93

**Deeply Rich Beef and Marsala
Stew** with Dijon Mustard / 95

Global Pantry Ingredients

Harissa, *p. 13*
Very Slow Tomatoes, *p. 25*
Za'atar, *p. 26*

Shopping Intel

Thicker Bread Broils Better.
The already-baked naan has to withstand a blast from the broiler, and if it's too thin it will burn to shattering shingles. Buy a naan with some body from an Indian or Middle Eastern bakery or shop. In supermarkets, we recommend the widely available Stonefire brand. In a pinch, thick pita will work, too.

Spice-Market Tomato Soup
with Naan Soldiers

ACTIVE TIME: 25 minutes
TOTAL TIME: 1 hour 25 minutes
SERVES 4

This simple but richly spiced soup uses our Very Slow Tomatoes for an intense tomato payoff, with a glug of cream at the end to smooth out the edges. The combo of harissa and za'atar brings an Arab spice basket glory to the party. Do not resist the urge to dunk the naan soldiers. Serve with a substantial side such as Roasted Cauliflower Salad with Quick-Pickled Raisins (page 62) for a hearty meal. Any leftover soldiers make a crunchy next-day snack (leave them out covered with a paper napkin), or break them into croutons.

FOR THE SOUP

2 tablespoons extra-virgin olive oil

1 medium onion, finely chopped

2 cloves garlic, minced

2 cups unsalted chicken stock

1 cup lightly packed Very Slow Tomatoes (page 25), chopped

1 can (28 ounces) diced tomatoes, preferably fire-roasted, undrained

1½ tablespoons harissa paste

1 teaspoon ground cumin

1 teaspoon paprika

FOR THE NAAN SOLDIERS

12 naan rounds or other thickish flatbreads (about 12 ounces)

2 tablespoons za'atar spice mix

3 tablespoons extra-virgin olive oil

FOR FINISHING

½ cup heavy cream

Kosher salt and freshly ground black pepper to taste

½ cup crumbled feta cheese

Your best extra-virgin olive oil, for garnish

1 To prepare the soup, heat a large, heavy saucepan over medium heat. Add the oil to the pan and swirl to coat. Add the onion and garlic; sauté until soft, about 4 minutes. Add the stock, both kinds of tomatoes, the harissa, cumin, and paprika; let bubble for 10 minutes.

2 Remove the soup from the heat and let cool to allow the flavors to marry, 1 hour (it will still be warm).

3 To prepare the naan soldiers, arrange an oven rack 6 inches below the broiler. Preheat the broiler to low.

4 Cut each naan round into 5 strips, each about ¾ inch wide (if using a larger piece of naan, cut soldiers to a handy length). Arrange the soldiers on two sheet pans. Mix the za'atar and olive oil in a small bowl; brush some of the oil mixture on each soldier, brushing and dabbing it on one side.

5 Place one sheet pan of the naan under the broiler and broil it, watching like a hawk after 1 minute, and remove when the soldiers are a toasty brown, about 2 minutes. Repeat with the second sheet pan of naan. Brush the soldiers with the remaining oil mixture.

6 When the soldiers are done, put the still-warm soup into a blender, add the cream, and blend on medium speed until the soup is smooth but still has texture—not completely creamy—about 15 seconds. Reheat the soup over medium heat until thoroughly heated, about 5 minutes, adding a bit more stock if it seems too thick. Season with salt and pepper. Ladle the soup into 4 bowls. Top each serving with 2 tablespoons feta and a drizzle of your best olive oil. Serve with 6 soldiers per bowl, with the rest of the soldiers in a basket in the center of the table.

Harissa's rich complexity brings depth to a simple soup.

Punched-Up Butternut Bisque
with Microwave-Crisped Prosciutto

ACTIVE TIME: 30 minutes
TOTAL TIME: 50 minutes
SERVES 4

Global Pantry Ingredient

Ají Amarillo Paste,
see Try This!, *p. 54*

Shopping Intel
Cheap Prosciutto Is A-OK.
When you're serving prosciutto as beautifully silky, buttery uncooked ham, nuanced with terroir, go for the best Italian stuff. But when you're microwaving it for a crunchy topping, inexpensive presliced domestic prosciutto works great—in fact, it's likely better.

If butternut squash soup often disappoints because it's too sweet, this recipe changes the game. A good dose of ají amarillo paste provides a punch of South American floral heat to counterbalance the sweetness. Savory sautéed leeks are blended in for an allium backnote, and—ta-da!—crispy prosciutto goes on top at the last second to add some salty, porky goodness in every bite. A note about the heat: Two tablespoons of the chile paste is right for a nice kick, while four is for chile-heads only.

You'll see that that the prosciutto is quickly crisped in the microwave, an underutilized kitchen tool we also deploy to crisp bacon bits for maple syrup on page 234. The same work in the oven takes much longer, though if you need to do it that way, bake on a parchment-lined sheet pan at 375°F for 12 to 15 minutes.

---

1 medium butternut squash (1½ pounds), halved lengthwise

2 tablespoons extra-virgin olive oil

1 teaspoon kosher salt

¾ teaspoon freshly ground black pepper, plus more for garnish

1 cup thinly sliced leeks

3 sprigs thyme

1 cup unsalted chicken stock

4 thin slices (½ ounce each) prosciutto

½ cup half-and-half

2 to 4 tablespoons ají amarillo paste

Toasted baguette slices, for serving (optional)

1 Preheat the oven to 450°F with a rack in the center. Line a sheet pan with aluminum foil.

2 Scoop out and discard the seeds and membranes from the squash halves. Brush the cut sides of the squash evenly with 1½ teaspoons of oil. Sprinkle with ¼ teaspoon each of salt and pepper. Arrange the squash, cut sides down, on the prepared pan. Bake until tender when pierced with a knife, 30 to 35 minutes. Remove the pan from the oven and turn the squash cut sides up. Cool slightly, about 5 minutes.

3 Meanwhile, heat the remaining 1½ tablespoons oil in a medium saucepan over medium-low heat. Add the leeks and thyme to the pan, and sprinkle with the remaining ¼ teaspoon salt. Cook until the leeks are tender and just starting to brown, about 8 minutes. Add the stock to the pan, scraping to loosen any browned bits on the bottom of the pan. Remove from the heat and let stand for 10 minutes. Discard the thyme.

4 Arrange 2 prosciutto slices on a layer of paper towels on a microwave-safe plate. Microwave on High until shriveled and crisp around the edges, 1½ to 2 minutes. Remove the prosciutto from the plate (it will crisp more as it cools). Repeat the process with the remaining 2 prosciutto slices.

5 Scoop the cooked squash from the skins and place the flesh in a blender; discard skins. Add the leek mixture, half-and-half, 2 tablespoons of ají amarillo paste, and the remaining ½ teaspoon salt and ½ teaspoon pepper. Remove the center piece from the blender lid (to allow steam to escape)

and cover the lid with a towel (to prevent splatters). Blend until completely smooth, 30 seconds to 1 minute. You may need to pause to push bigger chunks down from the top. Pour the pureed soup into the saucepan; heat over medium heat until thoroughly heated, about 2 minutes, taking care not to allow the soup to come to a boil. Whisk in more ají amarillo if you want more heat.

6 Ladle the soup evenly among 4 bowls. Garnish with additional black pepper, if desired. Lay 1 prosciutto slice atop each serving (or crumble it if you prefer).

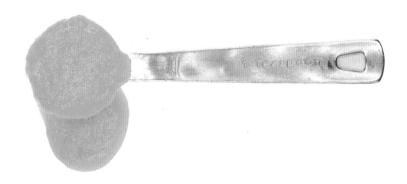

Ají amarillo paste has high, tart flavors that play against the sweetness of squash.

"Diner-Style" French Onion Soup:
An Easy and Almost One-Pot Way

ACTIVE TIME: 40 minutes
TOTAL TIME: 1 hour 40 minutes
SERVES 6

Here's a recipe that shortens the long caramelization of onions, in favor of a quicker browning reminiscent of flat-top cooking in a diner kitchen. We ditch the little onion soup crocks and finish everything in one pot—while still dishing out lots of deep, sweet onion flavor and cheesy goo. It's a loose riff on the French classic that you can get on the table in less than two hours, with much of that time being the soup doing its happy bubble on the stove. We've used two pantry umami stars—Marmite and miso—to speed the enrichment of the flavors.

---

6 tablespoons unsalted butter

4½ pounds yellow or white onions (6 to 8 large), halved and cut into thin half-moons

Hot water, as needed

3 cloves garlic, minced

1 tablespoon chopped fresh thyme

1 teaspoon Marmite

1 teaspoon white miso

½ teaspoon freshly ground black pepper

5 cups beef broth (see Flavor Booster)

½ cup dry marsala wine or full-bodied dry sherry (such as oloroso)

2 teaspoons sugar or to taste

½ teaspoon kosher salt or to taste

1 medium (12-ounce) baguette, cut into 1-inch slices

12 ounces Gruyère cheese or other hard melting cheese (such as Comté), shredded

1 Heat a large skillet *and* a Dutch oven over high heat for 3 minutes. Add 3 tablespoons butter to each; the butter should melt and sizzle and begin to smoke. Reduce the heat to medium-high, add half of the onions to each pan, and stir immediately. The onions will initially steam and exude water, then begin to fry and turn brown after about 5 minutes. Let them sit periodically and scorch a bit (but not burn), diner-style, before stirring again. Increase the heat if needed. Keep this up until the onions are quite dark brown, about 12 minutes, adding a bit of hot water if they begin to stick. Stir in the garlic (divvy it between the pans) during the last 2 to 3 minutes. Add the onions from the skillet to the Dutch oven, then stir in the thyme, Marmite, miso, black pepper, and 1 cup of broth. When the pastes are dissolved, add the remaining 4 cups broth and the marsala.

2 Reduce the heat to low and cover the Dutch oven. Adjust the heat over the next minute until you can maintain a medium bubble. Cook for 30 minutes, then uncover

Global Pantry Ingredients

Marmite, *p. 15*

Marsala, *p. 15*

Miso, *p. 16*

Key Technique

Diner-Style Onions. Rather than a very slow and gentle caramelization of such a large amount of onions, we imagine onions cooked on a flat-top of our favorite diner: scorched here and there at a higher temp, but not bitter, and doubly delicious. We use two pans here only to speed things up. With a bit of patience, you can do it in a single large Dutch oven.

Flavor Booster

Use Better Stock. Marmite and miso boost the meaty flavor. Another factor is the beef stock. After years of comparison tasting, we like low-sodium or unsalted Swanson stocks in general, but we're seeing more and more "artisan" stocks and bone broths. If you really want to splurge, buy some frozen demi-glace (extremely reduced beef stock, used in French sauces, sold in fancy food stores) and add a spoonful or two to taste. Miso and Marmite are salty, so when buying your beef broth, watch for sodium content on the labels; one fancy version contained 690 mg of sodium per cup, which (aside from being more than a quarter of the recommended daily intake) means you'd want to eliminate the extra salt added in Step 2, lest the broth become too salty.

and cook 30 minutes more. The onions should be soft; if not, boil a few minutes longer. Stir in the sugar and salt, and add more salt to taste if needed. If you want a bit more oniony sweetness, add a bit more sugar.

3 While the soup is bubbling, arrange the oven rack at a place that will accommodate the Dutch oven without touching the broiler element. Preheat the oven to 350°F. Arrange the bread slices on a sheet pan. Bake until lightly browned, about 10 minutes. Remove the bread from the oven and heat the broiler to high.

4 When the onions are soft, assemble the toasted bread slices on top of the soup to cover as much of the surface as possible. With a spoon, dunk each slice so the soup just runs across, or use a ladle to wet the tops. Spread the cheese evenly across the bread. Place the Dutch oven under the broiler. Broil until the cheese is brown and bubbly and crusty, 4 to 5 minutes.

5 Ladle the soup and cheese-topped bread into bowls. If needed, you can cut the cheese first with scissors before ladling.

Good marsala is nutty and slightly bitter, enriching the earthy onions.

Loads-of-Chicken–Flavored Soup

with Shrimpy Corn Wontons

ACTIVE TIME: 1 hour
TOTAL TIME: 1 hour
SERVES 4

Why bother making wontons at home when they're standard-issue inexpensive takeout? Because these are damn delicious, and our rotisserie chicken shortcut yields a heartier broth for the lovely wontons, which are sweet with corn and shrimp, smoky with a touch of bacon, and nutty from best-quality toasted sesame oil. Yes, the wontons involve about 45 minutes of contemplative kitchen Zen handwork (maybe enlist a partner, friends, or kids to help), but it's a simple, fun task rewarded by everyone at the table slurping and grinning at the result.

FOR THE SOUP

1 medium (2 to 3 pounds) rotisserie chicken

1 tablespoon neutral oil (such as canola)

2 carrots, diced

1 celery stalk with leaves, diced

1 medium onion, diced

2 quarts unsalted chicken stock (such as Swanson)

2 teaspoons Korean toasted sesame oil

1 teaspoon soy sauce

1 scallion, greens finely chopped, for serving

Chili crisp or chili oil, for serving

FOR THE WONTONS

1 slice Benton's bacon (or other smoky bacon), finely chopped

1 cup fresh corn kernels (about 1 ear)

1 teaspoon soy sauce

1 teaspoon Korean toasted sesame oil

½ pound frozen US-caught peeled and deveined shrimp, thawed, drained, and patted dry

1 tablespoon cornstarch, plus extra for dusting

1 scallion, finely chopped

1 package (3-inch square) wonton wrappers (at least 32 wrappers)

Salt, for cooking the wontons

1 To prepare the soup, debone the chicken, putting the bones and skin in a bowl and pulling the chicken meat into bite-size pieces. Put half of the meat in the fridge for the soup, and save the other half (in the fridge or freezer) for another use. Heat a large Dutch oven over medium heat. Add the neutral oil to the pan and swirl to coat. Add the carrots, celery, and onion; sauté 3 minutes or until soft. Add the chicken bones and skin; sauté 1 minute. Add the stock and bring to a simmer; simmer on a low bubble until the wontons are ready to cook, about 50 minutes.

Global Pantry Ingredients

Benton's Bacon, *p. 9*

Chili Crisp, *p. 10*

Korean Toasted Sesame Oil, *p. 14*

Soy Sauce, *p. 22*

Shopping Intel

Square Wonton Wrappers. The wrappers we use here are 3 inches square and found in the refrigerated section of most supermarkets, often near the tofu. (There are round wrappers in Asian markets, too, but the square ones make the shape seen here.) The wheat-flour wrappers come dusted with cornstarch and are remarkably strong and un-sticky, and will stay supple after filling for quite some time. The key to sealing them is a very firm pinch, with water as the sealant.

Freezing Intel

Wontons Freeze Well. If you make the recipe for two people, the leftover wontons can be dusted with a bit of cornstarch and put in a ziplock freezer bag or other container to freeze. Drop them frozen into boiling water—they'll need a little longer to cook than the fresh variety.

Flavor Booster

Add a Dash of Dashi. This is a chicken-based soup, but a tablespoon of Japanese dashi base—which we use in the recipe on page 88—nicely amps up the seafood flavor to echo the shrimpy wontons, if you like that sort of thing (we do).

2 To prepare the wontons, place the bacon in a small microwave-safe bowl. Microwave on High for 1 minute. Place the bacon and drippings, corn, soy sauce, sesame oil, and shrimp in a food processor; process to a paste in which you still see bits of corn and shrimp. Transfer the mixture to a medium bowl. Add the 1 tablespoon cornstarch and the scallion and mix thoroughly until completely blended.

3 Set up your wonton assembly station by dusting a sheet pan with cornstarch, filling a small bowl with water, and fetching a small basting brush. To make the wontons, put a wrapper on the counter in front of you so that it is square-shaped as you face it, not diamond shaped. Use the brush (or your fingertip) to moisten all four edges. Use a measuring spoon to put 1 slightly mounded teaspoon of filling in the center of the wrapper, then take the far side of the square and fold it toward you like a blanket, to cover the filling. Use your fingers to gently squeeze the air out from this rectangular packet, then press the wet edges together very firmly into the counter surface to seal them entirely. You will now have a half-size wonton in front of you with a bulge in the middle. Now make it into a neat little sitting-up packet by dabbing the two bottom corners with water. Pick up the packet and bring the wet corners together and pinch very firmly between your fingers to seal. Check all sides to make sure no gaps reveal filling; if you see a gap, pinch it shut. Put the wonton on the sheet pan and repeat.

4 When you've wrapped up about three quarters of the filling (at least 24 wontons), fill a large pot of water with 12 cups of water, add 1 teaspoon salt, and set it on the stove. Bring it to a boil while you finish making the wontons (if it boils before you're done, turn the heat down a bit).

5 Set the finished wontons near the stove. Use a colander to strain the broth into a large bowl (discard the solids). Clean out the soup pot and pour the broth back in it. Stir in the chicken meat and adjust the heat to low. Stir in the 2 teaspoons sesame oil and 1 teaspoon soy sauce.

6 To cook the wontons, drop them into the boiling salted water (it should be at a full boil) and cook them until they float, 3 minutes. Fish them out with a slotted spoon or spider strainer, and divide them among 4 large soup bowls. Ladle a quarter of the chicken and broth into each bowl of wontons, sprinkle with the chopped scallion, and serve with chili crisp or chili oil on the side for those who want a little heat.

7 Easy Steps to Perfect Wontons

1. Moisten all four edges of the wonton wrapper with water.

2. Use a measuring spoon to scoop up a slightly rounded teaspoon of filling.

3. Arrange the filling in the middle of the wrapper.

4. Fold the top half of the wrapper over the bottom half, then moisten the two bottom corners of the wrapper.

5. Bring the two moistened corners together and pinch firmly to seal.

6. Press all seams firmly to ensure the wonton is completely sealed.

7. Continue filling wrappers until you use up all the filling.

Global Pantry Ingredients

Mirin, *p. 16*

Miso, *p. 16*

Shichimi Togarashi, *see Try This!, p. 137*

Soy Sauce, *p. 22*

Tahini, *p. 24*

Shopping Intel

The Noodles. The best noodles for this are authentic ramen noodles from the Sun Noodle company (with several factories in the United States), sold frozen in Asian supermarkets in 11-ounce packages, enough for two bowls. If you can't find that, or another frozen ramen noodle, substitute fresh Asian noodles such as yakisoba or even fresh wonton noodles, available refrigerated in many supermarkets, often near the produce section. Package sizes vary, and noodles might cook to different yields; aim to use no more than 1¼ cups of cooked noodles in each serving so you'll have the right broth-to-noodle ratio.

Your Japanese Pantry. We've leaned on mirin, dashi soup base, soy sauce, and miso here, all umami-boosting ingredients from fridge and pantry (and used in many of our recipes), available in most good Japanese or Asian supermarkets or online. While you're at it, buy a jar of shichimi togarashi, the red pepper spice mix found in most ramen shops, to add heat at the table.

Brilliant Bowl of Ramen Pleasure
in Less Than an Hour

ACTIVE TIME: 35 minutes
TOTAL TIME: 35 minutes
SERVES 4

Spend much time scouting shops in the back alley shops of Tokyo and Osaka and you understand that there aren't dozens of varieties of what is surely the world's favorite noodle soup—there are *thousands*, with more riffs always bubbling away. This fast take on the ramen idea (no eight-hour simmering of pork bones, leave that to the pros) borrows a technique taught to us by Rich Landau, chef of the superb vegan restaurant Vedge in Philadelphia: scorching vegetables to bring out umami for a broth (using turnips in a ramen stock base is certainly unconventional, but yummy). For richness and creamy effect, we've borrowed from a bowl Scott swooned over in Tokyo, adding sesame paste to the broth. Except for the dashi used here, which contains tuna, this is vegan; if you want vegan, look for vegan "umami" broth base, often made with seaweed.

2 teaspoons neutral oil (such as canola)

4 ounces shiitake mushrooms, sliced

4 teaspoons light soy sauce or tamari, plus more as needed

¼ cup dashi broth concentrate (such as Yamaki Kappo Shirodashi or Marukin)

2 tablespoons tahini

1 tablespoon white or red miso

1 tablespoon minced peeled fresh ginger

2 cloves garlic, coarsely chopped

½ cup hot water

½ large onion, cut into small wedges

1 turnip (about 8 ounces), cut into small wedges

3 tablespoons mirin

2 packages (11 ounces each) frozen or fresh ramen noodles, or equivalent (see Shopping Intel)

2 cups fresh bean sprouts

1½ cups fresh or frozen corn kernels

½ cup thinly sliced scallion greens

½ cup thinly cut nori (seaweed) strips (optional)

Shichimi togarashi spice mix for the table (optional)

1 Heat a wok or large heavy-bottomed saucepan over medium-high heat for 1 minute (longer if using a pot). Add the oil to the pan and swirl to coat. Add the mushrooms; stir-fry for 1 minute. Add 1 teaspoon soy sauce; cook for another minute, then remove the mushrooms from the pan. Wipe down the wok with a paper towel to remove any excess oil.

2 Bring a large pot of water to a boil over high heat; this will be for the noodles.

3 Combine the dashi concentrate, tahini, miso, ginger, and garlic in a bowl with the hot water. Heat the wok or pot over high heat to shimmering-hot and add the onion and turnip pieces. Sear on all sides, letting the wedges sit untouched on the hot metal for a minute or so before turning so that very dark sides and edges develop. When scorched on all sides, about 4½ minutes, reduce the heat, add the dashi mixture and 2¾ cups more water, and boil vigorously for 5 minutes.

4 Pour the hot dashi mixture into a blender. Remove the center piece from the blender lid (to allow steam to escape); cover the lid with a towel (to prevent splatters). Blend on high speed until very smooth, 1 to 1½ minutes. Return the pureed dashi mixture to the wok, bring it to a simmer over low heat, and add the remaining 3 teaspoons soy sauce and the mirin. Adjust the broth to taste—if you like it saltier, add more soy.

5 Place the noodles in the boiling water and stir them with tongs to separate them and prevent them from sticking. Cook until al dente, about 4 minutes (this will depend on the type of noodle).

6 As the noodles cook, add the bean sprouts and corn to your simmering broth. When the noodles are done, drain them and divide them evenly among 4 large soup bowls; ladle the broth and vegetables evenly over the noodles. Sprinkle the scallions on one side of each bowl and sprinkle the nori, if using, on the other. Top with the mushrooms. Sprinkle with shichimi togarashi, if desired.

Lightnin' Fast Weeknight
Skillet Chili

ACTIVE TIME: 23 minutes
TOTAL TIME: 23 minutes
SERVES 4

Yes, you can have a savory, rich pot of chili in under 25 minutes. *And* a chili that has none of the dusty, morose, chili-powder flavor that comes with some spice-packet shortcut recipes. Premade pico de gallo brings a fresh, vibrant character. We bring out several other big-flavor guns: canned chipotles in adobo, canned fire-roasted tomatoes, and a fresh poblano.

---

1 tablespoon canola oil

1 cup finely chopped onion

3 cloves garlic, minced

1 medium poblano pepper, seeded and chopped

½ pound 90% lean ground beef

½ pound Mexican chorizo

1 teaspoon smoked paprika

1 teaspoon ground cumin

½ teaspoon kosher salt

1 cup fresh pico de gallo

¾ cup unsalted beef or chicken stock

1 tablespoon chopped canned chipotle chiles plus 1 tablespoon of adobo sauce

1 can (14.5 ounces) fire-roasted diced tomatoes, undrained

1 can (15.5 ounces) reduced-sodium kidney beans, rinsed and drained

⅓ cup sour cream or crumbled cheese such as queso fresco, for topping (optional)

Chopped scallions, for topping (optional)

Chopped fresh cilantro, for topping (optional)

Corn chips or crumbled tortilla chips, for topping (optional)

1 Heat a 10-inch cast-iron skillet or other straight-sided skillet over medium-high heat. Add the oil to the pan and swirl to coat. Add the onion, garlic, and poblano; sauté until softened slightly, 3 minutes. Crumble the beef and chorizo into the pan; sprinkle the meat with the paprika, cumin, and salt. Cook until the meat is browned, stirring frequently to crumble, about 5 minutes.

2 Stir in the pico de gallo, stock, chipotles, adobo sauce, tomatoes, and beans. Bring the mixture to a boil. Reduce the heat to low, and simmer for 5 minutes. Ladle the chili into bowls and top with your preferred toppings.

Global Pantry Ingredients

Chipotles in Adobo, *p. 10*
Mexican Chorizo, *p. 15*
Smoked Paprika, *p. 22*

Flavor Booster
Perkier Pepper. Instead of a bell pepper, we use a poblano. The dark green pepper (an ancho before it's dried) offers more depth, encompassing fruity, bitter, and sometimes fiery notes.

Shopping Intel
Fresh Is Best. Pico de gallo is a chopped mixture of tomato, cilantro, jalapeño, and lime, less wet than salsa, and the fresh stuff—usually found in the refrigerated part of the produce section in good supermarkets—is leaps and bounds better than anything you'll find in the inner aisles.

One-Pot Green Chili
with Rich, Falling-Apart Pork

ACTIVE TIME: 45 minutes
TOTAL TIME: 3 hours 30 minutes
SERVES 6

Many recipes for this satisfying Mexican-themed stew—a state favorite in New Mexico and Colorado—involve blister-roasting and peeling tomatillos and chiles on several sheet pans, but we wanted to see if a one-pot version would do it justice. Job done: The long, slow cook yields succulent pork, tangy gravy, and lovely heat, while Marmite, of all things, adds umami depth. Serve with warm tortillas (we love the corn variety for this), Mexican-style crema (see Try This! on page 94), chopped fresh jalapeños, and chopped cilantro for a Sunday football treat or a winter-chill comfort dinner.

---

3 tablespoons neutral oil (such as canola)

4 pounds boneless pork shoulder, cut into 1½-inch cubes, or 4½ pounds country-style pork ribs, deboned and cut into 1½-inch cubes

2 bunches cilantro, 1 whole, 1 chopped

2 jars (16 ounces each) roasted salsa verde or salsa verde (we like medium heat salsa, such as Herdez)

3 medium onions, quartered, and cut into ½-inch slices

1 large head garlic, cloves peeled and chopped

2 teaspoons Marmite

1 tablespoon ground cumin

1 teaspoon kosher salt

2 packs (13 ounces each) frozen, chopped, and roasted Hatch or other mild green chiles, thawed

Warm corn tortillas, crema, and chopped jalapeños, for serving

1 Preheat the oven to 275°F with the rack placed in the center.

2 Heat the oil in a large Dutch oven over medium-high heat. Batch-cook the pork so that the meat is separated in the pan, and brown thoroughly on one side, about 4 minutes. Flip it with a spatula and brown equally well on the opposite side, about 4 minutes more. You want to get a good crust on the meat (without burning it)—the flavor payoff is huge. Remove the pork from the pan.

3 While the pork browns, combine the bunch of whole cilantro with 1 jar of salsa verde in a blender or food processor and puree.

4 When the meat is done, add the onions and garlic to the pan and cook, stirring, to deglaze all the brown bits in the pan and

Global Pantry Ingredient

Marmite, *p. 15*

Shopping Intel

Seeking Salsa Verde. There are a zillion fancy and pricey green salsas, but all you need here is an inexpensive bottled variety whose first ingredient is tomatillos—Herdez from Mexico, widely available, works perfectly. We used the medium, but the heat-sensitive can substitute mild.

Heat in the Freezer. Chopped, roasted green chiles are found in the frozen-food section of many supermarkets. Hatch chiles are favored, but other varieties are available. Look for "fire-roasted" or similar claims on the label. Watch for spice levels—we used mild here, but you can find hotter. Or use five 4-ounce cans of roasted Hatch chiles found alongside other Mexican ingredients; but use half the amount of salt called for, adding more as needed at the end.

Try This!

Crema Mexicana. This belongs to a family of Mexican and Central American sour creams that vary by thickness, tang, saltiness, and color (some being colored a buttery yellow). They're luscious and can be a bit thinner than American sour cream, jiggly and shiny in the bowl. Look in the fridge sections of Hispanic markets and some national supermarkets. But check labels, for some brands have additives that are best avoided, like palm oils.

brown the onions, 2 minutes. Stir in the Marmite, cumin, and salt. Add the cilantro puree, the remaining jar of salsa verde, and the roasted chiles. Add the pork, stir, and bring the mixture to a boil. Remove from the heat.

5 Cover the pot, place the stew in the oven, and braise for 2 hours. Twenty minutes in, peek into the pot to make sure the stew is gently but not vigorously boiling; if it is boiling too hard, reduce the heat. (Keep checking every half hour.) After 2 hours, uncover the pot and continue to cook to thicken the stew, about 45 minutes.

6 Sample a piece of the meat; it should be tender and falling apart. If not, continue cooking, uncovered. When the meat is tender, remove the stew and garnish with the chopped cilantro. Serve with the tortillas, crema, and jalapeños on the side.

The added touch of salt in many silky Mexican sour creams goes perfectly with a meaty chili.

Deeply Rich Beef and Marsala Stew with Dijon Mustard

ACTIVE TIME: 37 minutes
TOTAL TIME: 3 hours
SERVES 6

The combination of properly good Sicilian marsala wine—not the cheap sweet American stuff—and best-quality Dijon mustard (one with richness and punch) yields one of the savoriest beef stews we've made. The flavor goes on and on, enveloping buttery soft chuck roast and lots of not-overcooked vegetables. On a day requiring extra comfort, spoon this over mashed potatoes; the double dose of spuds will do the trick.

---

2 tablespoons extra-virgin olive oil

2½ pounds boneless chuck roast, trimmed and cut into 1½-inch pieces

1 large onion, chopped

8 cloves garlic, smashed

2 tablespoons double-concentrated tomato paste

¾ cup dry Italian marsala wine

3 cups unsalted beef stock

5 tablespoons Dijon mustard

1 teaspoon kosher salt

1 teaspoon freshly ground black pepper

5 sprigs thyme

2 bay leaves

1 pound baby yellow potatoes, halved (or quartered if large)

12 ounces carrots, cut into 1-inch pieces

8 ounces cremini mushrooms, halved

1 Preheat the oven to 300°F with the rack arranged so that it will accommodate the Dutch oven without touching the broiler element.

2 Heat the oil in a Dutch oven over medium-high heat. Add half of the beef to the pan; cook until well browned, turning once or twice, about 8 minutes. Remove the beef from the pan and repeat the browning process with the remaining beef. Set the browned beef aside.

3 Add the onion to the pot; sauté 2 minutes. Add the garlic; sauté 1 minute. Stir in the tomato paste; cook 1 minute, stirring constantly. Stir in ½ cup marsala wine, scraping the bottom of the pan to loosen the browned bits; cook until about half of the liquid evaporates and the mixture is thickened, about 2 minutes. Stir in the browned beef, stock, mustard, salt, pepper, thyme, and bay leaves. Bring the mixture to a boil, then cover and remove from the heat.

4 Transfer the pot to the oven and braise for 1 hour.

5 Carefully remove the pot from the oven (leave the oven on) and stir in the potatoes, carrots, and mushrooms. Cover and return to the oven until the beef and vegetables are tender, about 1½ hours (it may take a few minutes more depending on the oven). Remove the pot from the oven, uncover, and stir in the remaining ¼ cup marsala wine. Discard the thyme sprigs and bay leaves before serving.

Global Pantry Ingredient

Marsala, *p. 15*

Flavor Booster
Creamy, Nose-Tingling Edge. The familiar brand of Dijon is good, but also try Maille, Inglehoffer, or Edmond Fallot brands, and if you can track down a jar of Amora in a French specialty shop (or online), you'll be using our absolute favorite—a creamy, spiky, vibrant mustard that's nonpareil in this stew.

Shopping Intel
Tomato Power in a Tube. For dishes that benefit from richness without cream, double-concentrated tomato paste is a godsend. It adds sweet tomato intensity without the thin acidity that would come from canned tomatoes. At the market, look for it near the canned tomatoes; it comes in a toothpaste-like squeezable tube.

Anchovies • Yuzu • Black Walnuts • Wondra • Sumac • Calabrian Chiles • Sorghu
Millet • Tabasco Sauce • Coconut Milk • Roasted Hazelnut Oil • Curry Leaves •
Sauce • Shrimp Paste • Worcestershire Sauce • Furikake • Sriracha • Saffron • Ban
Vinegar • Gochujang • Harissa • Marmite • Kecap Manis • Chili Crisp • Freeze-D
Strawberries • Tajín • Kimchi • Korean Toasted Sesame Oil • Dulce de Leche •
Sauce • Lemongrass • Whole Wheat Pastry Flour • Pomegranate Molasses • Mexi
Chocolate • Smoked Paprika • Chipotles in Adobo • Shichimi Togarashi • Makrut L
Leaves • Crema Mexicana • The Many Masalas • Capers • Mexican Chorizo • Mir
Oyster Sauce • Panko Breadcrumbs • Ras El Hanout • Andouille Sausage • Marsa
The Many Sambals • Benton's Bacon • Miso • Stone-Ground Grits • Tahini • Ghee • P
Sugar • Ají Amarillo Paste • Thai Curry Paste • Mustard Powder • Turmeric • Cultu
Butter • Kashmiri Mirch • Dried Porcini Mushrooms • Sweetened Condensed Mi
Anchovies • Yuzu • Black Walnuts • Wondra • Sumac • Calabrian Chiles • Sorghu
Millet • Tabasco Sauce • Coconut Milk • Roasted Hazelnut Oil • Curry Leaves •
Sauce • Shrimp Paste • Worcestershire Sauce • Furikake • Sriracha • Saffron • Ban
Vinegar • Gochujang • Harissa • Marmite • Kecap Manis • Chili Crisp • Freeze-D
Strawberries • Tajín • Kimchi • Korean Toasted Sesame Oil • Dulce de Leche •
Sauce • Lemongrass • Whole Wheat Pastry Flour • Pomegranate Molasses • Mexi
Chocolate • Smoked Paprika • Chipotles in Adobo • Shichimi Togarashi • Makrut L
Leaves • Crema Mexicana • The Many Masalas • Capers • Mexican Chorizo • Mir
Oyster Sauce • Panko Breadcrumbs • Ras El Hanout • Andouille Sausage • Marsa
The Many Sambals • Benton's Bacon • Miso • Stone-Ground Grits • Tahini • Ghee • P
Sugar • Ají Amarillo Paste • Thai Curry Paste • Mustard Powder • Turmeric • Cultu
Butter • Kashmiri Mirch • Dried Porcini Mushrooms • Sweetened Condensed Mi
Anchovies • Yuzu • Black Walnuts • Wondra • Sumac • Calabrian Chiles • Sorghu
Millet • Tabasco Sauce • Coconut Milk • Roasted Hazelnut Oil • Curry Leaves • I
Sauce • Shrimp Paste • Worcestershire Sauce • Furikake • Sriracha • Saffron • Bany
Vinegar • Gochujang • Harissa • Marmite • Kecap Manis • Chili Crisp • Freeze-Dr
Strawberries • Tajín • Kimchi • Korean Toasted Sesame Oil • Dulce de Leche •
Sauce • Lemongrass • Whole Wheat Pastry Flour • Pomegranate Molasses • Mexi
Chocolate • Smoked Paprika • Chipotles in Adobo • Shichimi Togarashi • Makrut Li
Leaves • Crema Mexicana • The Many Masalas • Capers • Mexican Chorizo • Mir
Oyster Sauce • Panko Breadcrumbs • Ras El Hanout • Andouille Sausage • Marsa
The Many Sambals • Benton's Bacon • Miso • Stone-Ground Grits • Tahini • Ghee • Pa
Sugar • Ají Amarillo Paste • Thai Curry Paste • Mustard Powder • Turmeric • Cultu
Butter • Kashmiri Mirch • Dried Porcini Mushrooms • Sweetened Condensed Mill

Rich and Hearty **Beef** and **Lamb**

Grilled Short Ribs: The Beefiest Beef in Beef Town, Part 1 / 98

Chuck Roast with Root Vegetables and Oyster Sauce Gravy / 101

BBQ Flanken-Cut Short Ribs with Garlicky Sweet Soy Glaze / 102

Damn Fine Meatloaf with Spicy Onion Glaze / 104

Hamburger Steaks with Rich Onion Gravy / 105

Ghee-Basted, Pan-Fried Grass-Fed Strip Steak: The Beefiest Beef in Beef Town, Part 2 / 106

Lamb Kebabs with Fragrant Pilaf / 107

Key Technique

Shortcut to Char. The beef grills for only a short time, 10 to 15 minutes, depending on the intensity of your grill. The brown sugar in the rub yields a hearty char in a short time.

Shopping Intel

Beautiful Beef in Bulk. These boneless short ribs may become your favorite "steak." They're intensely meaty, well marbled, and—when cooked to medium-rare—juicy and steak-like. Our favorite place to buy them is Costco. They're always beautifully marbled. They come in big quantities, of course, but you can cook extra, freeze extra, or save extra to use in a stew or braise, or thinly slice the raw meat for a stir-fry.

Grilled Short Ribs
The Beefiest Beef in Beef Town, Part 1

ACTIVE TIME: 10 minutes
TOTAL TIME: 50 minutes
SERVES 6

Brushing beef with umami-rich fish sauce before grilling is a flavor trick Ann came up with to amp up the beefiness and deepen all the savory goodness. A little brown sugar balances the salt. This is a rib purist's dish—no sauce slathered on or offered on the side, so serve it with something saucy like the Buttery Creamed Corn on page 262 or the Broiled Leeks with Pine Nut Sauce (page 242).

1½ tablespoons fish sauce

4 boneless beef short ribs (8 ounces each)

2 tablespoons brown sugar

2 large cloves garlic, grated on a Microplane

Neutral oil (such as canola), for coating the grill rack

¼ teaspoon flaky sea salt

1 Brush the fish sauce over all sides of the beef. Combine the brown sugar and garlic into a paste in a small bowl; rub the garlic paste over all sides of the beef. Let stand at room temperature while the grill heats, 20 to 45 minutes depending on the grill.

2 Heat your gas grill to medium-high (450°F to 475°F) or prepare your coals to maintain medium-high heat (gas will take 20 to 30 minutes; charcoal will take about 45 minutes).

3 Oil your grill rack and place the beef on it. Grill, flipping beef every 2 minutes, until a thermometer inserted in the thickest part of the ribs registers 125°F to 130°F, 10 to 12 minutes (this may take longer on some grills). Remove the beef from the grill; let the beef stand for 5 minutes, then slice diagonally across the grain. Arrange the slices on a platter; sprinkle with the flaky salt.

Chuck Roast
with Root Vegetables and Oyster Sauce Gravy

ACTIVE TIME: 28 minutes
TOTAL TIME: 4 hours 15 minutes
SERVES 6

Global Pantry Ingredient

Oyster Sauce, *p. 16*

Avoid This Mistake
No More Mushy Vegetables.
If you're resigned to soggy stews, the result here is a revelation. Meat of the chuck variety takes much longer than vegetables to tenderize, so we give it a head start. The vegetables are added only in the last hour or so.

From the moment the meat starts to brown on the stove, the kitchen fills with beefy aromas. The oyster sauce in the braising liquid kicks the effect up tenfold as the dish develops in the oven. The meat collapses into tenderness, the sauce melds into the stewy richness. This is perfect, simple, cool- and cold-weather comfort.

2 teaspoons kosher salt

1½ teaspoons freshly ground black pepper

1 boneless chuck roast (3 pounds)

2 tablespoons olive oil or canola oil

1½ cups unsalted beef stock

¼ cup oyster sauce

4 thyme sprigs

2 bay leaves

2 large onions, halved vertically and cut vertically into thick slices

6 cloves garlic, minced

1½ pounds Yukon Gold potatoes, unpeeled and cut into 2-inch chunks or wedges

1½ pounds turnips, cut into 2-inch chunks or wedges

1½ pounds carrots, cut into 2-inch-long pieces (any really thick pieces halved lengthwise)

1 Preheat the oven to 325°F with the rack placed in the center.

2 Heat a large Dutch oven over medium-high heat. Sprinkle ¾ teaspoon of salt and ½ teaspoon of pepper over the top of the roast; sprinkle the bottom with ¾ teaspoon of salt and ½ teaspoon of pepper. Add the oil to the pan and swirl to coat. Add the roast to the pan; cook until well browned on the bottom, about 5 minutes. Turn the roast over and cook until well browned, about 5 minutes.

3 Stir together the stock and oyster sauce in a 2-cup measuring cup. Pour the mixture over the browned roast in the Dutch oven, and tuck the thyme sprigs and bay leaves into the liquid. Scatter the onions and garlic over the roast. Continue to cook over medium-high heat until the liquid boils, 15 seconds to 1 minute, then cover the pot and place in the oven. Braise for 2 hours 45 minutes.

4 Remove the pot from the oven, uncover, and top the roast with the potatoes, turnips, and carrots. Cover the pot, return to the oven, and cook until the vegetables are tender when pierced with a knife, 1 hour to 1 hour 15 minutes.

5 Using long tongs, remove the roast to a large platter. This is a little tricky, and the roast will likely fall apart, but you'll need it in pieces to serve it anyway. Gently stir the vegetables into the cooking liquid; discard the thyme sprigs and bay leaves. Sprinkle the vegetables with the remaining ½ teaspoon salt and ½ teaspoon pepper; toss again gently to combine. Arrange the vegetables on the platter with the roast, or return the roast to the pot with the vegetables and serve.

Global Pantry Ingredients

Fish Sauce, *p. 11*

Kecap Manis, *p. 13*

Korean Toasted Sesame Oil, *p. 14*

Sriracha, *p. 23*

Shopping Intel

Flat Flanken Ribs. Unlike English-cut short ribs, flanken-style ones (aka cross-cut ribs) are sliced across the bones, so each rib contains some small, thin, cross-section bone pieces. The cut is a popular Korean barbecue option, so you'll have the best luck finding it at Asian markets that specialize in Korean foods. A stand-alone butcher may cut them for you. We also sometimes see them at Whole Foods.

BBQ Flanken-Cut Short Ribs
with Garlicky Sweet Soy Glaze

ACTIVE TIME: 6 minutes
TOTAL TIME: 36 minutes
SERVES 4

To use technical language, Ann's kids and husband went bonkers over these ribs, savoring their chewy texture and eat-with-your-hands fun. They're deeply beefy, with a glaze that's sweet, sticky, a little spicy, and very garlicky, from a trio of flavor juggernauts: kecap manis, sriracha, and fish sauce. We like to serve these with Asian rice (especially Korean new crop rice), kimchi, and crisp, thinly sliced cucumbers sprinkled with sesame seeds.

½ cup kecap manis

2 tablespoons rice vinegar

1 tablespoon Korean sesame oil

1 tablespoon fish sauce

1 teaspoon sriracha

3 medium cloves garlic, grated on a Microplane

2 pounds flanken-cut short ribs

Neutral oil (such as canola), for coating the grill rack

1 Heat your gas grill to medium-high (450°F to 475°F) or prepare your coals to maintain medium-high heat (gas will take 20 to 30 minutes; charcoal will take about 45 minutes).

2 Meanwhile whisk together the kecap manis, vinegar, sesame oil, fish sauce, sriracha, and garlic in a medium bowl. Place the ribs in a shallow dish or a large ziplock plastic bag. Add ½ cup of the kecap manis mixture and toss well to coat. Let stand at room temperature while the grill heats.

3 Place the remaining ¼ cup kecap manis mixture in a small bowl. Coat a grill rack with canola (or other neutral) oil. Remove the ribs from the marinade with tongs, shaking off and discarding the excess, and place them on the prepared rack. Grill, flipping and basting occasionally with the sauce in the bowl, until well-marked and lightly charred, about 10 minutes. Serve immediately.

Brilliant Leftovers

Spaghetti and Meatloaf. Here's a fantastic way to get a second meal out of this meatloaf if you double the recipe. Cut cold leftover meatloaf into 1-inch cubes, lightly dredge in all-purpose flour or rice flour, and pan-fry in olive oil to get a bit of crispness. Pour a very good unsweetened tomato ragù into the pan (Rao's is perfect), stir, and serve on spaghetti with a good grated Parmesan and crushed red pepper flakes. Half a loaf makes enough for four people.

Damn Fine Meatloaf
with Spicy Onion Glaze

ACTIVE TIME: 15 minutes
TOTAL TIME: 1 hour 15 minutes
SERVES 6

This is a succulent meatloaf with loads of savory flavor from an elixir of oyster sauce, Worcestershire, and soy. The onions in the topping are slightly scorched for added diner-style flavor, then mixed with ketchup and a good dose of sriracha for discernable heat along with tomatoey sweetness. Double the recipe for sandwich leftovers and a next-day spaghetti dinner (see Brilliant Leftovers).

FOR THE TOPPING

1 tablespoon canola or other neutral oil
1 medium onion, finely chopped
½ cup ketchup
¼ cup sriracha

FOR THE MEATLOAF

1 pound 80% lean ground beef
1 pound ground pork
1 cup panko breadcrumbs
½ cup ketchup
2 tablespoons oyster sauce
1 teaspoon garlic powder
1 teaspoon ground sage
2 teaspoons soy sauce
2 teaspoons Worcestershire sauce
2 large eggs, lightly beaten
Cooking spray

1 Preheat the oven to 325°F with the rack placed in the center.

2 To prepare the topping, heat the oil in a medium skillet over medium-high heat. Add the onion and cook, stirring occasionally, until the onion bits are browning or scorching about their edges, 5 to 6 minutes. Remove the pan from the heat. Stir in the ketchup and sriracha until well mixed.

3 To prepare the meatloaf, place the beef and pork in a large bowl. Top with the panko, ketchup, oyster sauce, garlic powder, ground sage, soy sauce, Worcestershire sauce, and eggs. Work the ingredients into the meat with your hands until thoroughly mixed but not pasty.

4 Coat a deep 9 × 5-inch loaf pan with cooking spray. Add the meat mixture to the pan, gently forcing it down to eliminate air pockets. Spread the topping evenly over the meat mixture. If your pan is smaller, reserve some of the meat to make a meatball or burger patty. Bake until an instant-read thermometer registers 155°F at the center of the meatloaf, 50 to 55 minutes. Remove from the oven and let stand for 10 minutes.

5 Carefully tilt the pan over a double layer of paper towels to drain any liquid. Cut the meatloaf into 6 thick slices (you can do this in the pan or transfer the meatloaf to a platter, using two spatulas to lift it out). Serve hot.

Hamburger Steaks
with Rich Onion Gravy

ACTIVE TIME: 30 minutes
TOTAL TIME: 30 minutes
SERVES 4

You're on a long back-roads drive—in Kansas, Mississippi, or Idaho. You're weary and neck-sore, the sun has set, and you're long past likely to find a good dinner. Then you spot a diner whose sign promises homestyle cooking. Remarkably, today's special is this, made of hand-formed "steaks" and flat-top browned onions. The meat has a seared crust; the gravy, thickened with Wondra (see Try This!), is a silky soliloquy about savory deliciousness. Well, that's the dream. The reality is that at least it's super-simple to make this plate of comfort at home. Mashed potatoes are legally mandated for a side dish (we like to run boiled, very tender, peeled Yukon Golds through a ricer and mix with warmed whole milk and a good bit of melted salted butter). Soft white dinner rolls wouldn't be a bad idea, either, for sopping. Maybe a soda, and fresh pie for dessert. All-American, yet global, too, what with the miso and panko.

1 pound 90% lean ground beef (preferably grass-fed)

¼ cup panko breadcrumbs

½ teaspoon kosher salt

½ teaspoon freshly ground black pepper

1 large egg, lightly beaten

3 tablespoons canola oil

1 medium onion, thinly sliced into rings

1 cup unsalted beef stock

2 tablespoons white miso

1 tablespoon Wondra flour (see Try This!)

1 Place the beef in a large bowl. Add the panko, salt, pepper, and egg. Mix well with your hands until thoroughly combined. Divide the mixture into 4 equal portions; shape each into a ½-inch-thick patty.

2 Heat a large cast-iron skillet over medium-high heat. Add 1 tablespoon of oil to the pan and swirl to coat. Add the patties to the pan. Cook until a nice crust forms, about 4 minutes, then turn with a spatula and repeat on the other side. Remove the patties from the pan.

3 Reduce the heat to medium. Add the remaining 2 tablespoons oil to the pan and swirl to coat. Add the onion; cook, stirring occasionally, until browned and soft, about 8 minutes.

4 Whisk together the stock, miso, and flour in a medium bowl until smooth. Pour over the onions in the pan. Bring to a boil; cook, stirring frequently, until thickened, 2 to 3 minutes. Nestle the patties into the gravy and cook until thoroughly heated, 2 to 3 minutes. Serve immediately with your favorite sides.

Global Pantry Ingredients

Miso, *p. 16*
Panko Breadcrumbs, *p. 17*
Wondra, *see Try This!*

Flavor Booster

Beef Up the Beefiness. A couple of tablespoons of white miso in the gravy takes it from mildly beefy to "OMG, that tastes like a whole side of beef concentrated into my skillet."

Try This!

Wondra. This is a one-trick pantry pony dating to 1963, but what a trick it is: "Pre-gelatinized" flour doesn't lump when stirred into liquids to thicken gravies, sauces, and soups, and yields a more flour-based mouthfeel than you'll get from, say, non-wheat thickeners like cornstarch. Look for the old-timey blue cardboard cylinder in supermarkets.

Wondra has a slightly gritty texture but magically dissolves without lumps.

Technique Tip

Sear Well and Don't Overcook. We start the steak stovetop to get a great sear and then pop it in the oven to finish cooking with gentler heat. A digital probe thermometer is your best insurance against an overcooked steak.

Shopping Intel

The Deal with Grass-Fed. Grass-fed beef is available at Whole Foods, increasingly at good meat counters in supermarkets, and from small butchers who focus on provenance. The standards for defining and certifying grass-fed beef vary, but generally the animal, after weaning, lives on foraged grasses rather than supplied food and isn't fattened on grains before slaughter. Grass-fed beef can be stronger in flavor but also leaner and tougher.

Cleanup Tip

Things Get Spattery. Pan-frying and basting are super-easy but generate enthusiastic spatters, so we move unneeded countertop items away from the stove for easy wiping up after and put the vent fan on its highest setting. The pan can smoke in the oven, too, so be ready to fetch it with sturdy mitts quickly after opening the oven door. And see the safety note about the hot pan in Step 3.

Ghee-Basted, Pan-Fried Grass-Fed Strip Steak
The Beefiest Beef in Beef Town, Part 2

ACTIVE TIME: 25 minutes
TOTAL TIME: 35 minutes
SERVES 4

When we were at *Cooking Light*, we bought a grass-fed steer from an environmentally conscious rancher. After it was butchered, the test kitchen experimented with all the cuts, figuring out optimal prep for meat that was much leaner than grain-finished beef. For strip steak, we settled on the classic restaurant-kitchen technique of pan-frying and butter-basting, which doesn't add much fat but does add much flavor. Here, funky-beefy ghee is swapped for butter, elevating the flavor beautifully.

---

1 grass-fed strip steak, about 20 ounces, at least 1½ inches thick

1 teaspoon kosher salt, plus extra as needed

2 tablespoons ghee

1 teaspoon finely chopped fresh rosemary

Freshly ground black pepper

1 Preheat the oven to 400°F with the rack placed in the center. Season the steak on both sides with the salt.

2 Heat a large cast-iron skillet over high heat for 3 minutes, or until you see the air over the pan shimmering. Add the ghee and swirl it around the pan to coat. Add the steak to the pan; cook until nicely browned, about 3 minutes. Flip it over and cook until nicely browned on the other side, another 3 minutes. Reduce the heat to medium-high and begin basting the meat by tilting the pan to spoon up ghee and pouring the ghee over the meat. Flip the steak a few times and continue basting for 6 minutes. If using a digital probe thermometer, insert it into the steak and put the pan in the oven.

3 Cook the steak in the oven until it reaches an internal temperature of 120°F (for medium-rare), about 10 minutes—possibly longer or shorter depending on your desired degree of doneness. Carefully remove the pan from the oven (it will be very hot!) and place it on the stovetop. *Put your oven mitt over the pan's handle to remind you that it's hot.* Transfer the steak to a cutting board.

4 Let the steak rest for 10 minutes. While it rests, add the rosemary to the hot pan and stir. Slice the steak against the grain and sprinkle with additional salt to taste and a few turns of fresh black pepper; drizzle the rosemary ghee from the pan over the slices.

Lamb Kebabs
with Fragrant Pilaf

ACTIVE TIME: 55 minutes
TOTAL TIME: 4 hours
SERVES 4

This sublime dish was Scott's favorite when he was a hungry teen living in Kabul: aromatic rice, dotted with sweet raisins and pine nuts, eaten with lamb that has big garlic oomph and char from the grill. This recipe is elevated by glorious saffron and made even meatier with ghee. Traditionally, kebabs made with meat from muttony fat-tailed sheep are grilled with extra bits of sizzling fat on the skewer. We use a cheaper, fattier lamb cut for a similar effect.

FOR THE LAMB

4 large cloves garlic, peeled

1 cup plain, tangy, thick full-fat Greek yogurt (no wimpy yogurt allowed)

1 teaspoon ground coriander

½ teaspoon kosher salt

1½ pounds bone-in lamb shoulder blade chops or other inexpensive lamb cut, cut into rough ¾-inch cubes

FOR THE PILAF

1 cup uncooked basmati rice

¾ teaspoon kosher salt

½ cup golden raisins

Very hot or boiling water, for soaking the raisins

2 tablespoons ghee (or butter if you don't have ghee)

2 medium carrots, cut into thin strips about 1½ inches long

1 medium onion, cut vertically into thin strips about 1½ inches long

½ teaspoon ground cumin

¼ teaspoon dried turmeric

¼ teaspoon ground cardamom

1 pinch saffron

Extra-virgin olive oil, for drizzling

Neutral oil (such as canola), for oiling the grill rack

¼ cup toasted pine nuts or toasted slivered almonds (see page 26)

1 To prepare the lamb, use a fine Microplane grater, garlic press, or mortar and pestle to produce a garlic paste. Combine the paste with the yogurt, coriander, and the salt in a large bowl to make a thick marinade. Add the lamb cubes and mix with your hands or a spoon until completely coated. Press the meat down into the bottom of the bowl and press a layer of plastic wrap on the surface of the meat to limit its exposure to the air. Marinate in the refrigerator for 3 hours.

2 Start preparing the pilaf when the lamb goes into the refrigerator. Place the rice in a fine-mesh strainer and rinse under cold water for 15 seconds, stirring with your fingers. Then drain the rice for 15 seconds, tapping the strainer on the edge of the sink to get as much water out as possible. Combine the rice, 1¼ cups water, and ½ teaspoon of salt in a small saucepan over medium-high heat. Bring to a boil, then reduce the heat to low, cover, and simmer until the liquid is absorbed and the rice is tender, 15 minutes. Remove from the heat

Just a few of these threads will transform a dish.

and let stand, covered, for 10 minutes. (If using a rice cooker, combine the rice, water, and salt and cook on the white rice setting.) When the rice is done, fluff with a fork and set aside at room temperature to cool.

3 Place the raisins in a medium bowl and add very hot or boiling water to cover; let stand at room temperature to plump.

4 Heat a medium skillet over medium heat. Add the ghee and heat until it melts. Add the carrots and onion to the pan; cook, stirring occasionally, until the vegetables begin to soften and the onion begins to become translucent, 2 minutes. Remove from the heat; stir in the cumin, turmeric, cardamom, and remaining ¼ teaspoon salt. Take the pinch of saffron between your finger and thumb and crush it by rolling it between your fingertips, letting the bits fall into the mixture. Drain the raisins and stir them into the mixture; cover the pan and set aside.

5 About 1 hour and 15 minutes before serving, preheat the oven to 300°F with the rack placed in the center. If using bamboo skewers, soak them in a pan of water.

6 As the oven heats, combine the rice and the onion-carrot mixture in an ovenproof casserole with a lid, or a Dutch oven, and stir thoroughly. Or, if your skillet is ovenproof and has a lid, stir the rice into the vegetable mixture in the skillet. Drizzle with a bit of olive oil, cover the pan with the lid (or aluminum foil, if you don't have a lid), and place the dish in the oven. Bake until the mixture is thoroughly heated and the flavors have married, 30 minutes to 1 hour.

7 About 30 to 45 minutes before cooking time, heat your gas grill to high (500°F to 600°F) or prepare your coals to maintain medium-high heat (gas will take 25 to 35 minutes; charcoal will take about 45 minutes). If using coals, when they are ready, spread them around the edge of the grill.

8 Remove the lamb from the fridge and, with the marinade still clinging to it, arrange 4 pieces on each skewer with the pieces touching each other and bunched toward the tip so each has a long handle; you should have at least 12 skewers. Place the skewers on a sheet pan and drizzle with olive oil on both sides.

9 Oil the grill rack with canola (or other neutral) oil. Place the meat part of the skewers over the heat, allowing the rest of the sticks to protrude over the side (the naked sticks can catch fire if they sit directly over the heat for too long). Grill with the lid open for 4 minutes or so until one side of the meat is charred about the edges, then turn. Continue to grill and turn until all parts are charred about the edges (if the kebabs stick, slide a metal spatula underneath them to loosen). Taste a piece—it should be medium rare or medium, depending on your taste. Total grill time is 8 to 12 minutes, depending on your heat source and how charred you like your meat (we like a good bit of char here). Remove to a serving platter.

10 Heap the rice on a platter and top with pine nuts. Serve with the kebabs.

Anchovies • Yuzu • Black Walnuts • Wondra • Sumac • Calabrian Chiles • Sorghu
Millet • Tabasco Sauce • Coconut Milk • Roasted Hazelnut Oil • Curry Leaves •
Sauce • Shrimp Paste • Worcestershire Sauce • Furikake • Sriracha • Saffron • Bany
Vinegar • Gochujang • Harissa • Marmite • Kecap Manis • Chili Crisp • Freeze-D
Strawberries • Tajín • Kimchi • Korean Toasted Sesame Oil • Dulce de Leche •
Sauce • Lemongrass • Whole Wheat Pastry Flour • Pomegranate Molasses • Mexi
Chocolate • Smoked Paprika • Chipotles in Adobo • Shichimi Togarashi • Makrut L
Leaves • Crema Mexicana • The Many Masalas • Capers • Mexican Chorizo • Mir
Oyster Sauce • Panko Breadcrumbs • Ras El Hanout • Andouille Sausage • Marsa
The Many Sambals • Benton's Bacon • Miso • Stone-Ground Grits • Tahini • Ghee • P,
Sugar • Ají Amarillo Paste • Thai Curry Paste • Mustard Powder • Turmeric • Cultu
Butter • Kashmiri Mirch • Dried Porcini Mushrooms • Sweetened Condensed Mi
Anchovies • Yuzu • Black Walnuts • Wondra • Sumac • Calabrian Chiles • Sorghu
Millet • Tabasco Sauce • Coconut Milk • Roasted Hazelnut Oil • Curry Leaves •
Sauce • Shrimp Paste • Worcestershire Sauce • Furikake • Sriracha • Saffron • Bany
Vinegar • Gochujang • Harissa • Marmite • Kecap Manis • Chili Crisp • Freeze-D
Strawberries • Tajín • Kimchi • Korean Toasted Sesame Oil • Dulce de Leche •
Sauce • Lemongrass • Whole Wheat Pastry Flour • Pomegranate Molasses • Mexi
Chocolate • Smoked Paprika • Chipotles in Adobo • Shichimi Togarashi • Makrut L
Leaves • Crema Mexicana • The Many Masalas • Capers • Mexican Chorizo • Mir
Oyster Sauce • Panko Breadcrumbs • Ras El Hanout • Andouille Sausage • Marsa
The Many Sambals • Benton's Bacon • Miso • Stone-Ground Grits • Tahini • Ghee • P,
Sugar • Ají Amarillo Paste • Thai Curry Paste • Mustard Powder • Turmeric • Cultu
Butter • Kashmiri Mirch • Dried Porcini Mushrooms • Sweetened Condensed Mi
Anchovies • Yuzu • Black Walnuts • Wondra • Sumac • Calabrian Chiles • Sorghu
Millet • Tabasco Sauce • Coconut Milk • Roasted Hazelnut Oil • Curry Leaves •
Sauce • Shrimp Paste • Worcestershire Sauce • Furikake • Sriracha • Saffron • Bany
Vinegar • Gochujang • Harissa • Marmite • Kecap Manis • Chili Crisp • Freeze-D
Strawberries • Tajín • Kimchi • Korean Toasted Sesame Oil • Dulce de Leche •
Sauce • Lemongrass • Whole Wheat Pastry Flour • Pomegranate Molasses • Mexi
Chocolate • Smoked Paprika • Chipotles in Adobo • Shichimi Togarashi • Makrut L
Leaves • Crema Mexicana • The Many Masalas • Capers • Mexican Chorizo • Mir
Oyster Sauce • Panko Breadcrumbs • Ras El Hanout • Andouille Sausage • Marsa
The Many Sambals • Benton's Bacon • Miso • Stone-Ground Grits • Tahini • Ghee • Pa
Sugar • Ají Amarillo Paste • Thai Curry Paste • Mustard Powder • Turmeric • Cultu
Butter • Kashmiri Mirch • Dried Porcini Mushrooms • Sweetened Condensed Mill

Pork Is an Umami Superstar

Grilled Pork Satay with a Sticky-Sweet Glaze / 112

Garlicky Citrus Grilled Pork with Sugar-Charred Pineapple / 115

Juicy Grilled Pork Tenderloin with a Tangy Basque Herb Sauce / 118

Rustic Tomato Galette with Smoky Bacon, Melty Cheese, and Sweet Onions / 119

Perfectly Creamy Cold-Pan Scrambled Eggs with Serrano Ham / 123

Umami-Rich Napa Cabbage Rolls Stuffed with Rice and Pork / 124

Luscious, Chewy Rice Cakes with Pork, Oyster Sauce, and Bok Choy / 128

Smoked Gouda Grits Bowl with Andouille and Tomatoes / 131

Global Pantry Ingredients

Kecap Manis, *p. 13*

Lemongrass, *p. 14*

Peanut Oil, *p. 18*

Sambal, *p. 21*

Soy Sauce, *p. 22*

Grilling Tip

Give Them Space. You want the satay to really char around the edges, and crowding the skewers together can prevent that. If your grill is small, it's better to cook in several batches so that maximum heat circulates around the meat.

Prep Tip

Get to the Heart. To prepare lemongrass for cooking, peel away and discard the tough outer leaves, revealing the pale yellow, more tender stalk. Trim off about ½ inch from the thicker root end, and cut the stalk to about 6 inches in length (discard the fibrous, tough top part—the thin part—or freeze to add aroma to stocks or soups).

Grilled Pork Satay
with a Sticky-Sweet Glaze

ACTIVE TIME: 50 minutes
TOTAL TIME: 1 hour 50 minutes
SERVES 6

This is a simplified version of one of the dishes that made Scott a food nut after he moved to Indonesia at age 10: sate babi, cooked at street stalls by vendors who furiously fanned the coals while the pork sizzled and smoked and sparks flew into the night air along with the sweet smells of caramelization and charring fat. Here, pieces of fatty pork shoulder or pork butt marinate for an hour or more in a mixture dominated by sweet soy and garlic. This is a chewier, cheaper cut, but each pork-a-licious bite is rendered sweetly intense by the kecap manis, with brilliant lemony-herbal undertones from the lemongrass. Serve with Our Best Shortcut to Homemade Peanut Sauce (page 18), rice, and sliced cucumbers (we like to add a side dish of stir-fried vegetables, too). Note that you'll need 24 bamboo skewers, 10 inches each, or a big bunch of flat metal skewers.

¾ cup coarsely chopped shallots (about 2 large)

2 tablespoons peanut oil or vegetable oil

1 tablespoon dark or light soy sauce

2 teaspoons sambal oelek

4 large cloves garlic, peeled

1 piece (6 inches) lemongrass, chopped into thin rings

1½ cups kecap manis

2½ pounds boneless pork shoulder or pork butt steaks

Neutral oil (such as canola), for coating the grill rack

Cooked white rice, sliced cucumber, and peanut sauce, for serving

1 Combine the shallots, peanut oil, soy sauce, sambal, garlic, and lemongrass in a small food processor or blender and puree until you have an almost-smooth paste. Alternatively, if you're feeling energetic, you can pound the mixture into a paste with a mortar and pestle, or chop everything finely with a sharp knife until it will yield a paste. Add 1 cup of kecap manis and pulse or stir until thoroughly combined.

2 Cut the pork into small cubes, about ½ to ¾ inch. Some pieces will be odd-shaped—no worries. Put the meat into a large ziplock bag with the kecap manis mixture; seal the bag and shake and knead for 30 seconds, until the pork is coated with the marinade. Put the bag on the counter, open, burp out the air, reseal, fold back until tight, and put in the fridge. After 30 minutes, turn the bag over and marinate for at least 30 minutes more (up to 2 hours).

3 While the pork marinates, put a half-inch of water in a sheet pan and soak the bamboo skewers.

4 About 30 to 45 minutes before cooking time, heat your gas grill to high (500°F to 600°F) or prepare your coals to maintain high heat (charcoal will take about 45 minutes). If using coals, when they are ready, spread them around the edge of the grill.

5 As the grill heats, skewer the pork cubes, 4 or 5 pieces per skewer, bunching the meat near the tip with the sides of the cubes touching. Put the pile of skewers on a sheet pan to transport to the grill. Put the remaining ½ cup kecap manis in a bowl with a barbecue brush and keep handy.

6 Oil the grill rack with canola (or other neutral) oil. Place the meat part of the skewers over the heat, allowing the rest of the sticks to protrude over the side (the naked sticks can catch fire if they sit directly over the heat for too long). Let one side of the pork char before turning the skewers. Baste the meat as you turn the skewers. Keep this up until all sides are charred and caramelized—10 to 15 minutes, though the cook time will vary depending on the heat of the grill. The meat should be cooked but not dry, the edges charred. If your grill is small, you may have to cook the satay in 2 or 3 batches. Use the warming rack on your grill if you have one, or place grilled kebabs, lightly covered with foil, in a warm oven.

7 Serve with white rice and sliced cucumbers, plus peanut sauce on the side for dipping.

Kecap manis, the gooey sweet soy of Indonesia, works wonders on the grill.

Garlicky Citrus Grilled Pork

with Sugar-Charred Pineapple

ACTIVE TIME: 50 minutes
TOTAL TIME: 5 hours 50 minutes
SERVES 8

This bright-flavored pork-steak party dish is inspired by the classic Puerto Rican roast, pernil. We like the cross-Atlantic addition of our beloved Banyuls vinegar for more depth and acidic edge. The marinated steaks are grilled alongside pineapple logs that are basted in a sweet, spicy liquid. For the marinade, a big mortar and pestle works if you like the arm workout, but a small food processor is ideal. Serve with rice and your favorite vinegary hot sauce, with a crunchy salad on the side.

FOR THE PORK

Zest of 1 large orange (about 1 tablespoon)

⅔ cup freshly squeezed orange juice (about 2 large oranges)

⅓ cup freshly squeezed lemon juice (about 2 large lemons)

3 tablespoons extra-virgin olive oil

1 tablespoon kosher salt

1 tablespoon dried oregano

2 teaspoons freshly ground black pepper

1 teaspoon Banyuls or sherry vinegar

10 large cloves garlic, peeled

3 pounds boneless pork shoulder steaks (about ¾ inch thick)

FOR THE GRILLED PINEAPPLE

⅓ cup freshly squeezed orange juice (about 1 large orange)

3 tablespoons brown sugar

2½ tablespoons freshly squeezed lime juice (about 1 large lime)

1 tablespoon honey

1 tablespoon olive or vegetable oil

1 teaspoon ground Hatch chile pepper, or other fragrant, medium-hot ground chile

Generous pinch of kosher salt

1 fresh pineapple

Olive oil, for basting the pork

Neutral oil (such as canola), for coating the grill rack

Cilantro leaves or sprigs, for garnish

1 Prepare the marinade for the pork: Place the orange zest, orange and lemon juices, olive oil, salt, oregano, pepper, vinegar, and garlic in a small food processor or blender; process until thoroughly mixed and no chunks of garlic remain. Pour the marinade into a 1-gallon ziplock bag and add the pork steaks. Seal the bag and toss the meat for 30 seconds until the steaks are completely coated. Then put the bag on the counter, open, burp out the air, reseal, roll the bag until tight, and put it in the fridge. Marinate for 5 hours (or 3 hours minimum if you're in a time crunch), turning the bag once every hour or so.

Global Pantry Ingredient

Banyuls Vinegar, *p. 9*

Flavor Booster

Elevating an Economy Cut. Five hours of marinating yields delicious citrus-infused pork flavor in a lower-cost cut. Zesting an orange with a fine Microplane grater releases maximum aromatics via the oils.

Visual Cue

A Little Pink Is Best. Long-revised pork safety rules allow steaks that are slightly pink in the middle, and tastier. When checking, look at the center of the chop, not the edge.

Shopping Intel

Not-Quite-Ripe Pineapple. Pineapples are often sold green and over-firm and need to be ripened at home for salads. For grilling, firm is OK, but feel for some give to the thumb when you squeeze at purchase. The basting liquid will add caramel sweetness as it cooks.

2 About 30 to 45 minutes before cooking time, heat your gas grill to high (500°F to 600°F) or prepare your coals to maintain high heat (charcoal will take about 45 minutes). If using coals, when they are ready, spread them around the grill.

3 To prepare the grilled pineapple, combine the orange juice, brown sugar, lime juice, honey, oil, ground chile, and salt in a large bowl and whisk until thoroughly mixed.

4 Cut the pineapple into logs: On a sturdy cutting board, cut the top and bottom ends off the pineapple. Then set the pineapple upright and cut off the outer skin, getting most—but not necessarily every trace—of the brown bits that extend into the fruit. Cut the pineapple in half vertically. Now take one half of the pineapple—still positioned vertically—and cut in half vertically to form 2 triangular logs. Cut away the core and cut the remaining fruit into 2 more logs. Repeat with the second half of the pineapple to yield 8 triangular logs total. You're not seeking perfection here—and don't cut away too much core at the expense of the fruit. It will all grill up nicely. Add the pineapple to the honey mixture in the bowl; set aside with a basting brush.

5 Remove the pork steaks from the bag and discard the marinade; place the pork on a sheet pan with tongs. Put the olive oil in a small bowl for basting the pork as it cooks.

6 When ready to grill, coat the grill rack with canola or other neutral oil. Place the pineapple logs on the prepared rack and grill, covered, until there are good grill marks on one side, 7 minutes. Baste the logs with the honey mixture and turn the pineapple with tongs. Now place the pork steaks on the grill beside the pineapple and grill, uncovered, without turning until the meat has a good char on one side, about 7 minutes. Brush the uncooked side lightly with oil and flip the meat. You may need to do this a few times until the meat is charred on both sides and slightly pink in the thickest part. Meanwhile, continue to baste and turn the pineapple (each baste adds flavor). The pineapple will take 20 to 25 minutes to cook, the pork will take about 15 minutes; they should finish cooking around the same time. (If one finishes before the other, place it on a warming rack in the grill or put it on a platter and cover with foil.)

7 Remove the pork to a platter. Pile the pineapple logs alongside and drizzle with any remaining basting liquid. Garnish the pork with cilantro.

**Global Pantry
Ingredients**

Banyuls Vinegar, *p. 9*

Piment d'Espelette, *p. 19*

Smoked Paprika, *p. 22*

Avoid This Mistake

No More Dry Pork. Despite being lean, tenderloin is reasonably forgiving, but the key is getting it off the heat when it reaches the USDA-approved 145°F. Use a meat or instant-read thermometer, and it will be juicy and just a bit pink.

Juicy Grilled Pork Tenderloin
with a Tangy Basque Herb Sauce

ACTIVE TIME: 20 minutes
TOTAL TIME: 40 minutes
SERVES 4

Here's Ann's go-to simple summer entrée, always gobbled up. It plays nicely with seasonal vegetables and doesn't heat up the kitchen. The sauce is our riff on *tximitxurri* (pronounced chee-mee-choo-ree), the Basque version of chimichurri. Piment d'Espelette, providing just a bit of heat, is worth seeking out not just for regional authenticity but also for its special fruity fire. The sauce is wonderfully sharp; you only need a little to perk up the pork.

FOR THE PORK

1 pork tenderloin (1¼ to 1½ pounds), trimmed

1 tablespoon olive oil

¾ teaspoon kosher salt

¾ teaspoon ground cumin

¾ teaspoon garlic powder

¾ teaspoon brown sugar

½ teaspoon smoked paprika

½ teaspoon freshly ground black pepper

FOR THE SAUCE

½ cup finely chopped fresh cilantro leaves and tender stems

¼ cup extra-virgin olive oil

1 tablespoon Banyuls or sherry vinegar

1 teaspoon piment d'Espelette

¼ teaspoon kosher salt

1 small clove garlic, grated on a Microplane

Neutral oil (such as canola), for oiling the grill

1 Heat your gas grill to medium-high (450°F to 475°F) or prepare your coals to maintain medium-high heat (gas will take 20 to 30 minutes; charcoal will take about 45 minutes).

2 To prepare the pork, brush it with the olive oil. Combine the salt, cumin, garlic powder, brown sugar, smoked paprika, and black pepper in a small bowl; rub the spice mixture evenly over all sides of the pork. Let the pork stand while the grill heats.

3 Meanwhile, prepare the sauce: Stir together the cilantro, olive oil, vinegar, piment d'Espelette, salt, and garlic in a small bowl. Set aside until ready to serve.

4 Coat the grill rack with canola (or other neutral) oil. Place the pork on the prepared rack, close the grill lid, and cook, turning every 4 or 5 minutes, until a thermometer inserted in the thickest part registers 145°F, about 20 minutes total. Remove the pork to a cutting board and let it stand for 5 minutes.

5 Cut the pork into 12 slices and serve with the sauce.

Rustic Tomato Galette

with Smoky Bacon, Melty Cheese, and Sweet Onions

ACTIVE TIME: 30 minutes
TOTAL TIME: 1 hour 50 minutes
SERVES 6

Pie pastry, perfectly flaky-meaty-savory because the fat is lard, embraces layers of properly ripe tomatoes, great American bacon, nutty cheese, and semi-caramelized onions in this delicious tart, which can be served warm or at room temperature. Paired with a chilled, fruity red wine and a crunchy salad, it's one of our favorite summer meals but will work year-round if you use those little, sweet grape tomatoes.

---

2 tablespoons unsalted butter

2 large white onions, halved vertically and thinly sliced into half rings

2 slices Benton's bacon or other salty, smoky, thick-cut bacon, cut into small bits

2 teaspoons chopped fresh thyme or oregano

4 medium ripe tomatoes or 1 pint grape tomatoes

Cooking spray

All-purpose flour, for dusting

⅓ Scott's Mom's Perfect Flaky Pie Pastry (recipe follows)

7 ounces Comté cheese or other melting cheese (see Shopping Intel), thinly sliced

1 large egg yolk

1 Preheat the oven to 375°F with the rack placed in the center.

2 Melt the butter in a large skillet over medium-high heat. Add the onions and bacon and cook, stirring occasionally, until the onions have somewhat softened, turned blond, and are dark brown here and there, about 18 minutes. Stir in the thyme and set aside.

3 Meanwhile, slice the stem end off the tomatoes and gently squeeze over the sink so most of the seeds and liquid drain out. If nothing comes out, poke your fingers or the knife tip into the cavities of the tomatoes. Cut the tomatoes into slices about ¼ inch thick. If using grape tomatoes, cut them in half lengthwise and squeeze out the seeds.

4 Coat an 18 × 13-inch sheet pan or baking sheet with cooking spray. Generously flour your counter and roll the pastry dough into a large, roughly shaped circle that's a bit wider than the short side of the sheet pan, about 15 inches. Don't stress: You really don't need a perfect circle for this! (For detailed rolling instructions, see page 120.) Fold the dough in half, place it on the pan, and unfold it into a circle that should nearly reach the edges of the shorter sides.

(For detailed rolling instructions, see page 120.)

Global Pantry Ingredient

Benton's Bacon, *p. 9*

Shopping Intel

Lard vs. Lard. National brands are found on the baking aisle and are very inexpensive. There are now small-brand versions of leaf lard (considered the finest variety of pig fat), but these are much more expensive. Look for those in Whole Foods and specialty food stores. Be cautious with house-rendered lard (manteca) in Latin food markets--it's delicious but can be very roast pork-y. If you're vegetarian, try a ratio of ⅓ butter, ⅔ shortening (and omit the bacon from this recipe).

Better Call Comté. Comté is a sweetish, rich French cheese that melts beautifully and has a funky quality that plays perfectly with bacon. Any cheese shop worth its salt should have it. In recent years, Costco has sold large wedges at great prices, too. If you can't find it, substitute a Swiss melting cheese such as Gruyère, Emmental, or Jarlsberg.

Technique Tip

Flaky Pastry Has Visible Blobs of Fat. When bringing the pastry together initially, and when rolling it out, you should see whitish streaks and blobs of fat in the dough. This is not undermixed. It's essential for flaky results.

Pastry Rolling Notes

• Out of the fridge, the cold dough can sometimes seem inclined to crack; if so, you can gently press it together while rolling it on a floured counter with your hands to soften it a bit (not flattening, just rolling).

• One-third of the pastry recipe works for the tomato galette here. To use it to make a two-crust dessert pie in a 9-inch pie plate, cut 1 dough ball into 2 pieces—⅓ for the top, ⅔ for the bottom.

• When using a rolling pin with this dough, be liberal with the flour on the counter and rolling pin. If the dough starts to stick, add more flour! Roll the dough a bit, rotate a quarter turn, roll some more, and repeat until you have a flat circle between ¼ and ⅛ inch thick. Periodically dust the circle with flour and flip it over as you roll it out. When the crust is large enough for your purpose, fold it in half and lift it onto the sheet pan, then unfold into a circle.

See visual step-by-steps for the pastry on p. 278.

5 Arrange the cheese planks in a circle on the pastry like you're laying a wood floor, with a 3- to 4-inch ring of pastry around the edge not covered. Then layer the onions over the cheese, and finally the tomatoes. If using grape tomatoes, arrange them with skin sides down. Fold one portion of the uncovered pastry up and lay it over the filling, then draw up a portion next to that, and so on, in successive overlapping folds, leaving the center of the tart uncovered.

6 Whisk together the egg yolk with 2 teaspoons of water in a small bowl. Brush the egg mixture over the dough (reserve any remaining unused egg mixture). Bake the tart until it's starting to brown (it will only be about halfway done at this point), about 30 minutes. Remove the tart from the oven and brush the dough with the remaining egg mixture. Bake until the pastry is well browned, about 30 minutes. Let stand for 20 minutes before cutting into wedges.

7 Serve hot or at room temperature (it's even great for breakfast, cold from the fridge, after a late night).

Scott's Mom's Super-Flaky Pie Pastry

ACTIVE TIME: 15 minutes
TOTAL TIME: 2 hours 15 minutes
MAKES 3 BALLS OF DOUGH FOR 3 LARGE 2-CRUST PIES

"Nothing to fear making homemade pastry if you use a light touch," noted Kay on her recipe card. Kay was Scott's mom, and she made famous pies from the great pastry tradition of southern Ontario, where she was born. Apple pie, of course, as well as wild raspberry, strawberry, Saskatoon berry, rhubarb, blueberry, and Christmas mince. The fat, Kay insisted, must be lard, giving a savory quality and irreproachable flakiness when baked to a beautiful brown.

---

5 cups (22½ ounces) all-purpose flour

1 tablespoon baking powder

1½ teaspoons table salt

1 pound lard, well chilled for at least 3 hours (preferably overnight)

1 medium lemon, juiced and strained

1 large egg, lightly beaten

1 Whisk together the flour, baking powder, and salt in a large bowl. Working quickly, cut the cold lard into 1-inch cubes, and drop the cubes into the flour mixture as you go, tossing to cover, keeping the cubes separate. When all of the cubes are in, use a pastry cutter to cut the flour and lard together so that the lard pieces are reduced to pea and small-marble size. You can also work the lard in quickly with your fingers.

2 Place the lemon juice into a 1-cup measuring cup and add ice water until you reach the 1-cup level. Pour the water mixture into a small bowl and beat in the egg until well combined. Pour this mixture over the flour mixture and stir with a large fork or spoon until it just comes together into a ball. It may be sticky. Put the ball onto a floured counter and gently knead until all of the flour is worked in and the dough holds together, but don't overwork. You will see blobs of fat in the dough: That's the goal. Divide the dough into 3 equal balls, cover tightly with plastic wrap, and refrigerate the dough you will use until ready to roll it out for a pie, at least 2 hours. Place extra wrapped dough balls in ziplock freezer bags and store in the freezer for up to 2 months.

Perfectly Creamy Cold-Pan Scrambled Eggs

with Serrano Ham

ACTIVE TIME: 6 minutes
TOTAL TIME: 6 minutes
SERVES 2

This recipe will completely elevate your egg game. Soft-scrambled eggs are creamy, comforting, and *so* easy to overcook—until you use the cold-pan trick. The eggs go into a small, unheated nonstick skillet with a pat of cultured butter, which adds way more pronounced sweet-cream, hint-of-tang buttery richness than regular butter. The burner is turned on and the gradual rise in temperature, with constant stirring for uniform curds, yields a consistent creaminess throughout. These eggs are made even more lovely with a side of salty ham. We opt for Spanish serrano, arguably the greatest of all European hams, but you can use prosciutto or, if you can find it, thinly cut salty American real country ham. Serve with biscuits or a crunchy toasted bread.

---

4 thin slices serrano ham

5 large eggs

2 tablespoons whole or 2% milk

¼ teaspoon kosher salt

2 tablespoons unsalted cultured butter

1 Portion your ham onto 2 serving plates and put the plates beside the stove. Crack the eggs into a medium bowl; add the milk and salt. Beat the mixture with a fork until no traces of translucent egg white streaks remain.

2 Pour the egg mixture into a small (8-inch) nonstick skillet or small saucepan (see Avoid This Mistake) off the heat; add the butter. Place the pan over medium-low heat. Cook, stirring and scraping constantly with a silicone spatula, drawing the less-cooked eggs toward the hotter middle of the pan, until the eggs are soft-scrambled, 3 to 5 minutes. As soon as the eggs are done—and that's just *before* they're absolutely done, since they will continue to cook off the heat—divide them between the plates and serve immediately.

Try This!

Cultured Butter. Fresh cream is innoculated with a live culture and left to ferment before churning, and the result is a creamier, richer, faintly tangy butter that we use in recipes in which buttery flavor is the star. One of our favorites is widely sold, Kerrygold Pure Irish Butter, while good food shops carry small-producer versions worth seeking out.

Avoid This Mistake

Small Pan for Proper Texture. A small nonstick skillet, about 8 inches in diameter, prevents the eggs from spreading into a too-thin layer that cooks too quickly. If you don't have that, a small, heavy-bottom saucepan will work if you keep the heat low (the flames should never lick up the sides of the pan if you're using gas) and stir constantly.

Shopping Intel

All Those Egg Claims. Taste and ethics agree: Hens need room to roam and forage for worms, bugs, and grass to yield the best-flavored eggs. We go for "pasture raised" and sometimes "free range," if the latter is accompanied by explicit claims (often including photos) of open-air hen lifestyle. "Cage free" isn't good enough.

Global Pantry
Ingredients

Chili Crisp, *p. 10*

Fish Sauce, *p. 11*

Korean Toasted
Sesame Oil, *p. 14*

Oyster Sauce, *p. 16*

Flavor Booster

The Other Pepper. The pork and rice filling features a good amount of ground white pepper, a variety favored by many Asian food cultures. Its brighter, grassier, less-hot character is a key to the flavor of the filling. Look for whole white peppercorns in Asian stores, or order online, and grind the usual way.

Size Matters

By Big, We Mean Big. Whether you're using napa or green cabbage, you need big leaves to encase the filling properly— and you want lots of leaf in every bite. For a napa cabbage, opt for a head that's at least a foot long; for a green cabbage, get the largest one you can find. You'll have leftover cabbage for a salad or stir-fry the next day.

Umami-Rich Napa Cabbage Rolls
Stuffed with Rice and Pork

ACTIVE TIME: 25 minutes
TOTAL TIME: 1 hour 40 minutes
SERVES 4

This delicious Asian-tilting riff on stuffed cabbage rolls uses fragrant jasmine rice, napa cabbage, and a brothy brown sauce enriched by oyster sauce and toasted sesame oil instead of a tomato-based one. A splash of fish sauce in the porky filling boosts the meaty-savory effect. The result is rich beyond compare, and ever-so-delicately sweet to match the cabbagey goodness. We love it with a dollop of chili crisp for extra crunchy umami and heat. Bonus: For anyone who has ever struggled with prying the leaves off a head of regular green cabbage, you'll be delighted with the ease of working with the napa variety—though we've provided instructions for both. See the images on page 127 for a visual assembly guide.

Cooking spray

1 large head napa cabbage or green cabbage

1 pound ground pork

1 cup cooked jasmine rice

⅔ cup thinly sliced scallions

1 tablespoon fish sauce

1 teaspoon freshly ground white pepper

½ teaspoon kosher salt

1 large carrot, shredded

2 cloves garlic, minced

1½ cups unsalted beef stock

¼ cup oyster sauce

1 tablespoon Korean toasted sesame oil

Chili crisp (optional)

1 Preheat the oven to 375°F with the rack placed in the center. Coat a 13 × 9-inch baking dish with cooking spray.

2 Prepare the cabbage: *If using napa cabbage,* remove 18 large leaves from the head of cabbage. Trim off 2 or 3 inches from the bottom of each leaf, where the vein is the thickest. Pile the leaves on a microwave-safe plate. Cover loosely with plastic wrap. Microwave on High for 5 minutes. Carefully uncover the plate and cool the cabbage slightly.

If using a large regular green cabbage, insert a short, sharp knife a couple of inches into the base of the cabbage and cut out a conical piece of the core. This makes removing the stiff outer leaves a bit easier. Follow the instructions in Step 2 to soften in the microwave.

3 Place the pork in a large bowl. Add the rice, scallions, fish sauce, pepper, salt, carrot, and garlic; mix well with your hands. Divide the pork mixture into 8 equal balls.

4 To stuff the leaves: *If using napa cabbage,* arrange 2 leaves on a work surface, with the narrower rib ends overlapping by an inch or two. Spoon one ball of filling into the center of the cabbage leaves. Fold the left leaf over the filling and roll over to the right side to enclose the filling in a cylinder. Arrange the filled leaves, seam side down, in the prepared baking dish. Repeat with the remaining cabbage leaves and filling to form 8 cabbage rolls (you should have a couple of extra leaves in case some tear or are too ratty looking).

If using regular cabbage, place a softened leaf before you with the thick stem part closest to you and a "wing" of the leaf on each side. Cut away a V-shaped notch of that thick stem part, 1 to 2 inches long, to make the leaf more pliable. Place the stuffing at the point of the notch so it's resting on the leaf between the wings. Fold the bottom of the cabbage leaf forward three-fourths of a turn, then fold in both wings of the leaf and finish rolling—as if you were rolling an egg roll. As you complete the cabbage rolls, place them in the prepared baking dish. You should have one extra leaf left over.

5 Whisk together the stock, oyster sauce, and sesame oil in a medium bowl; pour over the cabbage rolls. Cover the dish tightly with aluminum foil. Bake until the filling is thoroughly heated, the flavors are married, and the pork is cooked through, 1 hour. Uncover the dish and bake until the liquid is slightly thickened, about 15 minutes; the sauce will be more like broth than gravy. Serve with chili crisp on the side, if desired.

Proper toasted Korean sesame oil is incredibly nutty and somewhat tannic.

1. Arrange two leaves so that the rib ends overlap by an inch or two.

2. Spoon one portion of filling into the center, where the leaves meet.

3. Fold the left leaf over the filling.

4. Tuck the left leaf close to the filling and roll to the right side to form a cabbage roll.

Global Pantry Ingredients

Fish Sauce, *p. 11*

Korean Toasted Sesame Oil, *p. 14*

Oyster Sauce, *p. 16*

Shopping Intel

Better Rice Cakes. You'll find Korean or Chinese flat rice cakes (or ovalettes) in vacuum-sealed packages at Asian markets, either in the freezer section or refrigerated section. If possible, look for a brand that lists only rice and salt on the ingredient list for the best flavor. Many brands also contain ethyl alcohol, which has a teensy bit of a chemical-like aftertaste.

Buy the Fatty Stuff. Skip past lean ground pork here; you want meat with some fat in it for the best flavor and texture. We get ground pork at local Asian markets; it's always flecked with a good amount of fat. Or look for the cheapest ground pork option at the grocery store; it's typically the fattiest.

Luscious, Chewy Rice Cakes
with Pork, Oyster Sauce, and Bok Choy

ACTIVE TIME: 42 minutes
TOTAL TIME: 42 minutes
SERVES 4

For years and years, whenever Ann's kids caught sight of Korean rice cakes in the kitchen, they actually cheered. It's no mystery why. Rice cakes (sometimes called rice ovalettes) have an addictive texture that falls somewhere between that of mochi and a gummy bear. Somehow they manage to be softer than any properly cooked noodle, yet *so chewy* in a way that makes eaters swoon. Why they are not in heavier rotation in noodle-mad American kitchens is a mystery. But beware: Their main goal in life is to stick together—before, during, and after cooking. Your goal in life is to separate them until every surface makes contact with the sauce. The water-soak process here begins that job, as does using a big nonstick pan for the cooking, and energetic tossing of the cakes in the pan to get the sauce distributed. This is a lightly sauced dish to let the rice cakes and crunchy bok choy shine, but it is still deeply flavorful.

1½ pounds rice cake ovalettes

1 pound (3- to 4-inch) baby bok choy, halved lengthwise, or quartered larger baby bok choy

1 bunch scallions (about 8)

2½ tablespoons Korean toasted sesame oil

1 pound ground pork

6 cloves garlic, minced

1½ tablespoons brown sugar

1½ tablespoons fish sauce

¼ cup oyster sauce

1 teaspoon rice vinegar

1 Whether frozen or refrigerated, place the rice cakes in a large bowl and cover with cool water. Let stand for 5 minutes to start the separation process, then agitate with your hands and pry apart any cakes that are stuck together. Leave in water until ready to cook.

2 Bring a large Dutch oven full of water to a boil. Fill a large bowl with ice water and have it close to the stove. Add the bok choy to the boiling water; cook until just wilted, 1 to 2 minutes. Using a spider skimmer or slotted spoon, remove the bok choy to the bowl of ice water to stop the cooking, then transfer to a paper towel–lined plate. Keep the ice water in the bowl.

3 Drain the rice cakes and add to the boiling water. Boil until most of the rice cakes start to float, 2 to 3 minutes. Drain and place the rice cakes in the ice water. (It's fine if all the ice has melted already.)

4 Thinly slice the white and light green parts of the scallions. Cut the dark green tops into 1-inch pieces and keep separate.

5 Heat a large 12- to 14-inch nonstick skillet (don't even think of doing this in a wok; the rice cakes will stick) over medium-high heat. Add 1 tablespoon sesame oil to the pan and swirl to coat. Crumble the pork into the pan; cook until the pork starts to lose its pink color, about 2 minutes. Add the white and light green scallion slices and garlic; cook, stirring frequently, until the pork starts to brown, about 3 minutes. Add the brown sugar and fish sauce (be sure to turn the vent hood on); cook until the pork is well browned, about 4 minutes.

6 Whisk together the remaining 1½ tablespoons sesame oil, oyster sauce, 3 tablespoons water, and the vinegar in a bowl. Stir the sauce into the pork mixture. Drain the rice cakes and add to the skillet, along with the bok choy and scallion tops. Cook, stirring frequently, until thoroughly heated, about 3 minutes.

Oyster sauce instantly brings that familiar, beloved restaurant-dish flavor.

Smoked Gouda Grits Bowl

with Andouille and Tomatoes

Global Pantry Ingredients

Andouille Sausage, *p. 8*
Stone-Ground Grits, *p. 23*

ACTIVE TIME: 27 minutes
TOTAL TIME: 27 minutes
SERVES 4

These creamy, cheesy grits are special enough for an elegant dinner but homey enough for a Sunday morning with the fam. In fact, Ann makes this (or something like it, varying sausage or cheese) just about every weekend. Here we add a splash of strong coffee to the topping, à la Southern red-eye gravy; you won't taste coffee notes but instead a pleasantly intense flavor akin to the best brown gravy. Proper andouille, with its chewy texture and garlicky goodness, is important.

2 cups 2% reduced-fat or whole milk

3 tablespoons salted butter

½ teaspoon kosher salt

¾ cup plus 2 tablespoons uncooked white or yellow stone-ground grits

9 ounces andouille sausage, sliced

1½ cups halved grape tomatoes

½ cup sliced scallions

½ cup strong brewed coffee

3 ounces smoked Gouda cheese, shredded

1 Pour 2 cups of water into a medium, heavy saucepan. Add the milk, 2 tablespoons of butter, and the salt. Bring the mixture to a boil over medium-high heat. Whisking constantly, gradually add the grits. Reduce the heat to low or medium-low to maintain a gentle simmer. Cover the pan partially and cook the grits, whisking occasionally, until creamy and thick, about 20 minutes.

2 Meanwhile, melt the remaining 1 tablespoon butter in a medium skillet over medium heat. Add the andouille to the pan; sauté until browned, about 5 minutes. Remove the andouille from the pan. Add the tomatoes and scallions to the pan; sauté until the tomatoes start to soften, 3 to 4 minutes. Return the sausage to the pan and stir in the coffee. Cook until the liquid reduces by about half, about 2 minutes. Keep warm until the grits are done.

3 Remove the grits from the heat. Gradually add the cheese, whisking until the cheese melts. Serve the sausage mixture over the grits.

Key Techniques

Safeguard Against Lumps. Lumpy grits are a crying shame. You must work against them from the very beginning, then maintain: Whisk the liquid constantly as you slowly pour the uncooked grits into the pot, then whisk occasionally as they cook to their thickened state.

Creamy—Not Stiff. The familiar grits ratio is 1 part grits to 4 parts water. We add a little less grits, though, which delivers a creamier, less stiff consistency that mingles with the sauce beautifully.

Anchovies • Yuzu • Black Walnuts • Wondra • Sumac • Calabrian Chiles • Sorghu
Millet • Tabasco Sauce • Coconut Milk • Roasted Hazelnut Oil • Curry Leaves • F
Sauce • Shrimp Paste • Worcestershire Sauce • Furikake • Sriracha • Saffron • Bany
Vinegar • Gochujang • Harissa • Marmite • Kecap Manis • Chili Crisp • Freeze-Dr
Strawberries • Tajín • Kimchi • Korean Toasted Sesame Oil • Dulce de Leche • S
Sauce • Lemongrass • Whole Wheat Pastry Flour • Pomegranate Molasses • Mexic
Chocolate • Smoked Paprika • Chipotles in Adobo • Shichimi Togarashi • Makrut Li
Leaves • Crema Mexicana • The Many Masalas • Capers • Mexican Chorizo • Miri
Oyster Sauce • Panko Breadcrumbs • Ras El Hanout • Andouille Sausage • Marsa
The Many Sambals • Benton's Bacon • Miso • Stone-Ground Grits • Tahini • Ghee • Pa
Sugar • Ají Amarillo Paste • Thai Curry Paste • Mustard Powder • Turmeric • Cultu
Butter • Kashmiri Mirch • Dried Porcini Mushrooms • Sweetened Condensed Mil
Anchovies • Yuzu • Black Walnuts • Wondra • Sumac • Calabrian Chiles • Sorghu
Millet • Tabasco Sauce • Coconut Milk • Roasted Hazelnut Oil • Curry Leaves • F
Sauce • Shrimp Paste • Worcestershire Sauce • Furikake • Sriracha • Saffron • Bany
Vinegar • Gochujang • Harissa • Marmite • Kecap Manis • Chili Crisp • Freeze-Dr
Strawberries • Tajín • Kimchi • Korean Toasted Sesame Oil • Dulce de Leche • S
Sauce • Lemongrass • Whole Wheat Pastry Flour • Pomegranate Molasses • Mexic
Chocolate • Smoked Paprika • Chipotles in Adobo • Shichimi Togarashi • Makrut Li
Leaves • Crema Mexicana • The Many Masalas • Capers • Mexican Chorizo • Miri
Oyster Sauce • Panko Breadcrumbs • Ras El Hanout • Andouille Sausage • Marsa
The Many Sambals • Benton's Bacon • Miso • Stone-Ground Grits • Tahini • Ghee • Pa
Sugar • Ají Amarillo Paste • Thai Curry Paste • Mustard Powder • Turmeric • Cultu
Butter • Kashmiri Mirch • Dried Porcini Mushrooms • Sweetened Condensed Mil
Anchovies • Yuzu • Black Walnuts • Wondra • Sumac • Calabrian Chiles • Sorghu
Millet • Tabasco Sauce • Coconut Milk • Roasted Hazelnut Oil • Curry Leaves • F
Sauce • Shrimp Paste • Worcestershire Sauce • Furikake • Sriracha • Saffron • Bany
Vinegar • Gochujang • Harissa • Marmite • Kecap Manis • Chili Crisp • Freeze-Dr
Strawberries • Tajín • Kimchi • Korean Toasted Sesame Oil • Dulce de Leche • S
Sauce • Lemongrass • Whole Wheat Pastry Flour • Pomegranate Molasses • Mexic
Chocolate • Smoked Paprika • Chipotles in Adobo • Shichimi Togarashi • Makrut Li
Leaves • Crema Mexicana • The Many Masalas • Capers • Mexican Chorizo • Miri
Oyster Sauce • Panko Breadcrumbs • Ras El Hanout • Andouille Sausage • Marsa
The Many Sambals • Benton's Bacon • Miso • Stone-Ground Grits • Tahini • Ghee • Pa
Sugar • Ají Amarillo Paste • Thai Curry Paste • Mustard Powder • Turmeric • Cultu
Butter • Kashmiri Mirch • Dried Porcini Mushrooms • Sweetened Condensed Milk

Poultry, Mostly Chicken, Entirely Elevated

Finishing Tip

Last-Minute Broiling. Often, the chicken skin isn't quite browned and crisp enough after its bake, so we finish with a brief broil, carefully pulling the pan before burning can happen. The result is lovely color and even more flavor.

Revisiting One of the Great Chicken Recipes of All Time

ACTIVE TIME: 20 minutes
TOTAL TIME: 25 hours 30 minutes
SERVES 6

This is our homage to the culinary event that was Chicken Marbella in the 1980s, published in *The Silver Palate Cookbook*. It was a sensation, partly for the exuberant use of prunes, vinegar, wine, olives, and sugar, partly because it proved a fail-safe dinner-party hit. We've reduced the alarming amounts of sugar, added some Mediterranean zing with preserved lemon, greatly boosted the olives (because: olives), provided some anchovy umami, and simplified the prep using precut chicken thighs. If you have white-meat partisans in the house, you can include a couple of breasts, halved, and reduce the thigh count by four. Note that the longer you marinate the chicken, the tastier it will be—we recommend starting the night before if you can.

1½ cups pitted Castelvetrano olives (or 2 cups if you eliminate the optional kalamatas, below)

1 cup pitted prunes, halved

½ cup pitted kalamata olives (optional)

½ cup chopped preserved lemon

⅓ cup red wine vinegar

2 tablespoons chopped fresh oregano

2 tablespoons extra-virgin olive oil

1 teaspoon kosher salt

1 teaspoon freshly ground black pepper, plus more as needed

10 cloves garlic

8 oil-packed anchovies, chopped

12 air-chilled, skin-on, bone-in natural chicken thighs

1 cup dry white wine

2 tablespoons honey

¼ cup light brown sugar

1 The evening before (better) or early in the morning the day you plan to serve the chicken, combine the Castelvetrano olives, prunes, kalamata olives (if using), preserved lemon, vinegar, oregano, oil, salt, pepper, garlic, and anchovies in a large bowl; stir well. Add the chicken and toss until everything is nicely mixed, then cover the bowl and put it in the refrigerator. Chill until 90 minutes before serving, occasionally tossing the chicken for even marination.

2 Preheat the oven to 350°F with the rack placed one position up from the center.

3 Arrange the thighs in a sturdy baking dish large enough to lay all the thighs flat (or use two smaller pans); a 13 × 9-inch baking dish should work well. Spoon the prune mixture evenly over the chicken. Pour in the wine and drizzle the honey in ribbons over the thighs, then sprinkle the sugar over it all. Sprinkle a few turns of black pepper over the arrangement.

4 Bake, uncovered, until the chicken is done, about 1 hour and 15 minutes. Chicken is done if a thermometer inserted in the center registers at least 165°F, or the juices run clear when you cut deeply into a thigh in the middle of the pan with a sharp knife.

5 When done, tilt the pan and use a spoon to baste juice all over the chicken. If the chicken isn't browned enough, turn the broiler on high and broil the chicken on the same rack until nicely browned but not burnt, 2 to 3 minutes.

6 Remove the chicken to a serving platter and cover with aluminum foil to keep warm. Pour the sauce (with olives and prunes) into a medium or large skillet; cook on high heat, stirring frequently, until reduced by half, about 5 minutes. Pour the thickened sauce over the chicken and serve immediately.

Preserved lemons, especially the homemade variety on page 20, combine the best virtues of lemons and pickles.

Coca-Cola Chicken
with Crispy Togarashi Chicken Skins

ACTIVE TIME: 22 minutes
TOTAL TIME: 1 hour 37 minutes
SERVES 4

Coca-Cola chicken has Asian and American roots and involves cooking the bird in a sauce made from equal parts cola and ketchup. The basic ratio is intact here, but we've added some smoked paprika for more barbecue-flavor oomph. The additional twist is that we remove the skins from the chicken thighs (they would just get soggy when braised), dust them with a lovely store-bought Japanese spice blend, and roast separately for a crispy, complex accent. Serve this dish with rice, noodles, or mashed potatoes—something to soak up that sweet sauce. We use chicken thighs for their succulence, but you could use bone-in, skin-on breasts, too; cut them in half so they're thigh-size.

Cooking spray

8 bone-in, skin-on chicken thighs (3 to 3½ pounds)

2 teaspoons shichimi togarashi

1¼ teaspoons kosher salt

1 tablespoon canola oil

1 large yellow onion, sliced into ½-inch-thick rings

6 cloves garlic, smashed

½ teaspoon freshly ground black pepper

1 cup plus 2 tablespoons Coca-Cola

1 cup ketchup

2 tablespoons Worcestershire sauce

1 teaspoon smoked paprika

1 Place one oven rack in the upper third of the oven and one oven rack in the lower third. Preheat the oven to 400°F. Coat a 13 × 9-inch baking dish with cooking spray.

2 Line a large sheet pan with parchment paper. Remove the skins from the chicken thighs, scraping off any big pieces of fat that might come with them (discard fat). Flatten out the skins on the prepared sheet pan, bumpy side up, trying not to overlap them. Sprinkle evenly with 1 teaspoon of shichimi togarashi and ¼ teaspoon of salt. Set aside.

Shortcut Technique . . .
Just Cook 'Em. Many recipes for crispy chicken skin involve stacking two sheet pans with parchment paper between, so the skins are pressed into thin "chips." We skip the fuss, opting to keep the skins uncovered so they puff up a bit and have a texture similar to pork rinds.

. . . But Avoid This Mistake
Less Is More. When you season the raw chicken skins, the seasoning might seem sparse. Resist the urge to add more: The flavors concentrate as the skins cook and crisp.

Try This!
Shichimi Togarashi.
This Japanese spice blend is ubiquitous in ramen shops, offering a lovely mix of ocean-earth-and-fire qualities from sesame seeds, ground seaweed, sansho chiles, yuzu or other citrus peel, and a few other things. Look for it in Japanese and Asian stores and better supermarkets.

3 Heat a large skillet over medium-high heat. Add the oil to the pan and swirl to coat. Add the onion rings; sauté just until the onion begins to soften, about 3 minutes. Spoon the onion into the prepared baking dish; scatter the garlic in the dish. Sprinkle the meaty side of the chicken with ½ teaspoon of salt and the black pepper. Add the chicken to the skillet, meaty side down. Cook until just browned, 4 to 5 minutes. Arrange the chicken, browned side up, over the onion in the prepared dish. Add 2 tablespoons of cola to the skillet, scraping to loosen the browned bits. Pour over the chicken.

4 Whisk together the ketchup, the remaining 1 cup cola, the Worcestershire, smoked paprika, remaining 1 teaspoon shichimi togarashi, and remaining ½ teaspoon salt in a medium bowl. Pour the mixture evenly over the chicken. Cover the dish tightly with aluminum foil. Place the chicken mixture on the upper oven rack. Place the chicken skins on the lower oven rack. Bake for 30 minutes.

5 Uncover the chicken dish and return to the upper oven rack. Rotate the pan of chicken skins on the lower oven rack. Bake until the chicken skins are browned and crisp, not flabby, not burned, about 25 minutes. (Watch the skins: If some pieces brown early, remove them to a paper towel–lined plate.) Remove both pans from the oven and increase the oven temperature to 450°F.

6 Drain the chicken skins on a paper towel–lined plate. Remove the chicken thighs from the baking dish to a plate; tent with foil to keep warm. Return the sauce and onions in the baking dish to the oven. Bake until the sauce is slightly thickened, about 15 minutes. Plate the chicken with the sauce spooned over and the skins on top or on the side.

The seven ingredients in shichimi togarashi make it a more complex topping than simple chile powder, but it's still fiery.

Key Technique

Pound It Out. The secret to chicken breasts that don't dry out on the grill is pounding them to an even thickness, about ½ inch, so you don't have to wait for the thicker parts to cook while the thin areas wither into chicken leather.

Shopping Intel

Smaller Is Better. Boneless, skinless chicken breasts have ballooned out of control as if at the hand of plastic surgeons in Beverly Hills. Many weigh 12 ounces each, while some even reach a pound! That's too big for the bird and too big for the plate. To find reasonably sized 6- to 8-ounce breasts, look through the organic offerings. If you can only find large ones, cut them in half crosswise before pounding.

Grilled Chicken Breasts
with Chorizo Relish

ACTIVE TIME: 28 minutes
TOTAL TIME: 42 minutes
SERVES 4

This is the most successful chicken breast dish Ann has ever made for her family, who are generally lukewarm concerning America's Favorite Meat but were forced to try hundreds, if not thousands, of chicken breast dishes over the years as guinea pigs for Ann's magazine recipe testing. The cheeky idea of a meat relish, made from Mexican sausage further juiced with Basque peppers, to garnish the meat beneath was the clincher. All boredom is banished from the plate.

¼ cup extra-virgin olive oil

1½ teaspoons piment d'Espelette

1 teaspoon ground cumin

1 teaspoon kosher salt

4 boneless, skinless chicken breasts (6 to 8 ounces each)

4 ounces Mexican chorizo

½ cup diced yellow bell pepper

½ cup diced grape tomatoes

⅓ cup thinly sliced scallions

⅓ cup chopped fresh cilantro leaves

Neutral oil (such as canola), for oiling the grill rack

1 Heat your gas grill to medium-high (450°F to 475°F) or prepare your coals to maintain medium-high heat (gas will take 20 to 30 minutes; charcoal will take about 45 minutes).

2 Meanwhile, whisk together 3 tablespoons oil, the Piment d'Espelette, cumin, and salt in a pie plate or shallow bowl. Working with 1 chicken breast at a time, place the breast between 2 layers of plastic wrap or parchment paper; pound with a meat mallet or small, heavy skillet to an even thickness of about ½ inch. Place the pounded breasts in the oil mixture and toss to coat. Let stand at room temperature while the grill heats.

3 Heat a medium skillet over medium heat. Add the remaining 1 tablespoon oil and swirl to coat. Crumble in the chorizo and cook for 1 minute. Add the bell pepper; cook 3 minutes, stirring frequently. Add the tomatoes and scallions; cook for 1 minute. Remove from the heat and stir in the cilantro. Cover and keep warm.

4 When the grill is ready, oil the grill rack and arrange the chicken breasts on it. Close the grill lid and grill until a thermometer inserted in the center of the breasts registers 165°F, 5 to 6 minutes per side. Top the chicken with the relish and serve.

The Pleasures of Chicken and Rice

A Quicker Riff on the Hainanese Triumph, Part 1

ACTIVE TIME: 32 minutes
TOTAL TIME: 1 hour 25 minutes
SERVES 4

There have long been restaurants and food stalls in Singapore entirely devoted to Hainanese chicken rice, and that's where Scott first fell for this supreme Chinese meditation on the bird, in which poached chicken is served with chicken stock–infused rice, along with gingery-garlicky, soy, and sambal dipping sauces that are sometimes *also* flavored with chicken. The authentic recipe is rather involved, but Ann radically simplified it by using an Instant Pot and rotisserie chicken. The result, though certainly a somewhat cheeky adaptation, captures the flavors beautifully, right down to rice that's enticingly slick with a touch of schmaltz. We've added an American note with one of our favorite rice varieties, Carolina Gold.

Usually sold frozen, pandan leaves retain much of their aromatic power.

FOR THE STOCK AND MEAT

1 medium rotisserie chicken, chilled or at room temperature

1 tablespoon Korean toasted sesame oil

3 cups unsalted chicken stock

½ teaspoon kosher salt

4 scallions (green parts only)

4 (¼-inch-thick) slices peeled fresh ginger

2 lengths (8 inches each) pandan leaves, fresh or frozen (optional)

FOR THE GINGER-GARLIC SAUCE

3 tablespoons peanut oil

2 tablespoons grated or finely minced peeled fresh ginger

2 large cloves garlic, minced

¼ teaspoon kosher salt

FOR THE SWEET SOY SAUCE

3 tablespoons plus 1 teaspoon kecap manis

4 teaspoons soy sauce

FOR THE RICE

2 cups uncooked Carolina Gold rice (see Shopping Intel) or jasmine rice

2 tablespoons peanut oil or canola oil

1 tablespoon minced peeled fresh ginger

3 cloves garlic, minced

Sliced English cucumber and ½ cup sambal oelek, for serving

Global Pantry Ingredients

Kecap Manis, *p. 13*
Korean Toasted Sesame Oil, *p. 14*
Pandan Leaves, *see* Try This!
Peanut Oil, *p. 18*
Sambal, *p. 21*

Shopping Intel

A New Rice to Try. Carolina Gold rice is a long-grain white variety with a mild, clean, slightly sweet flavor and grains that remain fluffy and separate. We find it at Whole Foods, but there are several varieties online. If you don't have it, use a long-grain variety such as jasmine, well rinsed.

Try This!

Pandan, or screwpine, has some of the most difficult-to-describe flavors and aromas in global cooking: a sorta-creamy-vanilla-greenish-breadiness. It's beloved in both savory and sweet dishes. Look for pandan leaves, long and fibrous and usually frozen, in Southeast Asian food stores or stores like H Mart. Just toss leaves into soups or a pot of rice, and fish out after cooking. You may see tiny bottles of bright green pandan flavoring; it's artificial and yucky.

1 To prepare the stock and meat, pull the skin off the chicken and place in the Instant Pot. Cut the legs and thighs off and "massage" the meat off the bones with your fingers, retaining as many large pieces as possible while removing the cartilage. Put the bones and cartilage in the pot. Pull the breast meat off in whole pieces and slice crosswise into thick slices. Put the breast, leg, and thigh meat pieces in a bowl, add the sesame oil, and gently work the oil in so all pieces are coated. Cover the bowl and set aside. Pull the chicken carcass into pieces and add to the Instant Pot with the stock, salt, scallions, ginger, and pandan leaves (if using). Secure the lid in place and set the steam valve to Sealing. Set to Manual and cook at high pressure for 30 minutes.

2 Meanwhile, while the stock cooks, make the sauces. To prepare the ginger-garlic sauce, combine the oil, ginger, and garlic in a small skillet, then turn the heat to medium-low. Cook until the ginger and garlic are just golden but not browned, stirring frequently, about 2 minutes. Remove from the heat and stir in the salt. Pour into a small bowl.

3 To prepare the soy sauce, stir together the kecap manis and soy sauce in a small bowl.

4 When the stock cooking time is over, quick-release the pressure. Strain the stock through a sieve over a large bowl; discard the solids. Wipe the pot dry with a paper towel.

5 To prepare the rice, place it in a fine-mesh strainer. Rinse under cold water, then drain well by tapping the strainer on the side of the sink. Set the Instant Pot to Sauté. Add the oil to the pot, then add the ginger and garlic; sauté until lightly browned, about 3 minutes. Add the rice; cook, stirring constantly, until the rice is coated with oil, about 1 minute. Stir in $2\frac{1}{3}$ cups hot stock (reserve the remainder for another use).

6 Turn the Instant Pot off. Secure the lid in place and set the steam valve to Sealing. Set to Manual and cook at high pressure for 6 minutes. When the cooking time is over, allow the steam to release naturally for 10 minutes, then quick-release any remaining pressure. Fluff the rice with a fork. Arrange the rice, chicken, and sauces on a serving platter. Serve with cucumber and optional sambal, if desired. Alternatively, arrange the chicken, rice, and cucumbers on individual serving plates and serve sauces in communal or individual serving bowls.

The Pleasures of Chicken and Rice

A Big-Comfort Buttery Curried Weeknight Casserole, Part 2

ACTIVE TIME: 37 minutes
TOTAL TIME: 1 hour 7 minutes
SERVES 6

This recipe's origins lie with Ann's favorite way to eat leftover takeout Indian food—everything mixed with rice and tossed in the oven to make an old-timey "curry casserole." It has all the warming goodness of classic American comfort food but also the amped-up flavors we need today (we use a good dose of a good masala; no more quarter teaspoons of curry powder!). Broiling the chicken first gives it a hint of off-the-grill char. Baking the rice lets it soak up the sauce flavors while attaining those heavenly crispy edges. The fried onions on top are in no way "authentic" to a curry—but they're absolutely authentic to a great American casserole.

⅓ cup plain full-fat Greek yogurt

1½ tablespoons grated peeled fresh or frozen ginger

5 teaspoons butter chicken masala blend (or garam masala)

1¾ teaspoons kosher salt

½ teaspoon cayenne pepper

1 large clove garlic, grated on a Microplane

1 pound boneless, skinless chicken thighs, cut into bite-size pieces

6 tablespoons unsalted butter

1 large onion, finely chopped

1 teaspoon ground cumin

5 cloves garlic, minced

1 cup heavy cream

1 can (14.5 ounces) fire-roasted crushed tomatoes (such as Muir Glen)

2 pouches (8.5 ounces each) cooked basmati rice (about 3 cups)

Chicken stock, as needed

1 cup crispy French fried onions

Global Pantry Ingredient

Masala Spice Blend, *p. 15*

Flavor Booster

A Proper Masala. There are all kinds of dish-specific masalas (spice blends) at Indian markets or online (see page 15). The butter chicken masala blend makes capturing the flavor of its namesake dish effortless and easy. While this blend delivers the best flavor, in a pinch use any good, fairly mild garam masala.

1 Preheat the broiler to high with the oven rack about 4 inches below the element. Line a sheet pan with aluminum foil.

2 Stir together the yogurt, 1½ teaspoons of ginger, 2 teaspoons of masala blend, ¾ teaspoon of salt, the cayenne pepper, and grated garlic in a large bowl. Add the chicken; stir well to coat. Marinate at room temperature for 15 minutes.

3 Spread the chicken pieces out over the prepared sheet pan (the marinade will cling). Broil until the chicken starts to char in spots, about 5 minutes. Flip the chicken pieces over and broil until lightly charred, 5 to 6 minutes. Remove the pan from the oven, lower the oven rack to the center of the oven, and adjust the temperature to 400°F.

4 Meanwhile, melt 3 tablespoons of butter in a large skillet over medium-low heat. Add the chopped onion and ¼ teaspoon of salt; cook until tender, about 10 minutes, stirring occasionally. Stir in the cumin, minced garlic, and remaining 1 tablespoon ginger;

cook 2 minutes, stirring frequently. Add the remaining 1 tablespoon masala blend and ¾ teaspoon salt; cook until toasted and very fragrant, 1 minute, stirring constantly. Stir in the cream and tomatoes; cook 3 minutes, stirring frequently. Knead the rice pouches to separate the grains. Stir the rice and the chicken into the sauce mixture. If the mixture seems like it needs more sauce (you want it to make that ASMR-type smacking noise when you stir it), stir in a little stock.

5 Place the remaining 3 tablespoons butter in an 11 × 7-inch or 2-quart baking dish. Place the dish in the oven until the butter melts, about 5 minutes. (If the large skillet used in Step 4 is ovenproof, you can use it and stir the additional butter into the rice mixture.) Add the rice mixture to the baking dish. Bake until bubbly around the edges, 20 minutes. Sprinkle the casserole with the crispy onions; bake until the onions are browned, 10 minutes. Serve hot, straight from the baking dish.

If the masala blend contains whole spices, you may want to grind it with a mortar and pestle.

Spicy-Honey Popcorn Chicken

and the Crispiest Waffles Ever

ACTIVE TIME: 1 hour
TOTAL TIME: 1 hour
SERVES 5

This is gorgeous sweet-savory brunch, lunch, or dinner fare, both comforting and dazzling. If you go in knowing it's a slightly involved recipe—you're pretty much on the case for an hour, but the steps are logically laid out here—you'll have big fun producing savory waffles so crisp (from the generous use of cornstarch) that we don't know why we ever made them any other way. They're topped with bite-size fried chicken (the chicken having marinated in chili crisp, because why not?) that's topped with a luscious sambal-lively honey. Bonus idea: Eliminate the scallions in the waffle recipe and they are perfect with a butter–maple syrup topping for breakfast, or enjoy with the plum compote on page 185.

1 pound boneless, skinless chicken thighs, cut into small bite-size pieces

2 tablespoons chili crisp

4 teaspoons sugar

1½ teaspoons kosher salt

¾ cup honey

1 tablespoon sambal oelek

1 cup (4½ ounces) all-purpose flour

1⅓ cups (5⅓ ounces) cornstarch

1½ teaspoons baking powder

1⅓ cups whole milk

¼ cup unsalted butter, melted

2 tablespoons canola oil, plus more for frying

2 large eggs, lightly beaten

⅔ cup chopped scallions

Cooking spray

1 Place the chicken in a medium bowl. Add the chili crisp, 1 teaspoon sugar, and ½ teaspoon salt. Toss well to thoroughly coat the chicken. Marinate at room temperature for 30 to 35 minutes (as long as it takes you to get to Step 7).

2 Combine the honey, sambal, and ½ teaspoon salt in a small saucepan; cook over medium-low heat for 3 to 5 minutes, stirring occasionally, without boiling the mixture. Remove the pan from the heat and set aside. The sauce will thicken a bit as it sits.

Global Pantry Ingredients

Chili Crisp, *p. 10*
Sambal, *p. 21*

Pacing Tip

These Waffles Will Hold.
Don't worry that the waffles will go limp in a 250°F oven while you finish the dish. They won't: They'll hold their shattering texture for at least an hour when placed directly on the oven rack.

Equipment Info

Use What You've Got.
Ideally you'll want a standard round American (meaning not Belgian) waffle maker for these. If your waffle iron is a 9-inch square model, scoop ½ cup of batter in the direct middle of the waffle maker and close the lid; the waffles will end up imperfectly round with super-crispy edges.

Game Plan

Step-by-Step Does It. The steps are straightforward: Marinate the chicken, make the sauce, prep the batter, and get started on making the waffles, then alternate between cooking the last waffles and frying the chicken. If you have a kitchen buddy, have them attend the waffle iron while you fry.

3 Preheat the oven to 250°F with the rack placed in the center.

4 Whisk together the flour, ⅓ cup cornstarch, the baking powder, the remaining 3 teaspoons sugar, and ½ teaspoon salt in a large bowl. Whisk together the milk, butter, 2 tablespoons oil, and half of the beaten egg mixture (just eyeball it) in a medium bowl. Add the milk mixture to the flour mixture and stir just until combined. Stir in the scallions.

5 Heat a round 9-inch waffle iron to the highest setting. Coat the plates of the iron lightly with cooking spray. Scoop ½ cup batter in the center of the bottom plate; close the lid and cook until the waffle is well browned and very crisp, 3 to 4 minutes. Place the cooked waffle directly on the oven rack to keep warm. Repeat the process to yield 5 waffles.

6 After cooking the second or third waffle, pour oil into a large cast-iron skillet to a depth of ½ inch. Heat it over medium-high heat until it reaches 370°F on an instant-read thermometer (the temperature will drop a bit when you add the chicken).

7 Add the remaining beaten egg mixture to the marinating chicken mixture and stir well to coat (essentially turning the marinade into a batter). Place the remaining 1 cup cornstarch in a large ziplock bag. Scoop out the chicken mixture with your hands into the cornstarch bag, allowing any excess batter to stay behind. Seal the bag and shake well to coat the chicken with cornstarch. Knead the bag if there are large clumps of uncoated chicken.

8 Place a paper towel–lined plate near the stove. Drop about one-fourth of the chicken pieces into the hot oil. Adjust the heat to maintain the oil temperature between 350°F and 360°F. Fry the chicken until lightly browned (it won't deeply brown) and crisp, 4 to 5 minutes. Scoop out the chicken and drain on paper towels. Repeat the process in three more batches. Serve the chicken over the waffles, and drizzle with the honey sauce.

It's fun to experiment with any of the red-chile Southeast Asian–style sambals. We often add sugar to sambal oelek to cut its vinegar attack.

Simply the Best-est and Moist-est
Turkey Meatballs

ACTIVE TIME: 18 minutes
TOTAL TIME: 28 minutes
SERVES 4

Global Pantry Ingredient

Oyster Sauce, *p. 16*

We know what you're thinking: Meatballs made from ground turkey breast meat, aka culinary Superballs born in a nightmare elementary-school kitchen? Nope and no-how. These are moist, buttery-tasting, a little garlicky, and supremely satisfying. The key is the panade, an old French trick for adding a starchy mash to keep ground meat mixtures tender. True, the evaporated milk–bread combo does make the raw mixture alarmingly soft, so you'll need to scoop it onto the pan with a cookie scoop. Before the finishing touch under the broiler, they'll look a little like drop biscuits (which we kitchen nerds find hilarious). Don't be alarmed; just trust the process. The blast of heat on the oyster sauce glaze works flavor miracles, with some of the more browned bits boasting lightly charred notes. Serve with pasta and marinara sauce, in a hoagie roll with marinara, on a grain bowl, chopped on a pizza, or as a stand-alone entrée with mashed potatoes and green beans (à la meatloaf).

Cooking spray

2 ounces soft (but not squishy) white bread—such as Cuban bread, French bread (the squishy supermarket kind), bolillo, or hoagie rolls

⅔ cup evaporated milk

1 pound ground turkey breast

¼ cup chopped fresh parsley

1 teaspoon kosher salt

½ teaspoon freshly ground black pepper

½ teaspoon dried oregano

1 large clove garlic, grated on a Microplane

1 large egg, lightly beaten

1 tablespoon oyster sauce

1 Preheat the oven to 400°F with the rack placed in the center. Line a large sheet pan with aluminum foil; coat the foil with cooking spray.

2 Tear the bread into pieces and place in a food processor; pulse until coarse breadcrumbs form. Place the breadcrumbs in a large bowl and stir in the evaporated milk. Let stand until the breadcrumbs absorb the milk, about 5 minutes.

3 Crumble the turkey into the bowl, and add the parsley, salt, pepper, oregano, garlic, and egg. Combine the mixture with your hands until well blended. (The mixture will be very soft.) Using a 2-tablespoon cookie scoop, scoop the mixture onto the prepared pan to form 20 meatballs. (A spoon-and-silicone-spatula combination also works well.) Bake until a thermometer inserted into a few test meatballs registers 165°F, 8 to 10 minutes.

4 Remove the pan from the oven. Preheat the broiler to high. Stir together the oyster sauce and 2 teaspoons water in a small bowl and brush over the meatballs. (It will not seem like enough, but it's just the right amount.) Broil the meatballs until lightly browned, 1 to 2 minutes.

Key Technique

Give Them a Nice Tan. Meatballs or burgers made from ground turkey breast are sadly pale even when fully cooked. Our trick is to brush on diluted oyster sauce after baking and give them a quick tan under the broiler. Result: more color, more umami.

Flavor Booster

A Richer Sort of Milk. Old-timey evaporated milk in the panade has a concentrated, rich milkiness that rivals heavy cream—but with far less fat. Use leftovers to make a satisfying oatmeal or add to your coffee (as Ann's grandfather always did).

Anchovies • Yuzu • Black Walnuts • Wondra • Sumac • Calabrian Chiles • Sorghu
Millet • Tabasco Sauce • Coconut Milk • Roasted Hazelnut Oil • Curry Leaves •
Sauce • Shrimp Paste • Worcestershire Sauce • Furikake • Sriracha • Saffron • Ban
Vinegar • Gochujang • Harissa • Marmite • Kecap Manis • Chili Crisp • Freeze-D
Strawberries • Tajín • Kimchi • Korean Toasted Sesame Oil • Dulce de Leche •
Sauce • Lemongrass • Whole Wheat Pastry Flour • Pomegranate Molasses • Mexi
Chocolate • Smoked Paprika • Chipotles in Adobo • Shichimi Togarashi • Makrut L
Leaves • Crema Mexicana • The Many Masalas • Capers • Mexican Chorizo • Mir
Oyster Sauce • Panko Breadcrumbs • Ras El Hanout • Andouille Sausage • Marsa
The Many Sambals • Benton's Bacon • Miso • Stone-Ground Grits • Tahini • Ghee • P
Sugar • Ají Amarillo Paste • Thai Curry Paste • Mustard Powder • Turmeric • Cultu
Butter • Kashmiri Mirch • Dried Porcini Mushrooms • Sweetened Condensed Mi
Anchovies • Yuzu • Black Walnuts • Wondra • Sumac • Calabrian Chiles • Sorghu
Millet • Tabasco Sauce • Coconut Milk • Roasted Hazelnut Oil • Curry Leaves •
Sauce • Shrimp Paste • Worcestershire Sauce • Furikake • Sriracha • Saffron • Ban
Vinegar • Gochujang • Harissa • Marmite • Kecap Manis • Chili Crisp • Freeze-Dr
Strawberries • Tajín • Kimchi • Korean Toasted Sesame Oil • Dulce de Leche •
Sauce • Lemongrass • Whole Wheat Pastry Flour • Pomegranate Molasses • Mexi
Chocolate • Smoked Paprika • Chipotles in Adobo • Shichimi Togarashi • Makrut L
Leaves • Crema Mexicana • The Many Masalas • Capers • Mexican Chorizo • Mir
Oyster Sauce • Panko Breadcrumbs • Ras El Hanout • Andouille Sausage • Marsa
The Many Sambals • Benton's Bacon • Miso • Stone-Ground Grits • Tahini • Ghee • P
Sugar • Ají Amarillo Paste • Thai Curry Paste • Mustard Powder • Turmeric • Cultu
Butter • Kashmiri Mirch • Dried Porcini Mushrooms • Sweetened Condensed Mi
Anchovies • Yuzu • Black Walnuts • Wondra • Sumac • Calabrian Chiles • Sorghu
Millet • Tabasco Sauce • Coconut Milk • Roasted Hazelnut Oil • Curry Leaves •
Sauce • Shrimp Paste • Worcestershire Sauce • Furikake • Sriracha • Saffron • Ban
Vinegar • Gochujang • Harissa • Marmite • Kecap Manis • Chili Crisp • Freeze-Dr
Strawberries • Tajín • Kimchi • Korean Toasted Sesame Oil • Dulce de Leche •
Sauce • Lemongrass • Whole Wheat Pastry Flour • Pomegranate Molasses • Mexi
Chocolate • Smoked Paprika • Chipotles in Adobo • Shichimi Togarashi • Makrut L
Leaves • Crema Mexicana • The Many Masalas • Capers • Mexican Chorizo • Mir
Oyster Sauce • Panko Breadcrumbs • Ras El Hanout • Andouille Sausage • Marsa
The Many Sambals • Benton's Bacon • Miso • Stone-Ground Grits • Tahini • Ghee • P
Sugar • Ají Amarillo Paste • Thai Curry Paste • Mustard Powder • Turmeric • Cultu
Butter • Kashmiri Mirch • Dried Porcini Mushrooms • Sweetened Condensed Milk

Irresistible **Fish** and **Seafood** (Sustainable, Too)

Slow-Roasted Salmon
with Citrus-Olive Relish / 152

Stovetop-Smoked Salmon
with Miso Sauce / 154

Quick Pan-Fried Fish Curry
with Coconut Milk and
Curry Leaves / 156

Crispy Fried Catfish and
a Quick Chowchow / 159

Nice and Easy Crab Cakes
with Thai Curry Flavors / 160

Crabby Fried Rice with a
Fiery Sauce in the Thai Style / 161

Chile Shrimp with the
Creamiest Coconut Grits / 165

10-Minute Pan-Seared Scallops
with Yuzu Kosho Sauce / 167

Prep Pointer

Take the Chill Off. Let the fish sit out at room temperature for 30 minutes (as directed in Step 1) before it goes into the oven. It will cook more evenly.

Shopping Intel

Farmed Fish Works Fine. As with our stovetop-smoked salmon on page 154, high-quality, sustainable, farm-raised Atlantic salmon yields the luscious, unctuous texture that works so well with our relish. Buy from a good fish counter that promotes sustainable practices.

Leftover Tip

Prime Parsley. Flat-leaf (Italian) parsley, often overlooked, has punchy garden-green flavor and chewy texture. When you find yourself with a lot left over, you can use it—enhanced with extra-virgin olive oil and a dribble of good vinegar—as the main green in a tomato salad, or chopped into a bowl of whole grains, feta, preserved lemon, and pine nuts or black walnuts.

Slow-Roasted Salmon
with Citrus-Olive Relish

ACTIVE TIME: 12 minutes
TOTAL TIME: 55 minutes
SERVES 4

With its bright, briny citrus-olive relish—which really highlights the fermented lemony depth and supple texture of preserved lemons—this easy dish of silky, slow-cooked salmon is downright dinner party–worthy. If you've had the experience of overcooking salmon at a higher temp, this super-easy method is much more forgiving.

---

4 salmon fillets (6 ounces each), either skin-on or skinless

1 teaspoon kosher salt

½ teaspoon ground coriander

¼ teaspoon freshly ground black pepper

2 navel oranges

½ cup coarsely chopped pitted Castelvetrano olives

¼ cup fresh flat-leaf parsley leaves

¼ cup slivered red onion

2 tablespoons extra-virgin olive oil

1 tablespoon finely chopped preserved lemon

1 Arrange the salmon fillets in an 11 × 7- or 13 × 9-inch baking dish. Combine ¾ teaspoon of salt, the coriander, and pepper in a small bowl; sprinkle evenly over the salmon. Let the salmon stand at room temperature for 30 minutes.

2 Preheat the oven to 250°F with the rack placed in the center .

3 Cut the top and bottom off each orange so each stands upright on a cutting board. Slide your knife down the sides of the fruit to remove the peel and pith; turn the fruit over and remove any bits of peel and pith from the other side. Holding one orange over a medium bowl, cut between the membranes to extract supremes. Repeat with the remaining orange. Stir in the olives, parsley, onion, 1 tablespoon of oil, the preserved lemon, and remaining ¼ teaspoon salt. Let stand at room temperature until ready to serve.

4 Drizzle the remaining 1 tablespoon oil evenly over the salmon. Slow-roast the salmon until desired degree of doneness, 20 to 25 minutes for medium-rare. The fish might look uncooked, but test it with a fork to see if it's starting to flake.

5 Clean away any white albumin from the bottom of the fillets and transfer them to a platter. Spoon the orange relish over the fish and serve.

Visual Cue

A Little Bit Blackened Is Better.
Sugar in the miso glaze will
blacken around the edge of
the fish as it broils. Go for that
liminal perfection while being
eagle-eyed to remove the
salmon before it rushes into
simply burnt.

Stovetop-Smoked Salmon
with Miso Sauce

ACTIVE TIME: 25 minutes
TOTAL TIME: 3 hours 25 minutes
SERVES 4

We've always loved Alaska black cod
(sablefish) broiled with miso glaze,
first eaten long ago at Nobu in New
York and Tojo's in Vancouver, both
landmark Japanese restaurants in
their day. But black cod can be pricey
and hard to find in prime condition.
This showstopper, a pan-Pacific riff,
marinates less pricey salmon in miso,
raising the game by using a fast, easy,
jury-rigged stovetop smoker (for this,
you will need a disposable aluminum
foil pan and a quarter cup of unsoaked
wood chips—see photos). Hot-smoking
salmon like this is a method Scott
learned to love in New Zealand. The
salmon is finished under the broiler
while the marinade is elevated to a
sauce. Serve with a salad and rice
or a whole grain like freekeh, millet
(see Try This! on page 175), or farro.

1 tablespoon plus 2 teaspoons brown sugar

⅓ cup plus ¼ cup mirin

4 tablespoons white miso

1 teaspoon Korean toasted sesame oil

1 teaspoon light or dark soy sauce

4 fresh, sustainable salmon fillets
  (6 ounces each; see Shopping Intel
  on page 152)

Cooking spray

1 Whisk together the sugar, ⅓ cup mirin,
3 tablespoons miso, the oil, and soy sauce in
a small bowl until the miso has thoroughly
dissolved.

2 Combine the salmon in a large ziplock
bag with the marinade; seal, gently toss the
salmon until it's completely coated, then
burp the air out of the bag, fold it tight, and
marinate in the refrigerator for 3 hours.

3 Place an oven rack 6 inches below the
broiler and preheat the broiler to high.
Place a rack on the next rung down as
well, in case needed. Line a sheet pan with
aluminum foil, coat it with cooking spray,
and place it next to the stovetop smoker.

4 Remove the salmon from the bag and set
the bag aside (don't discard the marinade);
arrange the salmon on the surface of the
stovetop smoker pan opposite the wood
chips, with a little space between pieces.
Cover the pan tightly with foil. Turn on the
stove's overhead vent fan. Turn an electric
burner on high or a gas burner on medium
and let burn for 10 to 30 seconds or until
smoke begins to seep out from the foil.
Reduce the heat to medium-low and smoke
the salmon for 6 minutes. Remove the pan
from the heat, leave the foil cover on for an
additional minute, then carefully uncover.
At this point you can spritz the wood chips
with water to extinguish them. Remove the
salmon pieces to the prepared sheet pan.

5 Brush the salmon with a bit of the marinade, trying to avoid slopping it onto the pan itself. Put the rest of the marinade in a small saucepan. Place the salmon under the broiler and broil until the thin "tail" end and other edges begin to blacken without burning, 8 minutes. (If the salmon seems to be burning, put the pan on the rack below to continue cooking.) Remove the fish and poke the thickest part of one piece with the tip of a sharp knife to see if it is cooked; the flesh should be turning opaque but still slightly transparent, too—"medium rare." Broil or continue cooking on the lower rack for a few more minutes if needed.

6 While the salmon is broiling, whisk the remaining 1 tablespoon miso and ¼ cup mirin into the marinade and bring to a boil over medium-high heat; reduce the heat to medium-low and let bubble until it has the consistency of a thin caramel sauce, about 2 minutes. Reduce the heat to a low simmer.

7 When the salmon is done, transfer the fillets to serving plates with a large fish spatula, careful to keep the fish intact. Drizzle the sauce over the fillets and serve.

How to Fashion a Stovetop Smoker

1. Poke holes in an 11 × 7-inch aluminum pan, where the flame or burner will be.

2. Put ¼ cup dry culinary wood chips over the holes, spray cooking spray on the opposite side of the pan, and line up the salmon on sprayed area.

3. Seal the pan with aluminum foil and arrange the pan so that holes are over burner or flame. Salmon should not be over the burner; it can rest on the stove grate.

4. With the vent on, carefully open the foil to release smoke. Safely discard hot wood chips into a bowl of water, then discard. Save the smoker for another use.

Global Pantry Ingredients

Coconut Milk, *p. 10*

Curry Leaves, *p. 11*

Masala Spice Blend, *p. 15*

Peanut Oil, *p. 18*

Turmeric, *p. 24*

Shopping Intel

Sourcing Tilapia. Fish purists can be snooty about tilapia (some consider it the boneless, skinless chicken breast of the sea), but we like it for its mild flavor, firm texture, low price tag, wide availability, and easy cooking. Just make sure to choose a sustainable option; Monterey Bay Aquarium's Seafood Watch program's top recommendations are tilapia farmed in raceway systems in Peru or in ponds in Ecuador. We have been consistently impressed by the tilapia we get from Whole Foods.

Quick Pan-Fried Fish Curry
with Coconut Milk and Curry Leaves

ACTIVE TIME: 34 minutes
TOTAL TIME: 34 minutes
SERVES 4

One thing Scott loved when traveling in India and Bangladesh was a good fish curry in which the fish had been fried to gain a bit of a crust before its saucy immersion. This recipe is inspired by a style from the lovely west coast Indian state of Kerala, enriched with coconut milk and fragrant with fresh curry leaves—which are an essential ingredient. We use a purchased fish masala (spice mix) as a shortcut, which only requires finding said masala at an Indian food store—where the curry leaves should also be available in the refrigerated section. We used the Everest brand of fish masala, containing tamarind, coriander, chile, cumin, garlic, and more. Other fish masalas will also work fine. Serve with fragrant basmati rice.

2 small green chiles (such as Thai or bird's eye), seeded

2 medium onions, quartered

1 length (2 inches) fresh ginger, peeled and cut into small pieces

2 tablespoons cornstarch

2 tablespoons all-purpose flour

1 teaspoon ground turmeric

1 teaspoon kosher salt

1½ pounds tilapia fillets, cut in half lengthwise

4 tablespoons peanut oil, or neutral oil (such as canola)

2 tablespoons fish masala curry mixture (spice blend)

1 can (13.5 ounces) coconut milk (warm the can and shake before opening)

16 to 20 curry leaves

1 Place the chiles, onions, and ginger in a food processor or blender and process until a mushy paste results, about 30 seconds.

2 Mix the cornstarch, flour, turmeric, and ½ teaspoon salt on one side of a sheet pan, leaving the other side clean. Pat the tilapia fillets dry and press both sides into the cornstarch mixture firmly, shaking off the excess; set the coated fish on the clean part of the sheet pan. Heat 3 tablespoons of oil in a large, sturdy skillet over medium-high heat until shimmering, 2 minutes. Add the fish to the skillet and pan-fry until browned on the bottom (cook in batches to avoid crowding if using a smaller pan), about 2 minutes. Carefully turn the fish over with a spatula and cook until it flakes easily with a fork, a minute or two more. Place the fish back on the sheet pan (discard any remaining cornstarch mixture on it first).

3 Add the remaining 1 tablespoon oil to the skillet and swirl to coat. Add the onion paste; cook until the paste reduces and begins to fry and turns a pale yellow, about 5 minutes. Add the masala and continue to fry for another minute, stirring to combine. Reduce the heat to medium. Add the remaining ½ teaspoon salt, coconut milk, and curry leaves and simmer, uncovered, until the sauce has the consistency of a thick gravy, about 5 minutes. If the sauce is too thick, thin it with some hot water. Add the fish and simmer until the fish is thoroughly heated, about 2 minutes.

4 To serve, you don't have to remove the curry leaves, but tell eaters they don't have to eat them (no harm if they do).

Curry leaves should be bought fresh and are easily found refrigerated in Indian food shops.

Crispy Fried Catfish
and a Quick Chowchow

ACTIVE TIME: 40 minutes
TOTAL TIME: 40 minutes
SERVES 4

Piquant might be the best way to describe chowchow, the great Southern relish made from cabbage. It's tangy and sweet, with a pleasantly faint pungency and brilliant color that usually comes from turmeric and mustard seeds—both ingredients, incidentally, that are used in Indian pickles as well. It's often served with field peas or soup beans, or alongside a wedge of cornbread (see page 259). Here, it's used as a topper for crispy fried catfish.

FOR THE CHOWCHOW

2 cups thinly sliced green cabbage

½ cup finely chopped red bell pepper

½ cup finely chopped green tomato or tomatillo

⅓ cup thinly sliced shallots

¼ cup sugar

¼ cup white vinegar

½ teaspoon kosher salt

½ teaspoon yellow mustard seeds

½ teaspoon ground turmeric

FOR THE CATFISH

1 teaspoon kosher salt

½ teaspoon garlic powder

½ teaspoon ground turmeric

¼ teaspoon cayenne pepper

4 catfish fillets (6 ounces each)

¾ cup fine- or medium-ground yellow cornmeal

Canola oil for frying

1 To prepare the chowchow, cut the cabbage into pieces about 1½ inches long. Combine the cabbage, bell pepper, green tomato, shallots, sugar, vinegar, salt, mustard seeds, and turmeric in a small saucepan over medium-high to high heat. Bring the mixture to a boil; reduce the heat to medium-low and cook until the cabbage is just barely crisp-tender (it will soften more as the mixture stands), about 5 minutes. Remove the pan from the heat and cool for 15 minutes. Drain the chowchow. (You can prepare this ahead of time if you wish; the chowchow will keep in an airtight container in the fridge for up to 2 weeks.)

2 Meanwhile, to prepare the catfish, combine the salt, garlic powder, turmeric, and cayenne pepper in a small bowl until well mixed. Sprinkle the spice mixture evenly over the catfish. Pour the cornmeal into a pie plate or shallow bowl. Dredge the catfish in the cornmeal, pressing gently to coat both sides. Discard excess cornmeal.

3 Pour the oil into a large skillet to a depth of about ½ inch and heat over medium-high heat until the oil reaches 350°F to 375°F on an instant-read thermometer, 5 to 10 minutes. Carefully add the catfish to the oil and fry, turning once with a spatula, until well browned and the fish flakes easily when tested with a fork, 3 to 4 minutes per side. Drain the fish on paper towels.

4 Serve the catfish with the chowchow.

Global Pantry Ingredient

Turmeric, *p. 24*

Sustainability Note
Farmed in the States.
Although some international catfish sources sport sustainability certification, we like to support the American catfish-farming industry (there is also some wild-caught catfish from the Chesapeake Bay). We think it has a milder, more buttery flavor, while imported fish can have a muddier taste.

Seasoning Tip
Put It Where You Want It.
Instead of adding the seasoning to the cornmeal that we use for dredging the fish, we sprinkle it directly on the fish first, where it works harder and isn't shaken off.

Party On!
Everyone Loves a Fry-Up. For a fish-fry get-together, simply double all the ingredients, and fry the fish in batches (keep warm in a 200°F oven).

Nice and Easy Crab Cakes
with Thai Curry Flavors

ACTIVE TIME: 8 minutes
TOTAL TIME: 21 minutes
SERVES 4

Crab cakes should be mostly crab, right? We begin with the moister, stickier texture and richer, crabbier flavor of crab claw meat (rather than jumbo or lump) and add no starchy extenders, just an egg to help all the crabby goodness cling together under a buttery, crunchy panko coating. We nix the bother of making a sauce, instead folding lovely, warm, Southeast Asian spice-and-herb flavors right into the cakes via a convenient jarred Thai curry paste. These cakes make for a superb weekend lunch with a glass of cava or a spritzy 'ade and a green salad of your choosing.

⅔ cup panko breadcrumbs

¼ cup chopped fresh chives

¼ cup mayonnaise

2 tablespoons Thai red curry paste

1 large egg, lightly beaten

1 pound fresh crab claw meat

2 tablespoons unsalted butter

2 tablespoons canola oil

1 Place the panko on a plate or in a shallow bowl. Combine the chives, mayonnaise, curry paste, and egg in a medium bowl; gently fold in the crab. Divide the crab mixture into 4 equal portions, rolling each between your hands to form a ball. Roll each ball in the panko to coat.

2 Place the butter and oil in a large nonstick skillet and heat over medium heat until the butter melts and the pan is hot. Place the crab balls in the pan; flatten them slightly with a spatula to about a 1-inch thickness. Cook until browned on the bottom, about 5 minutes. Carefully turn the crab cakes over. They're delicate, but if they break apart, no worries; just push them back together. Cook until browned on the other side, about 5 minutes. Serve hot.

Panko brings so much more crunch than regular breadcrumbs.

Crabby Fried Rice
with a Fiery Sauce in the Thai Style

ACTIVE TIME: 25 minutes
TOTAL TIME: 25 minutes
SERVES 4

Every cook needs one or two fried rice dishes in their repertoire. This crab version, with its fish-sauce saltiness, was a go-to street-food treat when Scott backpacked through Thailand many years ago. It's pleasingly mild-flavored until, of course, you add a spoonful of the sharp, salty chile sauce served on the side—a version of the ubiquitous prik nam pla sauce—which livens things up as much as you dare. (For less heat, try substituting Fresno or serrano chiles instead of the little bird's eye variety, which will cut the Scoville firepower here by at least half, especially if you scrape out the seeds.) Serve a cooling, garlicky cucumber salad on the side. Check seafoodwatch.org for the latest intel on sustainable crab.

FOR THE SAUCE

3 tablespoons freshly squeezed lime juice

2 tablespoons fish sauce

1 tablespoon chopped fresh cilantro leaves

2 teaspoons sugar

2 red Fresno or green serrano chiles, seeded if desired, and sliced into thin rings (or use tiny bird's eye chiles for maximum heat)

2 cloves garlic, minced

FOR THE FRIED RICE

2 tablespoons fish sauce

1 tablespoon soy sauce (preferably light)

2 teaspoons sugar

4 cloves garlic, grated on a Microplane or mortared into a paste

3 medium shallots, cut into thin rings

4 cups cooked jasmine rice, chilled (1½ cups uncooked rice)

8 ounces fresh crab claw meat

½ cup finely chopped scallions

4 large eggs

¼ cup peanut oil or neutral oil (such as canola)

½ cup chopped fresh cilantro leaves and stems

Global Pantry Ingredients

Fish Sauce, *p. 11*
Peanut Oil, *p. 18*
Soy Sauce, *p. 22*

Rice Tips

Day-Old Rice Fries Better. Cold, day-old rice, or rice made in the morning and chilled, fries better than stickier fresh stuff. If it still seems sticky, you can work 2 teaspoons of neutral oil (such as canola), into the rice before you cook it to separate the grains.

Fry in Two Batches. Because the quantity of rice is quite large, we suggest dividing everything in half and cooking in two batches. Each only takes a few minutes. Batch one will keep fine in a warm oven, or even just covered on the counter.

1 To prepare the sauce, combine the lime juice, fish sauce, cilantro, sugar, chiles, and garlic in a small bowl; set aside.

2 To prepare the rice, preheat the oven to the warm setting. Meanwhile, whisk together the fish sauce, soy sauce, and sugar; divide evenly between 2 small bowls. Combine the garlic and shallots; divide evenly between 2 small bowls. Divide the rice, crab, and scallions into 3 separate piles on each of 2 plates. Gently crack 2 eggs into a small bowl so that the yolks remain intact; repeat with the remaining 2 eggs in another bowl.

3 Heat a wok or large skillet over medium-high heat for 2 minutes. Add 2 tablespoons of oil, swirl it in the wok for about 30 seconds, and add one portion of the garlic and shallots. Cook until fragrant and blond, but don't let the mixture burn, 1 to 2 minutes. Slip 2 eggs into the wok and gently break into large bits with a large spoon, flipping the bits without vigorously scrambling. When the eggs are just cooked, 1 to 2 minutes, stir in one portion of the rice and one portion of the soy sauce mixture; press the mixture up the sides of the wok or skillet a bit to capture the heat, and leave to cook until just starting to brown, about 1 minute. Then toss again and let cook until just starting to brown, about another 1 minute. Add one crab portion and one scallion portion and toss until the crab is thoroughly heated, 1 to 2 minutes. Remove the rice mixture to a large platter. Put the platter in the warm oven. Add the remaining oil to the wok, and repeat the process with the second batch. Add the second batch of rice to the warm platter.

4 Top the platter of rice with the chopped cilantro, and serve with the sauce on the side.

Chile Shrimp
with the Creamiest Coconut Grits

ACTIVE TIME: 52 minutes
TOTAL TIME: 52 minutes
SERVES 4

This dish by Ann, the Low Country shrimp-and-grits classic taken for a Singapore spin, inspired us to write this book. Fiery chile-sauced shrimp are spooned over the creamiest grits you'll ever eat. Because shrimp often overcook before they brown in the pan, we brine them with a bit of sugar and fish sauce, which accelerates the browning while preserving texture. If you want to stick a bit closer to the Singapore style, leave out the lime; for a hint of acidity, spritz away.

FOR THE SHRIMP

2 teaspoons sugar

2 teaspoons sambal oelek

1 teaspoon fish sauce

1 teaspoon soy sauce

1 teaspoon peanut or canola oil

1 pound large (26/30-count) peeled and deveined shrimp

FOR THE GRITS

1 stalk lemongrass

1½ cups coconut milk (warm the can and shake before opening)

1½ cups unsalted chicken stock

¾ teaspoon kosher salt

¾ cup stone-ground white or yellow grits

1 teaspoon sugar

FOR THE SAUCE AND GARNISHES

6 tablespoons salted butter

2 teaspoons to 2 tablespoons sambal oelek

1 teaspoon sugar (optional)

2 tablespoons sliced scallions

4 lime wedges (optional)

1 To prepare the shrimp, combine the sugar, sambal, fish sauce, soy sauce, and oil in a large ziplock bag; seal and squeeze the bag until everything is thoroughly combined. Add the shrimp to the bag and massage until the shrimp are covered with the mixture. Squeeze air out of the bag and seal the bag. Put in the fridge to marinate for 30 minutes.

Global Pantry Ingredients

Coconut Milk, *p. 10*

Fish Sauce, *p. 11*

Lemongrass, *p. 14*

Sambal, *p. 21*

Soy Sauce, *p. 22*

Sustainability Note
Go for US Shrimp. We prefer wild-caught US shrimp, usually white Gulf shrimp. Buy them in the large or jumbo size range—anywhere from 26 to 30 per pound to 16 to 20 per pound—because they tend to have enough meat to take a proper sear without becoming rubbery. There are other sustainable wild-caught varieties, such as the fantastic candy-like spot prawns caught on the West Coast, but their season is brief and distribution limited.

2 To prepare the grits, trim off the root and upper two-thirds of the lemongrass stalk; peel and discard the toughest outer leaves. Slice the bulb in half lengthwise; reserve one half for another use. Place the remaining bulb half on a cutting board. Crush it several times with the flat side of a chef's knife to bruise and release its aromas.

3 Combine the bruised lemongrass, 1¼ cups coconut milk, stock, and salt in a medium saucepan; bring to a boil over medium-high heat. Gradually add the grits, stirring constantly; reduce the heat to low and cook, covered, until tender and thick, stirring occasionally, about 20 minutes. Stir in the remaining ¼ cup coconut milk and the sugar. Cover and keep warm.

4 To prepare the sauce and cook the shrimp, heat a large nonstick skillet over medium-high heat. Add 1 tablespoon butter and swirl until it melts. Add half of the shrimp, dropping them into the pan so that each shrimp does not touch another. Sauté for a minute or so, checking with tongs to see if the shrimp are browning. Once they have browned, flip the shrimp over, sauté for another minute, then remove to a plate. Add another 1 tablespoon butter and repeat with remaining shrimp.

5 When the shrimp are all done, add the remaining 4 tablespoons butter to the skillet, stirring and scraping the pan as the butter melts to mix in the browned bits of shrimp on the bottom. Stir in the 2 teaspoons (or more) sambal and the sugar, if desired. Add the shrimp and stir until covered with the sauce.

6 Fish the lemongrass out of the grits, then serve the shrimp mixture over the grits. Sprinkle with the scallions and serve with lime wedges, if desired.

Fish sauce: Fishy straight from the bottle, it melds in and adds its ocean umami.

10-Minute Pan-Seared Scallops

with Yuzu Kosho Sauce

ACTIVE TIME: 10 minutes
TOTAL TIME: 10 minutes
SERVES 2

Global Pantry Ingredients

Coconut Milk, *p. 10*
Yuzu, *p. 25*

Scott's kids used to joke that a certain type of home-cooked dish was "restaurant quality," meaning it duplicated very good fancily plated things served in terribly expensive (for a family of four) New York restaurants. Scallops are the easiest seafood to make this way: Fast sear + simple sauce + nice plating = restaurant quality! Here, the juice of mollusks sweetens the cooking butter, and then the butter is elevated by the ethereal citrus goodness, chile heat, and slight fermented funk of yuzu kosho. Everything is knit together with a bit of rich coconut milk. Serve with an interesting salad, a good white wine, and crusty bread, and save some money by staying in.

2 teaspoons yuzu kosho

⅓ cup coconut milk (warm the can and shake before opening)

2 teaspoons canola oil

2 tablespoons unsalted butter, at room temperature

8 to 10 large dry scallops (¾ to 1 pound), depending on size, patted dry

1 Mix the yuzu kosho together with 1 tablespoon of coconut milk in a small bowl until you have a slurry, then add the rest of the coconut milk and whisk until thoroughly mixed.

2 Heat the oil in a large skillet over medium-high heat for 30 seconds, then add the butter and swirl until just starting to brown. Add the scallops (keeping space between them) and sear undisturbed for 1½ minutes. Check one scallop: It should be beautifully seared. When it is, flip and cook the scallops for another 1½ minutes without poking them. Put the seared scallops on 2 serving plates and remove the pan from the heat.

3 Add the coconut milk mixture to the pan, where it should bubble. Stir with a silicone spatula until mixed and heated through, 30 seconds to 1 minute. Drizzle the sauce over the plated scallops. Serve immediately.

Shopping Intel
Proper Scallop Buying.
Buy "dry" scallops at a good fish counter. These are not water processed, and they sear well. (Previously frozen dry scallops will work, just thaw them completely and pat them completely dry.) Avoid those tiny bay scallops in favor of big fat ones rated 10 to 15 per pound. If those are not available, cook something else!

Anchovies • Yuzu • Black Walnuts • Wondra • Sumac • Calabrian Chiles • Sorghu
Millet • Tabasco Sauce • Coconut Milk • Roasted Hazelnut Oil • Curry Leaves •
Sauce • Shrimp Paste • Worcestershire Sauce • Furikake • Sriracha • Saffron • Bany
Vinegar • Gochujang • Harissa • Marmite • Kecap Manis • Chili Crisp • Freeze-Dr
Strawberries • Tajín • Kimchi • Korean Toasted Sesame Oil • Dulce de Leche •
Sauce • Lemongrass • Whole Wheat Pastry Flour • Pomegranate Molasses • Mexi
Chocolate • Smoked Paprika • Chipotles in Adobo • Shichimi Togarashi • Makrut Li
Leaves • Crema Mexicana • The Many Masalas • Capers • Mexican Chorizo • Mir
Oyster Sauce • Panko Breadcrumbs • Ras El Hanout • Andouille Sausage • Marsa
The Many Sambals • Benton's Bacon • Miso • Stone-Ground Grits • Tahini • Ghee • P.
Sugar • Ají Amarillo Paste • Thai Curry Paste • Mustard Powder • Turmeric • Cultu
Butter • Kashmiri Mirch • Dried Porcini Mushrooms • Sweetened Condensed Mi
Anchovies • Yuzu • Black Walnuts • Wondra • Sumac • Calabrian Chiles • Sorghu
Millet • Tabasco Sauce • Coconut Milk • Roasted Hazelnut Oil • Curry Leaves •
Sauce • Shrimp Paste • Worcestershire Sauce • Furikake • Sriracha • Saffron • Bany
Vinegar • Gochujang • Harissa • Marmite • Kecap Manis • Chili Crisp • Freeze-Dr
Strawberries • Tajín • Kimchi • Korean Toasted Sesame Oil • Dulce de Leche •
Sauce • Lemongrass • Whole Wheat Pastry Flour • Pomegranate Molasses • Mexi
Chocolate • Smoked Paprika • Chipotles in Adobo • Shichimi Togarashi • Makrut Li
Leaves • Crema Mexicana • The Many Masalas • Capers • Mexican Chorizo • Mir
Oyster Sauce • Panko Breadcrumbs • Ras El Hanout • Andouille Sausage • Marsa
The Many Sambals • Benton's Bacon • Miso • Stone-Ground Grits • Tahini • Ghee • Pa
Sugar • Ají Amarillo Paste • Thai Curry Paste • Mustard Powder • Turmeric • Cultu
Butter • Kashmiri Mirch • Dried Porcini Mushrooms • Sweetened Condensed Mi
Anchovies • Yuzu • Black Walnuts • Wondra • Sumac • Calabrian Chiles • Sorghu
Millet • Tabasco Sauce • Coconut Milk • Roasted Hazelnut Oil • Curry Leaves • F
Sauce • Shrimp Paste • Worcestershire Sauce • Furikake • Sriracha • Saffron • Bany
Vinegar • Gochujang • Harissa • Marmite • Kecap Manis • Chili Crisp • Freeze-Dr
Strawberries • Tajín • Kimchi • Korean Toasted Sesame Oil • Dulce de Leche •
Sauce • Lemongrass • Whole Wheat Pastry Flour • Pomegranate Molasses • Mexi
Chocolate • Smoked Paprika • Chipotles in Adobo • Shichimi Togarashi • Makrut Li
Leaves • Crema Mexicana • The Many Masalas • Capers • Mexican Chorizo • Mir
Oyster Sauce • Panko Breadcrumbs • Ras El Hanout • Andouille Sausage • Marsa
The Many Sambals • Benton's Bacon • Miso • Stone-Ground Grits • Tahini • Ghee • Pa
Sugar • Ají Amarillo Paste • Thai Curry Paste • Mustard Powder • Turmeric • Cultu
Butter • Kashmiri Mirch • Dried Porcini Mushrooms • Sweetened Condensed Mill

Meat-Free Mains
for Breakfast, Lunch, and Dinner

Harissa, *p. 13*

Pomegranate Molasses, *see* Try This!

Avoid This Mistake

Pre-Combine Your Ingredients.
The pressed tofu is tossed
with cornstarch, garlic powder,
and salt before being crisped
in the pan. To ensure critical,
even distribution, stir these
ingredients together first, then
vigorously toss with the tofu
cubes to coat.

Shopping Intel

Less-Wet Tofu. Look for firm
tofu that's not packed in
water but in vacuum-sealed
packaging without added
liquid—it doesn't need to be
pressed before cooking. You'll
find it at Trader Joe's and many
large supermarkets. We also
tried an organic "super firm"
tofu that did have a bit of water
but was so dense that it worked
beautifully after pressing.

Try This!

Pomegranate Molasses.
This slow-cooked reduction
of pomegranate juice is
upliftingly zippy—and not
nearly as "dark"-flavored as
sugar-based molasses—with
a tannic cut you'll recognize
from munching fresh arils when
you struggled to pull them out
of their webby pomegranate
caves. It's widely used in Persian
and Middle Eastern cooking,
and not particularly expensive
given the source fruit. One of
our favorite brands, Al Wadi,
comes from Lebanon.

Virtuous Vegan Harissa Tofu Bowls
with Farro

ACTIVE TIME: 30 minutes
TOTAL TIME: 45 minutes
SERVES 4

Ann would get aggravated when her
family told her they didn't like tofu.
This dish cured that whine: When tofu
is well seasoned and perfectly crisped,
by damn, they *love* it. Firm bean curd
is pressed dry, then coated in seasoned
cornstarch and pan-fried till crisp-
edged and chewy within. A sweet-spicy
sauce—which borrows heat and tang
from Middle Eastern harissa and the
fruity joy of pomegranate molasses—
builds even more of a crust. No other
food takes on quite this crunchy-then-
chewy texture; each tofu cube is pure,
zingy pleasure.

---

1 package (14 ounces) extra-firm or
   super-firm tofu

1 pound broccolini, trimmed

1⅓ cups whole-grain farro

1½ tablespoons cornstarch

1 teaspoon kosher salt

½ teaspoon garlic powder

4 tablespoons extra-virgin olive oil

2½ tablespoons harissa paste or sauce

1½ tablespoons pomegranate molasses

½ teaspoon ground cumin

1 small red onion, cut into 8 wedges

1 Cut the tofu block lengthwise into
4 equal slabs. Arrange the slabs on a double
layer of paper towels. Top with more paper
towels, then a cutting board. Top with a
heavy skillet. Let stand to drain the water,
20 minutes. (You can skip this process if
you're using vacuum-sealed tofu.)

2 Meanwhile, bring a Dutch oven full of
water to a boil. Add the broccolini to the
pan; boil until crisp-tender, 2 to 3 minutes.
Using tongs, move the broccolini from the
pan to a colander. Rinse well with cold water.

3 Add the farro to the boiling water; cook
until al dente or to your liking, anywhere
from 20 to 45 minutes, depending on the
variety. Drain and set aside.

4 Cut each tofu slab into ¾- to 1-inch
cubes and place in a medium bowl. Combine
the cornstarch, ½ teaspoon salt, and the
garlic powder in a small bowl; sprinkle over
the tofu and toss well to coat, until there are
scant traces of the coating mixture on the
bottom of the bowl.

5 Heat 2 tablespoons of oil in a large nonstick skillet over medium-high heat. Add the tofu to the pan. Cook until nicely browned on one side, 3 to 4 minutes; then turn every 2 to 3 minutes, about 12 minutes total. You don't have to brown all 6 sides, but you'll find as you go that the crust development accelerates, and that's what you want—go by look more than time. (Taste one tofu cube at this point and remember this method when you want an even simpler, non-harissa-sauced dish that will convert anyone to the appeal of tofu.) Reduce the heat to medium. Combine the harissa and pomegranate molasses in a small bowl and add to the pan. Cook, tossing the tofu in the mixture, until the sauce is absorbed and the tofu is coated and browned, about 2 minutes. Remove the tofu from the pan.

6 Add 1 tablespoon oil and the cumin to the pan; cook until fragrant, about 30 seconds. Stir in the farro. Cook until thoroughly heated, 2 to 3 minutes. Stir in ¼ teaspoon salt. Divide the farro mixture evenly among 4 shallow bowls. Divide the tofu evenly among the bowls.

7 Meanwhile, heat another skillet over medium-high heat. Add the remaining 1 tablespoon oil and swirl to coat. Add the onion and broccolini. Cook until the vegetables begin to char, about 3 minutes, then turn the vegetables and continue cooking until the onion is just done, about 3 minutes. Sprinkle with the remaining ¼ teaspoon salt. Divide the vegetables evenly among the bowls.

Pomegranate molasses is tangy, fruity, and concentrated.

The Creamiest Vegetarian Curry
with Paneer

ACTIVE TIME: 34 minutes
TOTAL TIME: 45 minutes
SERVES 4

Global Pantry Ingredients

Ghee, *p. 12*
Kashmiri Mirch, *see* Try This!, *p. 180*
Masala Spice Blend, *p. 15*

Though our quicker riff on a classic Indian vegetarian curry uses some shortcut tricks, it gets within reach of the beautiful flavors of a traditional preparation. This is basically a one-pot "gravy" in which milky paneer cheese and toasted nuts are added for chew just before serving. The luscious texture comes from pureed raw cashews, the creamiest of all the nuts. One flavor-boost method we like is to toast a few extra whole spices before using a well-chosen masala spice mix (see The Right Spice Mix). Toasting adds tremendous fragrance and depth and takes less than two minutes.

You'll want to have all of the ingredients, measured and chopped, by the stove before you begin cooking; it makes the recipe a breeze to pull together. Eat this with soft, buttered white rolls for a sopping-lunch in the Mumbai street-food style, or with basmati rice for a comforting bowl with a simple cucumber salad (vinegar, salt, sugar, chopped cilantro) on the side.

2 tablespoons ghee

1 cup raw cashews

1 teaspoon cumin seeds

½ teaspoon cardamom seeds

1 bay leaf

2 cloves garlic, finely chopped

1 inch peeled fresh ginger, finely chopped (or, if frozen, grated)

1 large onion, chopped

1 tablespoon pav bhaji masala (or a good garam masala)

1 teaspoon kosher salt

1 teaspoon ground hot chile pepper, Kashmiri mirch if you have it

1½ pounds large tomatoes, chopped

½ cup half-and-half

8 ounces paneer, cut into 1-inch cubes

1 Heat a large nonstick skillet or heavy-bottomed pot (a Dutch oven will work) over medium heat for 1 minute. Add 1 teaspoon of ghee and ½ cup of raw cashews; sauté, stirring frequently, until the nuts are browned (but not burned) on both sides, 2 to 3 minutes. Put the nuts on a plate and turn the heat to low.

Shopping Intel
Seek Out This Cheese. Paneer is a milky, chewy, fresh Indian cheese that doesn't melt. It's gradually finding its way into the dairy or cheese cases of larger supermarkets but can reliably be found, fresh or frozen, in Indian food stores, which also offer dozens of masala mixtures. If you don't eat dairy, a very firm tofu will work.

The Right Spice Mix
A Street Food Masala. Pav bhaji masala is a fairly simple spice mix—chile, fennel, coriander, cumin, a few more—used in a wildly popular Bombay street food, pav bhaji. Basically, it's a yummy vegetable gravy eaten with soft bread or rolls. Ask for this masala in Indian food stores; several versions are available online.

2 Add the cumin seeds, cardamom seeds, and bay leaf to the pan and toast until fragrant, stirring constantly, about 30 seconds. Add the remaining 5 teaspoons ghee and stir in the garlic and ginger; sauté until they are soft and golden, 90 seconds. Bump the heat to medium-low. Add the onion and sauté until it is nicely golden and translucent, about 6 minutes. Add the masala, salt, and ground chile pepper and sauté an additional minute. Add the tomatoes and the remaining ½ cup raw cashews and simmer, covered, for about 15 minutes. Occasionally lift the lid and break up the tomatoes with a spoon, stirring to make sure the mixture isn't sticking. If the mixture isn't bubbling, turn the heat up a bit.

3 Remove the bay leaf, then spoon the tomato mixture into a blender, add ½ cup water, and puree on high until very smooth, about 45 seconds. Pour back into the pan over low heat, stir in the half-and-half and paneer, and let the mixture gently bubble until the cheese is hot, about 3 minutes—be careful to make sure it doesn't stick.

4 Put the curry in a serving bowl and top with the toasted nuts.

Milky-tasting ghee is every bit as delicious as, but entirely different from, olive oil.

Double-Crispy Spicy Eggplant
on Cumin-Scented Millet

ACTIVE TIME: 45 minutes
TOTAL TIME: 45 minutes
SERVES 4

This dish is inspired by one of Ann's favorite treats, found on many pan-Chinese restaurant menus. Fantastically crispy eggplant "batons" are tossed with tingling Szechuan spices and topped with fresh cilantro and scallions. One shortcut here is the use of chili crisp, some versions of which offer both heat and Szechuan-style numbing tingle as well as a crunchy chew that amplifies the crisp texture of the eggplant. (You can add crushed Szechuan peppercorns if your crisp lacks the tingle.) The whole dish is made even more fragrant and hearty on a bed of millet, a traditional grain of China that, once cooked, has the appearance of couscous and a texture and flavor similar to quinoa.

FOR THE MILLET

1 tablespoon canola oil

1 teaspoon cumin seeds

¾ cup uncooked millet

½ teaspoon kosher salt

FOR THE EGGPLANT

Canola oil for frying

3 medium Japanese eggplants
(6 to 7 ounces each; in a pinch, globe eggplants will work)

⅔ cup cornstarch

2 tablespoons chili crisp
(or 3 if you love the heat!)

½ teaspoon kosher salt

¼ cup thinly sliced scallions, for serving

2 tablespoons chopped fresh cilantro, for serving

1 To prepare the millet, heat the oil in a small saucepan over medium-high heat for 1 minute. Add the cumin seeds; cook until very fragrant, about 30 seconds, being careful not to let them burn. Add the millet; cook until lightly toasted and fragrant, 2 to 3 minutes, stirring frequently. Stir in 1¼ cups water and the salt. Bring to a boil; cover, reduce the heat to low, and simmer until tender and not starchy, 25 to 28 minutes. Remove from the heat and let stand, covered, for 10 minutes. Fluff with a fork.

Global Pantry Ingredients

Chili Crisp, *p. 10*
Millet, *see* Try This!

Try This!
Millet. Millet is a delicious, often overlooked, mild-flavored, gluten-free whole grain (actually a seed) that humans have enjoyed for 7,500 years in Asia and Africa. There are hundreds of varieties, often just called "millet" on whole-grain shelves or online.

Key Techniques
Don't Dry Your Batons. We tested several different ways of making the crispy eggplant—using different flours, an egg coating, and a wet batter. In the end, the best method was simply to dredge the eggplant in cornstarch. To get the cornstarch to stick, we rinse the eggplant but do not pat it dry, leaving a scant film of water.

Mind Your Temp. Frying is not difficult if you maintain proper temperature so the food expels steam while forming a crust rather than absorbing oil. This is critical with spongy eggplant. Use an instant-read thermometer, and don't crowd the pan. The temp will drop after a batch, so adjust the burner up and then down again, before adding the next batch. Keep cooked eggplant warm in a low oven.

2 Prepare the eggplant while the millet cooks. Pour the oil to a depth of ½ inch in a large, deep cast-iron skillet or heavy pot such as a Dutch oven. Heat over medium-high heat until the oil reaches 350°F; adjust the heat to maintain the oil temperature.

3 While the oil heats, peel the eggplants and cut lengthwise into quarters; cut quarters crosswise into roughly 3-inch-long pieces. Place the eggplant pieces in a colander or strainer; rinse and allow to drain for a minute. Place the cornstarch in a pie plate or other shallow dish. Dredge half of the eggplant in the cornstarch, turning to coat.

4 Place a paper towel–lined plate near the skillet. Shake off the excess cornstarch from the eggplant pieces before you add them to the hot oil. Fry the eggplant, turning occasionally, until lightly browned and crisp, about 3 minutes. Drain on paper towels and repeat with the remaining eggplant.

5 Carefully add 1½ tablespoons of hot frying oil to a wok or another large skillet; heat over medium-high heat. Stir in the chili crisp, then add the fried eggplant and salt. Toss until the eggplant is coated. Serve immediately over the millet; sprinkle with the scallions and cilantro.

The original Chinese chili crisp, left, created a craze, and now there are dozens of varieties globally.

How to Build a
Damn Fine Veggie Burger

ACTIVE TIME: 25 minutes
TOTAL TIME: 25 minutes
SERVES 4

We haven't really got on the pricey fake-meat burger bandwagon because, as meat eaters, we like our veggie burgers to taste like what they are: humble beans and grains, crisp-fried and extra flavorful here with the addition of a pantry superstar, smoked paprika. Humble, but not *earnest*: We slather on creamy mayo (preferably our Umami Mayo on page 179), which helps lock our favorite fun burger topping onto the bun—crunchy potato sticks. Look for cardboard canisters of said sticks in the potato chip aisle of most supermarkets.

⅔ cup old-fashioned oats

1 can (15 ounces) low-sodium black beans, rinsed and drained

1 teaspoon garlic powder

1 teaspoon smoked paprika

2 teaspoons Marmite

¼ teaspoon kosher salt

1 large egg

1 cup cooked farro

2 tablespoons canola oil

½ cup Umami Mayo (recipe follows) or store-bought mayo

4 multigrain hamburger buns

4 slices (½ inch thick) tomato

1 cup canned potato sticks

4 lettuce leaves

1 Place the oats in a food processor; pulse until finely chopped, 6 to 8 times. Add the beans; pulse until chopped, about 4 times. Add the garlic powder, smoked paprika, Marmite, salt, and egg; process until well blended. Remove the blade from the processor; add the farro and stir in with a spatula (so you don't have to use—and wash—a separate bowl).

2 Heat a large nonstick skillet over medium heat. While the pan heats, pat the bean mixture into an even layer in the food processor. Score the mixture with your spatula to divide it evenly into quarters. Scrape up one quarter of the mixture at a time and shape into a bun-size patty (3½ to 4 inches in diameter). Place the patties on a plate or a piece of wax or parchment paper.

3 Add the oil to the hot pan and swirl to coat. Add the patties to the pan; cook until browned and slightly crisp on the outside, about 3 minutes per side. Spread 1 tablespoon mayo over each side of each bun. Top the bottom half of each bun with 1 tomato slice, 1 patty, and ¼ cup potato sticks. Arrange lettuce on top bun halves. Bring buns together to assemble the burgers.

Global Pantry Ingredients

Marmite, *p. 15*
Smoked Paprika, *p. 22*

Texture Tips
Get Thee Behind Me, Mushy Burger. A bean burger should be firm and crisp-edged. Here oats integrate the mixture while cooked farro adds body and provides chewy bits in every bite. The potato sticks give you truckloads of bonus crunch.

Time-Saver
Precooked Farro Works Fine. It only takes 25 or 30 minutes to cook farro, but pouches of precooked farro can be found at stores like Target, near the pouches of precooked rice.

Umami Mayo

ACTIVE TIME: 6 minutes
TOTAL TIME: 6 minutes
MAKES ABOUT 1 CUP

This isn't a gimmick. The notorious English yeast spread Marmite adds a mysterious savory note to homemade mayo that one taster likened to "the dark, crispy edges of roasted potatoes." That in turn boosts the umami quality of a burger, and it's terrific on our black bean burgers, as well as any other sandwich. Making this mayo is quick and easy with a mini food processor. If using an immersion or stick blender, beware of overmixing, as this can cause the mayo to separate or "break."

1 large egg yolk (use pasteurized if you're concerned about eating raw egg)

2 teaspoons freshly squeezed lemon juice

1½ teaspoons Marmite

1 teaspoon Dijon mustard

¼ teaspoon table salt

1 cup neutral oil (such as canola, grapeseed, or avocado)

Place the egg yolk in a mini food processor. Top with the lemon juice, Marmite, mustard, and salt; pulse until combined, 3 to 4 times. Slowly drizzle in the oil through the opening in the lid, pulsing almost constantly, until emulsified and thick. If your processor doesn't have a hole, remove the top periodically to add the oil. Transfer to an airtight container. It will keep in the refrigerator for up to 1 week.

Global Pantry Ingredient

Marmite, *p. 15*

Adds savory goodness, but we still don't spread it on toast with butter, mind you . . .

Try This!

Kashmiri Mirch. This is a medium-hot, somewhat bitter ground chile pepper rather like a top-quality hot paprika, used for both spice and deep red color. You'll find it in Indian supermarkets or online. In this recipe, we use it along with a boxed garam masala containing coriander, cumin, turmeric, black pepper, mustard, cardamom, cloves, nutmeg, and asafetida. See page 15 for more on masala blends.

Prep Tip

Set Those Whites. To get the egg white properly cooked, we cook this dish with the lid on, so still-runny yolks gain a slight white-ish film when the eggs are done. You can pretty up each serving this way: Dole egg and tomato into serving bowls and then gently break a yolk with a fork to loosen some yellow.

Flatbread Tip

Finding Frozen Parathas. Look for frozen parathas in your local Indian supermarket or Trader Joe's. The layered flatbreads can be placed directly on a hot unoiled griddle while still frozen. They puff and brown to a rich treat—crispy outside, soft within.

Shakshuka!
With a Nod to India

ACTIVE TIME: 26 minutes
TOTAL TIME: 30 minutes
SERVES 4

Eggs cooked in tomato with aromatic spices make a dish famous in North Africa and the Middle East as well as—in different form—India. Our version is a bright, happy, Mediterranean-Indian mash-up. It brings toasty mustard seeds, garam masala spice, ghee, and curry leaves to the party for a vibrant dish that's even more delicious served with Indian breads.

---

1 teaspoon yellow mustard seeds

3 tablespoons ghee

1 tablespoon minced or grated peeled fresh ginger

1 clove garlic, minced or grated

1 red bell pepper, diced

½ medium onion, minced

1 tablespoon garam masala

1 teaspoon Kashmiri mirch, hot paprika, or other ground hot chile pepper

½ teaspoon kosher salt

2 cans (14 ounces each) fire-roasted diced tomatoes, undrained

8 to 12 curry leaves

½ cup hot water (optional)

4 large eggs

½ cup minced fresh cilantro

8 parathas (see Flatbread Tip), or 4 pitas

1 Heat a large skillet over medium heat for 1 minute. Add the mustard seeds and toast until they are aromatic and popping, 1 to 2 minutes. Add the ghee, ginger, and garlic; cook until fragrant, stirring constantly, 30 seconds to 1 minute. Add the bell pepper and onion; cook, stirring frequently, until soft, about 5 minutes.

2 Add the garam masala, Kashmiri mirch, and salt and cook until very fragrant, stirring frequently, about 2 minutes. Add the tomatoes and curry leaves and cook until the tomatoes start to break down, about 3 minutes more. If the mixture is thicker than a watery gravy, add ½ cup hot water. Carefully crack the eggs into the tomato sauce and cover the pan; cook until the yolks have a white film and are cooked, but the yolks are still wobbly, about 5 minutes.

3 Remove the pan from the heat and use a large spoon to scoop out egg and sauce into 4 shallow bowls. To make the dish prettier, break each egg yolk gently with a fork. Garnish with a bit of cilantro and serve with your chosen bread.

Try This!

The Soul of Corn Flavor.
Masa harina, which differs
from other corn flours or
cornmeal because of its
treatment with limewater
(an ancient practice among
the indigenous people of
Latin America), has incredibly
corny depth and makes
pancakes that evoke the joy
of tamales, arepas, and corn
tortillas. You'll find it in most
large supermarkets, either
on the baking aisle or in the
international foods section—
and of course in any Latin
food market.

Key Technique

Luxurious Hot Butter Bath.
We fry eggs to over-easy
in salted cultured butter,
spooning the butter over
the eggs as they cook so
they're bathed in all that
goodness. No need for
extra salt because the butter
seasons them perfectly.

Savory Corn-on-Corn Pancakes
with Butter-Basted Eggs

ACTIVE TIME: 30 minutes
TOTAL TIME: 30 minutes
SERVES 4

Breakfast, brunch, lunch, dinner:
The flavor–texture combination of
corn-flour pancakes, spicy-crunchy
fresh corn, and unctuous butter-based
eggs—with a nice hit of tang from
the lime-and-chile Mexican blend
called Tajín—is a wake-up call for the
tastebuds at any time. These super-
fluffy pancakes are gluten-free yet
require no specialty flours. The corn
topping is inspired by esquites, the
salad version of Mexican street corn.
Note that these flapjacks are versatile,
too. Sweet tooths should try them on
their own with maple syrup or a fruit
compote; no need to alter the batter
recipe.

FOR THE PANCAKES

2 cups (7½ ounces) masa harina
   (either white or yellow)

1 teaspoon baking soda

½ teaspoon kosher salt

2 cups whole buttermilk

¼ cup salted cultured butter,
   melted

2 large eggs

FOR THE CORN

1 tablespoon salted cultured butter

2 cups fresh corn kernels

¼ cup chopped scallions

¼ teaspoon kosher salt

1 large jalapeño pepper, seeded and
   minced

¼ cup crumbled cotija cheese or
   queso fresco

¾ teaspoon Tajín seasoning

FOR THE EGGS

¼ cup salted cultured butter

4 large eggs

1 To prepare the pancakes, whisk together the masa harina, baking soda, and salt in a large bowl. Whisk together the buttermilk, melted butter, and eggs in a medium bowl.

2 Heat a large nonstick griddle or nonstick skillet over medium heat. Pour the buttermilk mixture into the masa harina mixture; stir until well combined. Scoop the batter by quarter-cupfuls onto the griddle or skillet; cook until lightly browned on the bottom, 3 to 4 minutes. Turn the pancakes over and cook until browned on the bottom, 3 to 4 minutes. Repeat the process in batches if needed (loosely cover the cooked pancakes with aluminium foil to keep warm). Add a splash of buttermilk to the batter if it gets too thick.

3 While the pancakes cook, prepare the corn by heating a medium skillet over medium heat. Add the butter and swirl until melted. Add the corn, scallions, salt, and jalapeño; cook until the corn is crisp-tender, about 3 minutes. Remove from the heat and sprinkle with the cotija and Tajín. Spoon into a bowl and wipe out the pan with a cloth.

4 To prepare the eggs, melt the butter in the skillet over medium-low heat. Crack the eggs into the pan and allow the whites to just start setting, about 30 seconds. Slightly tilt the pan so that you can gather some butter in a spoon. Spoon the butter over the eggs repeatedly as they cook to over-easy doneness, about 2 minutes. Serve the corn mixture and eggs over the pancakes.

The zing of lime and chile lifts and brightens the corn topping.

Tender Multigrain Walnut Pancakes
with Plum Compote

ACTIVE TIME: 15 minutes
TOTAL TIME: 45 minutes
SERVES 4

Thick, soft, and fluffy: These are the qualities we demand from a pancake. But more: We want them a bit hearty, too, from whole grains. All virtues are possible when you use whole wheat pastry flour (see Try This!). They have nutty flavor and an alluring creamy interior, too. Although we have often made them with pecans, here we go for bigger earthy-rich flavor, using toasted black walnuts. The final touch is a fragrant, tart plum compote. With or without nuts, there's a good chance these will be your favorite all-round pancakes, because they're simply fabulous with warm maple syrup and a rivulet of melted butter, too.

FOR THE COMPOTE

8 medium red or black plums (about 1¼ pounds), pitted and each cut into 6 wedges

1 tablespoon honey, plus extra as needed

¼ teaspoon ground cardamom (optional)

¼ teaspoon kosher salt

1 tablespoon unsalted butter, cut into small pieces

Hot water (optional)

FOR THE PANCAKES

1 cup (4½ ounces) whole wheat pastry flour

1 cup quick-cooking oats

1½ tablespoons sugar

1½ teaspoons baking powder

½ teaspoon baking soda

½ teaspoon kosher salt

1¾ cups whole buttermilk, plus extra as needed

2 tablespoons unsalted butter, melted

1 large egg

½ cup coarsely chopped toasted black walnuts (see page 26)

Cooking spray

1 To prepare the compote, preheat the oven to 400°F with the rack placed in the center. Place the plums in an 11 × 7-inch baking dish. Drizzle with the honey; sprinkle with the cardamom, if desired, and the salt. Scatter the chopped butter over the plums. Bake until just tender, 20 minutes. Stir the mixture, and bake until very soft and juicy, an additional 5 minutes. Keep an eye on them, and if they begin to dry out, add a bit of hot water and stir. Remove from the oven and let the mixture cool while you make the pancakes. If the compote is too tart, stir in another tablespoon of honey.

Try This!
Whole Wheat Pastry Flour. No more brick-like results! Whole wheat pastry flour is a revelation: whole grain goodness in a much more finely milled flour, suitable for delicate cakes and pastry. The key: It's made from soft white wheat. Look for it in natural food stores; Whole Foods has a good 365 brand version that is our go-to choice.

Make-Ahead Tip
Making Mornings Easier. You can cook up the pancakes, allow them to cool completely, and stack them between pieces of wax or parchment paper. Freeze them in a ziplock freezer bag for up to 2 months. Thaw in the microwave for 30 seconds to 1 minute. You can also make the compote ahead and stash it in the fridge for 2 or 3 days.

Simple Substitution
No Quick Oats? You can pulse regular rolled oats in a food processor to break them up a bit, or soak in the buttermilk for 10 minutes before adding to the rest of the batter.

2 To prepare the pancakes, whisk together the flour, oats, sugar, baking powder, baking soda, and salt in a large bowl. Whisk together the buttermilk, melted butter, and egg in a medium bowl. Add the buttermilk mixture to the flour mixture; mix just until combined. The batter should be thick but pourable; if you need more liquid, add a splash of buttermilk. Fold in the black walnuts.

3 Heat a griddle or large nonstick skillet over medium heat. Coat the griddle or skillet with cooking spray, keeping the pan away from any open flame (cooking spray yields more consistent results than butter). Spoon ¼ cup batter per pancake onto the griddle or pan. Cook until the tops of the pancakes are dotted with bubbles, about 3 minutes. Flip the pancakes over; cook until browned on the bottom and done. To test for doneness, place your fingers on top of a pancake and nudge it, like you're trying to wake someone up. If you feel a lot of movement or sliding, the pancake is still raw in the center; you want it to feel firm. Remove the cooked pancakes from the pan and repeat the process with the remaining batter. Serve the pancakes with the compote.

If you fall for the earthy flavor of black walnuts, you'll always have a bag in the freezer.

Oaty McOatface!

ACTIVE TIME: 20 minutes
TOTAL TIME: 20 minutes
SERVES 2

The silly name of this bowl of oaty goodness honors a 2016 incident that proved that, for once, the social-media hive mind of the internet is not entirely evil. The British government polled for suggestions to name an expensive polar exploration research ship. The overwhelming winner was *Boaty McBoatface*. The agency involved eventually called the ship the *Sir David Attenborough* but—bless the British sense of humor—retained the popular name for a little yellow onboard autonomous submersible that is now prowling the ocean floor in aid of climate change research. Our oatmeal takes a childhood favorite flavor combo—PB&J—and gives it scientific nobility in the form of a tangy grape compote on top of peanutty oatmeal (easily made with peanut butter powder), the whole thing cooked in that miracle of technology, the microwave. Thyme adds a hint of woodsy, savory richness to the compote, if you choose to add it, but you can omit it for a more faithful homage to grape jelly.

FOR THE COMPOTE

1½ cups seedless red grapes

2 tablespoons golden raisins

1 tablespoon unsalted butter

2 teaspoons balsamic vinegar

2 teaspoons brown sugar

½ teaspoon fresh thyme leaves (optional)

⅛ teaspoon kosher salt

FOR THE OATS

⅔ cup quick-cooking toasted steel-cut oats (such as Coach's Oats)

¼ teaspoon kosher salt

⅓ cup unsweetened peanut butter powder

1 tablespoon brown sugar

1 tablespoon butter

1 To prepare the compote, toss together the grapes, raisins, butter, vinegar, sugar, thyme (if using), and salt in a medium microwave-safe bowl. Microwave, uncovered, on High for 3 minutes; stir the mixture. Microwave on High for another 3 to 4 minutes until the grapes are shriveled and a few start to burst. Cool slightly as the oats cook.

2 To prepare the oats, stir together the oats, 2 cups water, and the salt in a large microwave-safe bowl; make sure the bowl is large enough to account for the oatmeal bubbling up as it cooks. Microwave, uncovered, on High until creamy and thick, 4 to 6 minutes. If the oats seem too thick, add hot water and stir until you get the desired texture. Stir in the peanut butter powder, sugar, and butter. Divide the oats between 2 bowls; top with the compote.

Global Pantry Ingredient

Peanut Butter Powder, *p. 18*

Shopping Intel

These Oats Are Among the Best Oats. We have a soft spot for Coach's Oats, quick-cooking steel-cut oats that are toasted for superior flavor, invented by a small company in the early '90s. Today they're found most easily on Amazon, sometimes in Costco, or by searching for the company itself on Google. There are several other versions of quick-cooking steel-cut oats, but Coach's have powered many a family breakfast in Alabama and Colorado.

Anchovies • Yuzu • Black Walnuts • Wondra • Sumac • Calabrian Chiles • Sorghu
Millet • Tabasco Sauce • Coconut Milk • Roasted Hazelnut Oil • Curry Leaves •
Sauce • Shrimp Paste • Worcestershire Sauce • Furikake • Sriracha • Saffron • Bany
Vinegar • Gochujang • Harissa • Marmite • Kecap Manis • Chili Crisp • Freeze-Dr
Strawberries • Tajín • Kimchi • Korean Toasted Sesame Oil • Dulce de Leche •
Sauce • Lemongrass • Whole Wheat Pastry Flour • Pomegranate Molasses • Mexi
Chocolate • Smoked Paprika • Chipotles in Adobo • Shichimi Togarashi • Makrut L
Leaves • Crema Mexicana • The Many Masalas • Capers • Mexican Chorizo • Mir
Oyster Sauce • Panko Breadcrumbs • Ras El Hanout • Andouille Sausage • Marsa
The Many Sambals • Benton's Bacon • Miso • Stone-Ground Grits • Tahini • Ghee • P
Sugar • Ají Amarillo Paste • Thai Curry Paste • Mustard Powder • Turmeric • Cultu
Butter • Kashmiri Mirch • Dried Porcini Mushrooms • Sweetened Condensed Mi
Anchovies • Yuzu • Black Walnuts • Wondra • Sumac • Calabrian Chiles • Sorghu
Millet • Tabasco Sauce • Coconut Milk • Roasted Hazelnut Oil • Curry Leaves •
Sauce • Shrimp Paste • Worcestershire Sauce • Furikake • Sriracha • Saffron • Bany
Vinegar • Gochujang • Harissa • Marmite • Kecap Manis • Chili Crisp • Freeze-Dr
Strawberries • Tajín • Kimchi • Korean Toasted Sesame Oil • Dulce de Leche •
Sauce • Lemongrass • Whole Wheat Pastry Flour • Pomegranate Molasses • Mexi
Chocolate • Smoked Paprika • Chipotles in Adobo • Shichimi Togarashi • Makrut L
Leaves • Crema Mexicana • The Many Masalas • Capers • Mexican Chorizo • Mir
Oyster Sauce • Panko Breadcrumbs • Ras El Hanout • Andouille Sausage • Marsa
The Many Sambals • Benton's Bacon • Miso • Stone-Ground Grits • Tahini • Ghee • P
Sugar • Ají Amarillo Paste • Thai Curry Paste • Mustard Powder • Turmeric • Cultu
Butter • Kashmiri Mirch • Dried Porcini Mushrooms • Sweetened Condensed Mi
Anchovies • Yuzu • Black Walnuts • Wondra • Sumac • Calabrian Chiles • Sorghu
Millet • Tabasco Sauce • Coconut Milk • Roasted Hazelnut Oil • Curry Leaves •
Sauce • Shrimp Paste • Worcestershire Sauce • Furikake • Sriracha • Saffron • Bany
Vinegar • Gochujang • Harissa • Marmite • Kecap Manis • Chili Crisp • Freeze-Dr
Strawberries • Tajín • Kimchi • Korean Toasted Sesame Oil • Dulce de Leche •
Sauce • Lemongrass • Whole Wheat Pastry Flour • Pomegranate Molasses • Mexi
Chocolate • Smoked Paprika • Chipotles in Adobo • Shichimi Togarashi • Makrut L
Leaves • Crema Mexicana • The Many Masalas • Capers • Mexican Chorizo • Mir
Oyster Sauce • Panko Breadcrumbs • Ras El Hanout • Andouille Sausage • Marsa
The Many Sambals • Benton's Bacon • Miso • Stone-Ground Grits • Tahini • Ghee • P
Sugar • Ají Amarillo Paste • Thai Curry Paste • Mustard Powder • Turmeric • Cultu
Butter • Kashmiri Mirch • Dried Porcini Mushrooms • Sweetened Condensed Mill

Totally Satisfying Sandwiches

Mexican Chorizo, *p. 15*

Flavor Booster

Use All the Cilantro. We are big fans of using cilantro stems, not just the frilly, leafy parts. The stems have more flavor than the leaves, without ever tasting bitter (like parsley stems do).

Mexican Chorizo and Ground Pork Burgers
with Messy-Good Fixin's

ACTIVE TIME: 35 minutes
TOTAL TIME: 45 minutes
SERVES 4

With a bigger-than-usual meat patty topped with mashed avocado and fresh pico de gallo, these burgers are a double handful of drippy good fun. Mexican chorizo does the heavy lifting, flavor-wise, along with a bounty of fresh cilantro in both meat and pico. As for the cheese, American is the platonic ideal for burgers—salty, creamy-melty, and, well, what burgers need in order to taste like burgers.

¾ cup chopped cilantro leaves and stems

½ cup finely chopped tomato, seeded if desired

¼ cup finely chopped onion

1 tablespoon freshly squeezed lime juice

¾ pound ground pork

¾ pound Mexican chorizo

¾ teaspoon kosher salt

1 medium ripe avocado, pitted and peeled

1 medium clove garlic, grated on a Microplane

4 onion rolls or other hamburger buns

Neutral oil (such as canola), for oiling the grill rack

4 slices white American cheese

1 Heat your gas grill to medium-high (450°F to 475°F) or prepare your coals to maintain medium-high heat (gas will take 20 to 30 minutes; charcoal will take about 45 minutes).

2 While the grill heats, combine ¼ cup of cilantro, the tomato, onion, and lime juice in a small bowl; set aside.

3 Combine the pork, chorizo, ½ teaspoon salt, and the remaining ½ cup cilantro in a medium bowl, stirring well with your hands until the ingredients are fully incorporated. Divide the mixture into 4 equal portions, and shape each into a ½-inch-thick patty. Set the patties aside.

4 Mash the avocado with a fork in a small bowl; stir in the garlic and remaining ¼ teaspoon salt. Set aside.

5 Place the roll halves on the grill rack, cut sides down; grill until toasted, 30 seconds to 1 minute. Remove from the grill. Oil the grill rack and arrange the patties on the rack; close the grill lid and grill until well-marked on the bottom, about 5 minutes. Turn the patties over, close the grill lid, and grill until almost done, about 4 minutes (the patties should look crusty on the outside and feel firm when poked). Top each patty with 1 cheese slice; close the grill lid and grill until the cheese melts, about 1 minute.

6 Arrange 1 burger patty on the bottom half of each roll; top the patties evenly with the avocado mixture and the tomato mixture. Place the tops of the rolls on the burgers.

Shortcut Birria-Inspired
Beef Dip Sandwiches

ACTIVE TIME: 25 minutes
TOTAL TIME: 1 hour 20 minutes
SERVES 4

Traditional birria dishes involve long simmering of meat in a homemade chile broth. We use two time-saving tricks to put our riff within weeknight reach: We cook the meat in an Instant Pot, and use enchilada sauce and canned chipotle chiles, both easily found in any decent supermarket. The results aren't traditional, but they're delicious for a satisfying dinner sandwich that offers the special joys of the dip.

---

2 tablespoons canola oil

1½ pounds boneless chuck roast, cut into 2-inch cubes

2 cups finely chopped white onion

4 large cloves garlic, minced

1 cup unsalted beef stock, plus extra as needed

1¼ cups canned Hatch red enchilada sauce

1 tablespoon chopped canned chipotle chile

1 tablespoon adobo sauce (from can of chipotle chiles)

1 teaspoon ground cumin

½ teaspoon kosher salt

¼ cup chopped fresh cilantro

4 bolillo rolls, telera rolls, or soft French rolls, split in half

1 large ripe avocado, pitted, peeled, and thinly sliced

1 Set an Instant Pot to Sauté. Add 1 tablespoon of oil to the pot and swirl to coat. Add the beef to the pot. (If the pot is on the smaller side, do this in 2 batches.) Cook until well browned on the bottom, about 5 minutes. Turn the beef over and brown on the opposite side, about 5 minutes. Remove from the pot.

2 Add the remaining 1 tablespoon oil to the pot, and swirl to coat. Add 1 cup of onion and the garlic; sauté until just starting to soften, about 3 minutes.

3 Turn the Instant Pot off. Add the stock, scraping the bottom of the pot to loosen the browned bits. Stir in the enchilada sauce, chipotle, adobo sauce, cumin, and salt. Return the beef to the pot. Secure the lid in place and set the steam valve to Sealing. Set to Manual and a cook at high pressure for 40 minutes.

4 While the beef cooks, place the remaining 1 cup onion in a strainer; rinse well with cold water and drain well. Combine the rinsed onion and cilantro in a small bowl and set aside.

5 When the Instant Pot cook time is over, carefully quick-release pressure. Remove the beef from the pot with a slotted spoon to a shallow bowl or pie plate. Shred the meat with 2 forks and stir in ⅓ cup sauce from the pot. Divide the beef mixture evenly among the rolls; divide the avocado and onion mixture evenly among the rolls. Serve with the remaining sauce for dipping. If the sauce is a bit thick for dipping, stir in a little beef stock or hot water.

Global Pantry Ingredient

Chipotles in Adobo, *p. 10*

Flavor Booster
Smoke from a Can. The flavor of the convenient enchilada sauce used here is amped further by the addition of smoky canned chipotle chiles and some of the rich adobo sauce they're packed with.

Shopping Intel
Where to Find Bolillo Rolls. You'll have the best luck finding torpedo-shaped bolillo rolls at a Mexican or Latin foods grocery store. Some large supermarkets make them, too. In some parts of the country, look for Portuguese rolls as a good substitute. Soft French rolls will do in a pinch. The idea is to avoid anything too chewy or firm, so skip past the baguettes and ciabattas in favor of softer, soak-things-up buns.

Grill Tips

Gently Help Them Turn.
The fairly soft ground meat clings tentatively to the skewers, especially round skewers, and can stick to the grill, so when handling don't just abruptly lift a dog: Coax the meat with a metal spatula to flip and turn it. If a skewer comes completely off, just keep grilling the runaway kebab.

Get a Proper Char. This is not a case where you're trying to get the kebab off the heat the instant it's cooked to medium rare. Nor does the meat turn from red to pink to gray inside: It's basically gray from the get-go because of all the spices. The longer you cook, the more char and chew in the final dog—and that's the goal.

Heat Index

Those Small Green Fire Bombs.
Tiny green Thai-style chiles, now fairly widely available, can be super-hot. We use only one in the meat mixture and one in the chutney, but feel free to add more to either or both if your diners are heat-heads. Or divide the chutney and process half with an extra chile. In a pinch, sub in jalapeños. For a milder kebab, seed the chile or use only half.

Kebab-Dogs
with Spicy Ketchup, Fragrant Chutney, and Onions

ACTIVE TIME: 45 minutes
TOTAL TIME: 1 hour
SERVES 5 (2 dogs each)

Charred and fiercely spiced seekh kebabs, made from ground meat and grilled in long sausage-like lengths, were one of Scott's favorite street-food treats on trips to Pakistan when he was in high school. We didn't invent the kebab-dog idea here, but we've jazzed it up with global pantry versions of hot dog fixin's: a spicy, mustardy ketchup and a chutney subbing for relish. You'll need ten 10-inch bamboo or flat metal skewers; if using bamboo, soak them for 1 hour before putting them on the grill so they don't ignite.

FOR THE SEEKH KEBABS

1 cup cilantro leaves

1 tablespoon garam masala (preferably an aromatic Punjabi or Pakistani style)

1 teaspoon ground cumin

½ teaspoon freshly ground black pepper

½ teaspoon kosher salt

½ teaspoon ground ginger

½ teaspoon ground allspice or cloves

2 cloves garlic, peeled

1 medium onion, quartered

1 green Thai-style chile (or 2 if you like it hot)

½ cup panko breadcrumbs

1 pound 80% lean ground beef

Neutral oil (such as canola), for oiling the cutting board, meat, and grill rack

FOR THE SPICY KETCHUP

½ cup Heinz or other favorite ketchup

2 teaspoons mustard powder

2 teaspoons Kashmiri mirch or other ground hot chile pepper

2 teaspoons garam masala

FOR THE PUNCHY GREEN CHUTNEY

2 cups coarsely chopped cilantro leaves

1½ cups fresh mint leaves

2 teaspoons neutral oil (such as canola)

½ teaspoon sugar

1 green Thai-style chile

Juice of 1 lime

1 tablespoon plain, thick yogurt or mayo

FOR SERVING

10 hot dog buns

1 medium onion, medium diced (hot dog–stand style)

1 To prepare the seekh kebabs, place the cilantro, garam masala, cumin, pepper, salt, ginger, allspice, garlic, onion, and chile in a food processor; process until you have a smooth paste, about 30 seconds. Place the paste in a medium bowl; add the panko and mix well. Add the beef and work energetically with your hands until the beef begins to get pasty—the visual cue is the appearance of a slight stringiness or filament quality in the meat. Keep working a bit longer. This consistency helps the mixture retain its sausage-shape integrity as it grills. Chill the meat mixture for 30 minutes or up to 2 hours.

2 Heat your gas grill to high (500°F to 600°F) or prepare your coals to maintain high heat (charcoal will take about 45 minutes). If using coals, when they are ready, spread them around the edge of the grill.

3 Meanwhile, prepare the spicy ketchup: Stir together the ketchup, mustard powder, Kashmiri mirch, and garam masala in a small bowl; cover and set aside.

4 Make the chutney: Rinse out the food processor and pat dry. Combine the cilantro, mint, oil, sugar, chile, and lime juice in the processor. Process to a coarse paste, about 20 seconds. Put in a small strainer and press out most of the liquid. Mix with the yogurt; cover and set aside.

5 Lightly oil a cutting board. Put the chilled meat on it and mold the meat into a rectangle that's about twice as wide as it is long. Oil a sheet pan or platter to receive the skewers. Divide the meat rectangle into 10 long pieces, and roll each blob with your hands and on the board into a piece slightly longer than a hot dog (6½ to 7 inches). Take a skewer and press it into the meat so that only the tip of the skewer extends from the end, sinking the skewer halfway down into the meat, then pinching the meat closed around the skewer and rolling the meat on the board until you have a piece of even length and thickness. Repeat with the rest. If any of the "dogs" are uneven, borrow some meat from the other skewers. Brush the meat with oil on all sides. If you're not ready to grill, cover the kebabs with plastic wrap and return to the fridge.

6 Oil the grill rack and place the kebabs directly over the heat, keeping the exposed bamboo skewers off the end of the grill if possible. Close the lid and grill until one side is well charred, about 5 minutes, then begin to turn the kebabs (see Grill Tips) to cook all sides—the total time will be 15 to 18 minutes depending on the grill.

7 Swipe one side of each bun with a generous dollop of the spicy ketchup, the other with the chutney. Add a kebab and top with the chopped onion.

Dried mustard in the ketchup adds backbone.

Global Pantry Ingredients

Gochujang, *p. 13*

Kashmiri mirch,
  see Try This!, page 180

Korean Toasted
  Sesame Oil, *p. 14*

Soy Sauce, *p. 22*

Sriracha, *p. 23*

Key Technique

For Crumblier Beef. Dropping a hunk of ground beef straight from the package into a skillet begins a battle royale if your goal is meaty crumbles. Try this: Crumble the beef with your hands into the hot pan. It will still need breaking up, but much less.

Ground Beef Bulgogi Sloppy Joes
with Fiery Napa Slaw

ACTIVE TIME: 25 minutes
TOTAL TIME: 25 minutes
SERVES 4

We love a messy handful like this amped-up global version of the American classic. Ground beef gets the Korean barbecue flavor treatment with soy sauce, brown sugar, garlic, sesame oil, and a hint of gochujang so that it's saucy, sweet, and salty. Meanwhile, the spicy, mayo-dressed slaw keeps the sandwiches from veering *too* sweet. You can always make a small batch of no-chile slaw for the timid of palate. For a fun riff, use the meat and slaw for tacos instead of joes.

---

2 tablespoons mayonnaise

1½ tablespoons freshly squeezed lime juice

1 tablespoon sriracha

¾ teaspoon crushed red pepper flakes

¼ teaspoon kosher salt

3 cups thinly sliced napa cabbage

¼ cup slivered red onion

1 tablespoon Korean toasted sesame oil

1 pound 90% lean ground beef
  (preferably grass-fed)

4 cloves garlic, minced

½ cup chopped scallions

½ cup unsalted chicken stock

2 tablespoons brown sugar

2 tablespoons light or dark soy sauce

1 tablespoon gochujang paste

1 teaspoon cornstarch

4 sesame seed–topped hamburger buns,
  toasted

1 Whisk together the mayonnaise, lime juice, sriracha, crushed red pepper, and salt in a medium bowl. Add the cabbage and onion and toss well to coat. Let stand at room temperature while the beef cooks.

2 Heat a medium or large skillet over medium-high heat. Add the oil to the pan and swirl to coat. Crumble the beef into the pan and sprinkle with the garlic. Cook until the beef is browned, mashing frequently with a fork to crumble into small, sloppy joe–style bits, about 5 minutes. Stir in the scallions and cook 2 minutes.

3 Whisk together the stock, sugar, soy sauce, gochujang, and cornstarch in a bowl. Add the mixture to the pan. Cook, stirring frequently, until thickened, 2 to 3 minutes. Spoon about ½ cup beef mixture on the bottom half of each bun. Top each sandwich with about ½ cup slaw and the top half of the bun.

Sipper Suggestions
Fizz It Up Fancy-Like.
This is the perfect dish
for a dry Crémant d'Alsace
sparkler or a dry Spanish
cava or, if you can find it,
Costco's Kirkland brand
Champagne.

Superfast Smoked Chicken Sandwich
with Alabama White Sauce

ACTIVE TIME: 17 minutes
TOTAL TIME: 17 minutes
SERVES 4

The combination of vinegar-tangy, peppered mayonnaise and succulent smoky chicken is Alabama's great contribution to barbecue, made famous by Big Bob Gibson, who started selling smoked meat out of his home in Decatur in the 1920s and later opened a restaurant that's still extant. It's a genius flavor combo, almost mellow, which isn't something one says about most barbecue. Here we use the stovetop smoking hack on supermarket rotisserie chicken to get these glorious sandwiches on the dinner table in under 20 minutes!

½ cup mayonnaise, preferably Duke's

2 tablespoons white vinegar

1 teaspoon freshly ground black pepper

½ teaspoon kosher salt

½ teaspoon garlic powder

½ teaspoon Worcestershire sauce

½ teaspoon Tabasco or other hot sauce

1 small, warm rotisserie chicken

4 large hamburger buns

4 leaves iceberg lettuce

1 Whisk together the mayonnaise, vinegar, pepper, salt, garlic powder, Worcestershire, and Tabasco in a small bowl and place in the fridge to chill for 15 minutes.

2 Pull the chicken meat and skin off the bones, keeping the meat chunky (discard the skin and bones). Break the breasts into 3 or 4 pieces.

3 Set up a stovetop smoker as shown on page 155 and smoke the chicken on the heat for 4 minutes. Turn off the heat and let the chicken smoke for an additional 2 minutes. Remove the chicken to a platter or bowl.

4 Lay the buns open on the counter for assembly. Put ¼ of the chicken meat on each bottom bun, then spoon lots of sauce over the chicken (it's thin and will drip out the sides). Add the lettuce, close the buns, and serve.

Tabasco is still one of the best choices for a splash of pungent chile heat.

Chicken Salad Sandwiches

with Preserved Lemon, Dried Apricots, Moroccan Spices, and Black Walnuts

ACTIVE TIME: 10 minutes
TOTAL TIME: 10 minutes
SERVES 4

Another global-pantry riff on an American lunch-counter standard. There's an indulgent amount of mayo for creamy texture, preserved lemon for tang, tender dried apricots to sing sweet notes against the lemon, black walnuts and celery for crunch, and a lovely background of complex spice. It's good enough for a summer dinner with a garden tomato salad and a glass of iced tea or lively white wine. The rotisserie chicken factor makes it a fast solution for any day you need chicken-salad satisfaction in a hurry (just chop the meat and pop in the fridge on a plate to quickly cool it). If you're cooking for a crowd, double the recipe.

¼ cup chopped dried apricots

¾ cup Umami Mayo (page 179) or regular mayo

½ cup toasted black walnuts or regular walnuts, chopped

¼ cup minced celery

2 tablespoons coarsely chopped preserved lemon or 1 teaspoon lemon zest

1 tablespoon minced onion

½ teaspoon ras el hanout

2 cups coarsely chopped skinless white- and dark-meat rotisserie chicken (about half a chicken), at room temperature

8 slices favorite hearty sandwich bread, or baguette or focaccia sufficient for 4 sandwiches

Butter (optional)

1 Place the apricots in a small microwave-safe bowl with 2 tablespoons water; microwave on High for 1 minute to soften. Drain the water and let the apricots cool while you make the rest of the salad.

2 Combine the mayo, walnuts, celery, lemon, onion, and ras el hanout in a large bowl. Add the apricots when warm, not hot, and mix in the chicken.

3 Toast and butter (if desired) your sandwich bread and spread evenly with the chicken salad, or spread on a baguette or focaccia and serve.

Global Pantry Ingredients

Black Walnuts, *p. 9*
Preserved Lemon, *p. 19*
Ras El Hanout, *p. 20*

Leftover Tip

The Other Half of the Chicken. If you used half of a rotisserie chicken to make our Loads-of-Chicken–Flavored Soup with Shrimpy Corn Wontons (page 85), this is the perfect next-day use for the other half. If you buy a whole chicken for this, use the bones, skin, and remaining meat to make the soup that's on the wonton recipe page.

Super Croque!

ACTIVE TIME: 33 minutes
TOTAL TIME: 33 minutes
SERVES 4

We think this is the ultimate brunch sandwich—a combination of the French croque madame (ham, Gruyère, bread, with a fried egg on top) and croque monsieur (in which the bread is milk-soaked, as with French toast). The crowning touch is a dredge in panko that yields extra-crunchy texture in every bite. It's so satisfying that we dispense with the complication of a béchamel sauce. Arugula adds a gorgeous peppery touch. Smaller appetites will find a half sandwich (with a full egg) plenty satisfying. One note about prepping the eggs: Although lacy, crispy-edged eggs fried at high temperature are absolutely delicious, they're not ideal here. Gentler cooking keeps the egg soft all over, a textural yin to the yang of the super crunchy panko coating on the sandwich.

---

1 cup whole milk

8 large eggs

½ teaspoon kosher salt

½ teaspoon ground nutmeg, preferably freshly ground

1½ cups panko breadcrumbs

8 teaspoons Dijon mustard

8 slices (1½ ounces each) thick-sliced brioche-style sandwich bread

8 ounces thinly sliced deli ham

4 ounces cave-aged Gruyère cheese, shredded

5 tablespoons unsalted butter

1 cup baby arugula

1 Preheat the oven to 200°F with the rack placed in the center.

2 Whisk together the milk, 4 eggs, salt, and nutmeg in an 11 × 7-inch baking dish. Spread the panko onto a plate. Spread 1 teaspoon of the mustard over each bread slice. Layer 2 ounces of the ham and about ¼ cup of the cheese over each of 4 bread slices, mustard side up; top with the remaining bread slices, mustard side down.

3 Heat a large nonstick skillet over medium-low heat. Melt 2 tablespoons of butter in the pan. Carefully place 2 sandwiches in the milk mixture; allow to stand about 30 seconds on each side to absorb the liquid. Carefully lift the sandwiches out of the milk mixture and dredge on both sides with the panko. Place the sandwiches in the pan; cook until browned and toasted, 5 to 6 minutes on each side. Keep the sandwiches warm in the oven. Repeat the process with the remaining 2 sandwiches.

4 Meanwhile, fry the remaining eggs: Heat a large skillet over medium-low heat. Melt the remaining 1 tablespoon butter in the pan, swirling to coat. Crack the remaining 4 eggs into the pan; cook until the whites are set and the yolks are still runny, about 5 minutes, or to your desired degree of doneness.

5 Place each sandwich on a plate; top with ¼ cup arugula and 1 fried egg. Serve immediately.

Global Pantry Ingredient

Panko Breadcrumbs, *p. 17*

Flavor Booster

Aged Cheese Is Best. Regular Gruyère cheese is sweet and nutty and quite lovely. Cave-aged Gruyère, though, is a flavor bombshell, tasting of browned butter, caramel, and hazelnuts—with an irresistible salty edge.

Avoid This Mistake

Prevent the Rubbery Beasties.
It's shockingly easy to overcook
shrimp to rubber dog-toy
texture. We sidestep disaster
with a gentle poach, adding
the shrimp to boiling water and
immediately removing the pot
from the heat. After just a few
minutes in the hot tub, they're
done. And tender.

Shopping Intel

Upgrade Your Buns.
Look for brioche hot dog
buns (preferably top-split,
in a nod to the Northeast)
in your grocery store's bakery
section. They bring rich,
buttery goodness. If you
can't find them, butter buns
from the regular bread aisle
will do.

Shrimp Rolls
with Yuzu Kosho Mayo

ACTIVE TIME: 15 minutes
TOTAL TIME: 15 minutes
SERVES 4

Here's a bit of heresy: Right after
eating lobster rolls at some of the most
famous shacks in Maine, Scott made
Ann's shrimp rolls for the first time and
declared them *better*. The reason, he
deduces, is that while a bold addition
like yuzu kosho seems transgressive on
lobster, it works beautiful magic with
shrimp. And you don't have to take
out a second mortgage to feed four
people.

---

1 pound large peeled and
    deveined shrimp

3 tablespoons mayonnaise
    (preferably Duke's or our
    Umami Mayo on page 179)

2 teaspoons yuzu kosho

2 teaspoons freshly squeezed lime juice

2 tablespoons thinly sliced chives

Kosher salt (optional)

1 tablespoon salted butter, melted

4 top-split brioche hot dog buns

1 Bring a large saucepan of water to
a boil. Add the shrimp to the pan, and
immediately remove from the heat. Cover
and let stand until the shrimp are opaque
and done, 2 to 3 minutes. Drain and rinse
the shrimp with cold water. Drain well.
Chop the shrimp.

2 Whisk together the mayonnaise, yuzu
kosho, and lime juice in a medium bowl.
Add the shrimp and chives; stir well to
combine. Taste the mixture and add salt
if needed (some shrimp is plenty salty on
its own). Drizzle one quarter of the melted
butter down each bun crevice, then stuff
the shrimp mixture into the buns.

Yuzu kosho is a citrus-chile-salt flavor bomb.

The Ebi Filet-O

Our Version of the Best McDonald's Sandwich in the World

ACTIVE TIME: 25 minutes
TOTAL TIME: 25 minutes
SERVES 4

We're longtime champions of the McDonald's Filet-O-Fish as a brilliant sandwich when it arrives just made, with its crisp-edged block of pollock, spongy steamed bun, and—a genius, oddball choice for a seafood sammy—half-slice of processed cheese. Turns out the shrimp version in Japan, called Ebi Filet-O, is far better: Actual chunks of shrimp in a shrimpy-sweet patty with crunchy exterior, tangy sauce, and a good bun. Our version here delivers a full 4 ounces of shrimp, a robust panko crust, and a zingy sauce made with yuzu kosho and good old jarred tartar sauce.

½ cup ketchup

½ cup tartar sauce

1 teaspoon yuzu kosho, or 1 teaspoon freshly squeezed lime juice and 1 teaspoon sriracha or chili crisp

1 pound large peeled and deveined shrimp, fresh or frozen, thawed

1 teaspoon garlic powder (optional)

1 teaspoon rice flour or cornstarch

1½ cups neutral oil (such as canola)

2 large eggs, lightly beaten

1 cup panko breadcrumbs

4 brioche hamburger buns, or similar

2 slices American cheese (optional)

2 cups very thinly sliced or shredded napa cabbage or iceberg lettuce

1 Stir together the ketchup, tartar sauce, and yuzu kosho in a medium bowl and set aside.

2 Chop 6 shrimp into chunks and put them in a small bowl. In a mini food processor or food processor, process the remaining shrimp until you have a coarse but still slightly chunky paste. Mix the paste with the shrimp chunks, garlic powder (if using), and rice flour.

Shrimp Intel

Frozen Are OK. Large, peeled US-caught sustainable shrimp (often from the Gulf) in a 1-pound bag work well, but after thawing make sure you drain completely and then vigorously pat dry with paper towels.

Frying Tip

Two at a Time, Uses Less Oil. If you have a smaller cast-iron pan or similar sturdy pan, 1½ cups of oil will come at least halfway up the sides of the patties, which is fine for this sort of frying. The first two patties will keep well in a warm oven while you fry the second pair.

3 Heat a medium or large skillet over high heat, add the oil, and adjust the burner until the oil reaches 350°F to 360°F on a frying thermometer. (If you'll be cooking in batches, preheat the oven to 200°F.)

4 Place the eggs in a shallow bowl and spread the panko onto a dinner plate; place both near the stove. Place an empty plate near the stove. Form the shrimp mixture into 4 equal patties the diameter of the buns. The mixture will be quite loose but should hold together; if they don't, stir in a teaspoon of cornstarch and reform. Carefully dip each patty in the eggs, turning to coat. Place both sides of the patty on the panko to coat, then use your hands to coat the sides of the patty with crumbs; you may have to reform the patty a bit but should end up with a totally panko-coated patty. Put each crumbed patty on the empty plate.

5 Place 2 patties in the hot oil—be aware that the oil may spatter a bit as they cook. Fry until the bottom of the patty is browned, about 3 minutes, then carefully flip with a spatula and cook on the other side. If working in batches, put the cooked patties on a paper towel and then on a sheet pan in the oven.

6 Spread a generous dollop of the sauce on the top half of each bun. Top the bottom half of each bun with a patty, half of 1 slice of cheese (if using), the cabbage, and the other half of each bun.

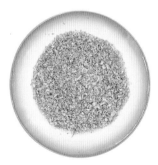

Panko makes the shrimp coating doubly crunchy.

Hot Dog and Bubbles Party!

It works this way: Everyone brings a bottle of dry sparkling wine—extra points for real Champagne—or a top-shelf bubbly nonalcoholic refresher. You stock some beer, sodas, and seltzers for the non-wine-drinkers, and supply wieners and buns and the fired-up grill.

Following is our favorite way to prep the dogs—a spiralization method to maximize weenie surface area for good char—and a range of condiments, jazzed up via the global pantry. All of the toppings recipes that follow make enough for 12 dogs and can be made a couple of hours ahead of time (reheat the onions and chili in the microwave for a couple of minutes before serving).

A few to-dos: Make small tent cards to label the toppings. Spiralize the wieners ahead of time, and butter and toast your buns when grilling, or beforehand if that's easier. A large green salad and potato salad round out the jolly feast. For dessert, bonus points if you make a clutch of the frozen bars and pops on pages 289–293, or a couple of the no-churn ice cream pies on page 286. Purchase recyclable plates, napkins, and cutlery. Gather lots of washable plastic or glass drinking glasses. Then: Party on!

---

12 hot dogs, spiralized (see below)

Neutral oil (such as canola), for oiling the grill rack

12 hot dog buns

Toppings as desired

1 Heat your gas grill to medium-high (450°F to 475°F) or prepare your coals to maintain medium-high heat (gas will take 20 to 30 minutes; charcoal will take about 45 minutes).

2 Oil the grill rack. Arrange the hot dogs on the grill rack. Grill, turning frequently with tongs, until lightly charred all over, 8 to 10 minutes.

3 Serve the hot dogs in the buns with toppings as desired.

Global Pantry Ingredients

Benton's Bacon, *p. 9*

Chipotles in Adobo, *p. 10*

Kecap Manis, *p. 13*

Kimchi, *p. 13*

Korean Toasted Sesame Oil, *p. 14*

Preserved Lemon, *p. 19*

Other Toppings

A mustard array: Set out a pot of Colman's Original English Mustard (or make your own with Colman's powder, water, salt, sugar, vinegar, and whatever spices you like) or a hot German mustard, plus a good Dijon, and round things out with old-school yellow mustard for ballpark dog fans.

Crunchy onion bits: Buy a jar of fried shallots or onions at an Asian supermarket, or sub in some crispy fried onions from the supermarket (the ones near the canned green beans), crushed a bit to sit easily on the dogs.

Spicy chili crisp and onions: Finely chop raw onions and stir in chili crisp to taste for a crunchy, spicy topping.

Suggested wines: We hold this truth to be self-evident: Inexpensive dry cavas from Spain and lots of other sparklers are just fine. Virtually every good winemaking area from Oregon to New Zealand makes tasty fizzy and dry bottles for under $15. But Champagne still rules, of course. It's as good and jolly with hot dogs as it is with foie gras.

How to Spiralize the Dogs

When Ann tested six wiener grilling methods for the Kitchn website a few years ago, the spiralizing method won. It increases the surface area via a corkscrew cut that runs the length of the dog—elongating the wiener, creating lots more edges to char, and adding nooks and crannies for the toppings to fill. All you need is a long wooden skewer or two and a cutting board. Push the skewer through the length of the dog, near the center; if you mess up and come out the side, simply pull out the skewer and try again. Make a spiral cut all the way down the dog, turning it as you go and cutting all the way down to the skewer. Carefully pull out the skewer and continue with more wieners.

6 Spiral-Dog Toppings

Smoky Bacon Ketchup

ACTIVE TIME: 3 minutes
TOTAL TIME: 11 minutes
MAKES ABOUT 1½ CUPS

This is a scaled-up version of the bacon ketchup on page 234, with the bacon bits added at the last minute for crunch.

---

4 slices Benton's bacon, or other very smoky, salty, thick-cut bacon

1 cup Heinz ketchup, or your favorite

1 Chop the bacon into small bits by cutting narrow strips lengthwise with a sharp knife, then crosscutting into bits. Put the bits in a sturdy, microwave-safe bowl and microwave on High until crisp bits reside in a pool of rendered bacon fat, 4 to 5 minutes.

2 Fish out the bacon bits and drain on paper towels, breaking them up if agglomerated. Whisk the fat into the ketchup until it's glossy. When ready to serve, put the ketchup in a serving bowl and strew the bits on top.

Relish in the Style of a Banh Mi

ACTIVE TIME: 5 minutes
TOTAL TIME: 5 minutes
MAKES ABOUT 1 CUP

Sweet, salty, crunchy, tangy—a loose flavor homage to the pickle often found on Vietnamese sandwiches.

½ cup coarsely chopped fresh cilantro

2 tablespoons sugar

2 tablespoons rice vinegar or white vinegar

1 tablespoon neutral oil (such as canola)

1 teaspoon kosher salt

1 large carrot, cut into 1-inch-thick chunks (about 1 cup)

1 length (4 inches) daikon radish, cut into 1-inch chunks (about 1⅓ cups)

Place all ingredients in a food processor and process until chunky but spoonable. Put in a fine-mesh strainer and drain off excess liquid for a few seconds by gently tossing the relish over the sink.

A Sweet and Tangy Relish

ACTIVE TIME: 4 minutes
TOTAL TIME: 4 minutes
MAKES ABOUT 1 CUP

We like a hot dog relish that two-steps between sweet-pickly and tangy-salty-garlicky. Voilà.

---

1 cup sweet pickle chips

⅓ cup coarsely chopped preserved lemon

2 tablespoons extra-virgin olive oil

1 clove garlic, grated on a Microplane

Place all ingredients in a mini food chopper or food processor and process until you have a relish consistency, about 30 seconds. You will likely need to stop halfway through to scrape the sides and push down the relish with a spatula.

Kimchi Coleslaw

ACTIVE TIME: 10 minutes
TOTAL TIME: 10 minutes
MAKES ABOUT 2 CUPS

Classic mayo slaw funkified with the great Korean cultured pickle, then deepened with toasted sesame oil.

⅓ cup mayonnaise (preferably Duke's)

1 tablespoon Korean toasted sesame oil

1 teaspoon sugar

½ teaspoon kosher salt

2 cups finely shredded or thinly sliced napa cabbage

¾ cup finely chopped scallions

½ cup finely chopped kimchi

Whisk together the mayonnaise, oil, sugar, and salt in a medium bowl. Add the cabbage, scallions, and kimchi; toss gently to coat.

Good kimchi is far funkier than sauerkraut.

For Extra Points
Want Cheese with Your Chili Dog? Grate firm, dry cotija cheese until you have a cup, then stir in ¼ cup of finely chopped cilantro (if desired) and serve in a bowl beside the chili.

A Zesty Chipotle Chili for Coney Dog Fans

ACTIVE TIME: 20 minutes
TOTAL TIME: 20 minutes
MAKES ABOUT 3 CUPS

Hot dog chili made spicy, earthy, and good with chipotles and cumin.

---

2 tablespoons neutral oil
(such as canola)

1 pound 90% lean ground beef

1 large onion, minced

½ cup ketchup

½ teaspoon ground cumin

½ teaspoon garlic powder

½ teaspoon ground chile pepper
(optional, for extra heat)

1 can (7.76 ounces) chipotle sauce
(such as La Costeña)

1 Heat a large skillet over medium-high heat for 2 minutes. Add the oil, wait a minute, and crumble in the beef, separating it into small bits by hand as you go. Cook the beef, breaking it up with a spatula or fork until even and fine in texture and lightly browned, 5 minutes. Add the onion and cook until the onion is softened, another 4 minutes.

2 Stir in ½ cup of water, the ketchup, cumin, garlic powder, chile pepper (if using), and chipotle sauce; cook until the mixture is thick, 5 to 7 minutes.

Kecap Manis Onions

ACTIVE TIME: 15 minutes
TOTAL TIME: 15 minutes
MAKES ABOUT 2 CUPS

These have the sweetness of caramelized onions, but maintain some body and a wee bit of crunch.

---

4 tablespoons unsalted butter

4 large white or yellow onions,
cut in half lengthwise and then sliced crosswise into thin half-moons

½ cup kecap manis

Heat your largest skillet on high heat for 1 minute (or heat a Dutch oven for 2 minutes). Add the butter and warm until just bubbly and melted. Add the onions and fry, stirring frequently, until they are starting to brown or char around the edges, about 7 minutes. Add ½ cup of water and continue to cook until the water boils off, about 2 minutes, then add another ½ cup and repeat, about 2 more minutes. Reduce the heat to low, add the kecap manis, and stir to coat all the onions, cooking until the mixture is thick and glossy, 2 to 5 minutes.

Sweet Indonesian soy is a shortcut to rich, dark flavors.

Avocado Toast
with Zingy Furikake Gremolata

ACTIVE TIME: 8 minutes
TOTAL TIME: 8 minutes
SERVES 2

Does the world need another avocado toast? Certainly, when it's capped with our herby, orangey, furikake-laced gremolata. It's such a simple touch that adds tons of flavor and intrigue. If your furikake contains a hint of wasabi, all the better.

---

2 medium-thick (1-inch) slices sourdough bread

⅓ cup coarsely chopped fresh flat-leaf parsley

1½ tablespoons furikake

2 teaspoons grated orange zest

1 small garlic clove, grated on a Microplane

1 large ripe avocado, pitted, peeled, and cut in half

¼ teaspoon kosher salt

1 Toast or broil the bread to your desired level of doneness.

2 Combine the parsley, furikake, orange zest, and garlic in a small bowl; toss well to combine the gremolata. Place an avocado half on each piece of toast; mash with a fork onto the toast. Sprinkle the salt and the gremolata evenly over the toasts.

Global Pantry Ingredient

Furikake, *p. 12*

Shopping Intel
Seek Out Real Bread. We've been taken in once too often by supermarket sourdough loaves that show lackluster crumb and no sign of sourdough flavor. Support your local artisan baker. You can slice the loaf and stash leftovers in the freezer in airtight bags for weeks.

Flavor Booster
Switch Up the Citrus. Gremolata is traditionally made with parsley, garlic, and lemon zest. Here, we go with floral, slightly sweet orange zest, which pairs beautifully with the earthy seaweed and toasted sesame seeds in the furikake.

Choose a furikake blend that speaks to you; you'll often see them flavored with sesame, chiles, wasabi, shiso, or yuzu.

Anchovies • Yuzu • Black Walnuts • Wondra • Sumac • Calabrian Chiles • Sorghu
Millet • Tabasco Sauce • Coconut Milk • Roasted Hazelnut Oil • Curry Leaves •
Sauce • Shrimp Paste • Worcestershire Sauce • Furikake • Sriracha • Saffron • Bany
Vinegar • Gochujang • Harissa • Marmite • Kecap Manis • Chili Crisp • Freeze-Di
Strawberries • Tajín • Kimchi • Korean Toasted Sesame Oil • Dulce de Leche •
Sauce • Lemongrass • Whole Wheat Pastry Flour • Pomegranate Molasses • Mexi
Chocolate • Smoked Paprika • Chipotles in Adobo • Shichimi Togarashi • Makrut Li
Leaves • Crema Mexicana • The Many Masalas • Capers • Mexican Chorizo • Mir
Oyster Sauce • Panko Breadcrumbs • Ras El Hanout • Andouille Sausage • Marsa
The Many Sambals • Benton's Bacon • Miso • Stone-Ground Grits • Tahini • Ghee • P
Sugar • Ají Amarillo Paste • Thai Curry Paste • Mustard Powder • Turmeric • Cultu
Butter • Kashmiri Mirch • Dried Porcini Mushrooms • Sweetened Condensed Mi
Anchovies • Yuzu • Black Walnuts • Wondra • Sumac • Calabrian Chiles • Sorghu
Millet • Tabasco Sauce • Coconut Milk • Roasted Hazelnut Oil • Curry Leaves •
Sauce • Shrimp Paste • Worcestershire Sauce • Furikake • Sriracha • Saffron • Bany
Vinegar • Gochujang • Harissa • Marmite • Kecap Manis • Chili Crisp • Freeze-Dr
Strawberries • Tajín • Kimchi • Korean Toasted Sesame Oil • Dulce de Leche •
Sauce • Lemongrass • Whole Wheat Pastry Flour • Pomegranate Molasses • Mexi
Chocolate • Smoked Paprika • Chipotles in Adobo • Shichimi Togarashi • Makrut Li
Leaves • Crema Mexicana • The Many Masalas • Capers • Mexican Chorizo • Mir
Oyster Sauce • Panko Breadcrumbs • Ras El Hanout • Andouille Sausage • Marsa
The Many Sambals • Benton's Bacon • Miso • Stone-Ground Grits • Tahini • Ghee • P
Sugar • Ají Amarillo Paste • Thai Curry Paste • Mustard Powder • Turmeric • Cultu
Butter • Kashmiri Mirch • Dried Porcini Mushrooms • Sweetened Condensed Mi
Anchovies • Yuzu • Black Walnuts • Wondra • Sumac • Calabrian Chiles • Sorghu
Millet • Tabasco Sauce • Coconut Milk • Roasted Hazelnut Oil • Curry Leaves •
Sauce • Shrimp Paste • Worcestershire Sauce • Furikake • Sriracha • Saffron • Bany
Vinegar • Gochujang • Harissa • Marmite • Kecap Manis • Chili Crisp • Freeze-Dr
Strawberries • Tajín • Kimchi • Korean Toasted Sesame Oil • Dulce de Leche •
Sauce • Lemongrass • Whole Wheat Pastry Flour • Pomegranate Molasses • Mexi
Chocolate • Smoked Paprika • Chipotles in Adobo • Shichimi Togarashi • Makrut Li
Leaves • Crema Mexicana • The Many Masalas • Capers • Mexican Chorizo • Mir
Oyster Sauce • Panko Breadcrumbs • Ras El Hanout • Andouille Sausage • Marsa
The Many Sambals • Benton's Bacon • Miso • Stone-Ground Grits • Tahini • Ghee • P
Sugar • Ají Amarillo Paste • Thai Curry Paste • Mustard Powder • Turmeric • Cultu
Butter • Kashmiri Mirch • Dried Porcini Mushrooms • Sweetened Condensed Mill

Noodles, Pasta, Pizzas, and Breads

Capers, *p. 10*
Very Slow Tomatoes, *p. 25*

Visual Cue

Lightly Does It. The ravioli is not heavily, wetly sauced in this recipe. The jammy tomatoes and salt-bomb capers add perfect pops of flavor when scant, and the Pecorino adds just the right hint of funky cheese.

Knife Pointer

Thin and Sharp Rules. The garlic and shallots are sliced as thin as possible, and a properly sharp, thin knife such as a Japanese nakiri—indispensable for most vegetable work, see page 297— will work wonders in seconds.

Flavor Booster

Crispy Capers. This simple trick never fails to add pops of bright brininess and irresistible crunch to a dish (as we do on the toasts on page 41). Pour about 1 cup olive oil into your smallest saucepan to reach a depth of ⅓ to ½ inch. Heat the oil over medium until it reaches 350°F on a thermometer. Carefully add ¼ cup salt-cured capers (rinsed well, drained, and patted dry) to the oil and fry until browned but not blackened, 2½ to 3 minutes. Remove the capers to a paper towel to crisp up. You won't need all the fried capers or their oil here; use the extra capers to top a salad and add the remaining caper oil to the dressing.

Ravioli

with Very Slow Tomatoes, Crispy Capers, and Caper Oil

ACTIVE TIME: 20 minutes
TOTAL TIME: 20 minutes
SERVES 2

If you have a batch of our Very Slow Tomatoes (page 25) in the fridge or freezer, this dish is a snap. It's a lovely simple dinner for two, with salty caper crunch accenting the tomato goodness, and very speedy if you use a good fresh ravioli from your favorite source. You can easily double the recipe to serve 4, but keep the same amount of caper oil; you won't need more. Frying the capers only takes a few minutes.

¾ cup Very Slow Tomatoes (page 25), thawed if frozen

¼ cup caper oil plus 1 tablespoon crunchy fried salt-cured capers (see Flavor Booster)

1 large or 2 medium shallots (about 3 ounces total), very thinly sliced crosswise

1 large clove garlic, very thinly sliced

8 ounces fresh, mildly flavored large ravioli, such as ricotta and spinach (about 10 ravioli)

Extra-virgin olive oil for drizzling

¼ cup grated Pecorino Romano cheese

1 Bring a large pot of lightly salted water to a boil over high heat.

2 Pile the tomatoes on a cutting board and go at them with a sharp knife, cutting crosswise and pulling back into a heap until you have a jammy consistency.

3 Heat a medium skillet over medium heat. Add the caper oil (reserve the capers) and swirl to coat the pan. Add the shallots— fluffing them with your fingers into rings as you drop them into the pan—and the garlic. Sauté, stirring occasionally, until the shallot rings are translucent and begin to yellow— but not brown—about 5 minutes.

4 Add the ravioli to the boiling water and cook according to the package directions.

5 Add the tomatoes to the skillet and stir, adding a bit of pasta water to break up the mixture. When the ravioli are done, use a slotted spoon to transfer them to the skillet. Don't empty the water pot yet. Use a bit more pasta water, a tablespoon at a time, if needed and toss or stir the ravioli to thoroughly coat. (You're not looking for a wet, loose sauce. You want a thick mixture that just clings.) Divide the ravioli mixture between 2 plates, drizzle with olive oil, dust with Pecorino, and top evenly with the capers.

Hazelnutty Pasta Aglio e Olio

ACTIVE TIME: 20 minutes
TOTAL TIME: 20 minutes
SERVES 4

Pasta aglio e olio (with garlic and oil) is one of the simplest, most soul-satisfying dishes you can make—a big bowl of oil-slicked noodles, fragrant with garlic. Thanks to roasted hazelnut oil, a game-changing pantry ingredient, our version is even more delicious, with notes of sweet-toasty hazelnuts permeating each bite. If you haven't already toasted some hazelnuts, do so before undertaking this dish (see the deep-toasting notes on page 26). No need for cheese or herbs here: They would just overpower the double-nutty effect. Use vermicelli if you can't find the angel hair pasta.

---

12 ounces uncooked angel hair pasta

1 tablespoon neutral oil (such as canola)

½ cup plus 4 teaspoons roasted hazelnut oil

4 large cloves garlic, thinly sliced lengthwise

¼ teaspoon crushed red pepper flakes

Kosher salt to taste

¼ cup chopped toasted, skinned hazelnuts

1 Bring a large pot of lightly salted water to a boil over high heat. Add the pasta and cook until al dente, about 4 minutes. Quickly scoop out and reserve 1⅓ cups pasta cooking water; drain the pasta immediately, and toss with the neutral oil.

2 While the pasta is cooking, combine ⅓ cup of hazelnut oil with the garlic and red pepper flakes in a large skillet or sauté pan over medium heat. Cook, stirring occasionally, until the garlic just barely starts to turn golden, 2 to 3 minutes.

3 Add ¾ cup of reserved pasta water to the pan and increase the heat to medium-high. Boil until the liquid reduces by about half and the mixture looks emulsified, almost like a shaken vinaigrette, about 3 minutes. Reduce the heat to medium-low. Add the drained pasta to the pan and toss with tongs until well coated. Add additional reserved pasta water as needed to keep the pasta moistened. Season to taste with salt.

4 Divide the pasta evenly among 4 shallow bowls. Drizzle 1 teaspoon of the remaining hazelnut oil over each serving, and sprinkle 1 tablespoon of the toasted nuts over each.

Global Pantry Ingredient

Roasted Hazelnut Oil,
p. 20

Avoid This Mistake
Go Easy Salting the Water. The sauce for the pasta is made up mostly of its cooking water, reduced and emulsified with the oil. Adding a handful of salt at the start will overpower the beautiful nuances of the hazelnut oil; we use no more than 2 teaspoons.

Key Technique
Boil, Boil Away. Because the sauce for pasta aglio e olio is little more than pasta water and oil, the key to getting it to cling to the noodles is a hard boil in Step 3, making the sauce, until it emulsifies; simmering won't get you there.

Key Technique

Smaller Smashes Better. Smashing dramatically opens up a cucumber so that it takes the flavors of the dressing into crags and crevices. Mini cukes are infinitely crunchier in this type of application. They usually come in 1-pound bags in the produce section.

To smash the cukes, trim off and discard a small slice from each end. Arrange 1 cucumber on a cutting board. Place the flat side of a chef's knife on top and press down on the knife with your body weight until you feel the cucumber give; it should break into 3 or 4 lengthwise pieces. Pull the pieces apart if they're still connected and cut them crosswise into ½- to 1-inch pieces. Repeat with the remaining cucumbers.

Shopping Intel

Buy Fresh Noodles. Fresh Asian wheat noodles, often containing eggs, preferably about the thickness of spaghetti, deliver the chewy-tender texture you want here. These may be called lo mein, but sometimes also yaki soba, which refers to a Japanese fried-noodle dish made with Chinese-style noodles. You'll find them chilled at the market, often adjacent to the produce section.

Cold Sesame Noodles
with Smashed Mini Cukes

ACTIVE TIME: 22 minutes
TOTAL TIME: 22 minutes
SERVES 4

Another much-loved restaurant dish that's so easy at home: chewy noodles coated with a rich, nutty sauce and topped with super-crunchy cucumbers. It answers all the cravings—it's flavor-packed, with contrasting textures that make it irresistible. Unsweetened powdered peanut butter instantly yields a smoother, silkier sauce with more concentrated flavor than does the goopy jarred stuff. You might think of a cold noodle dish as summertime eating, but trust us: It's a killer dish year-round, with enough chile heat to warm things right up.

3 tablespoons plus 2 teaspoons Korean toasted sesame oil

5 teaspoons rice vinegar

4 teaspoons sambal oelek

1 teaspoon kosher salt

2 medium cloves garlic, grated on a Microplane

12 ounces mini (Persian) cucumbers, smashed (see Key Technique)

½ cup unsweetened peanut butter powder

2 tablespoons soy sauce

2 teaspoons brown sugar

2 teaspoons grated peeled fresh or frozen ginger

12 ounces fresh Chinese egg noodles (see Shopping Intel)

⅓ cup chopped scallions

¼ cup chopped dry-roasted peanuts

1 Whisk together 2 teaspoons each of the toasted sesame oil, vinegar, and sambal in a medium bowl. Add ½ teaspoon of salt and 1 garlic clove and whisk to combine. Add the smashed cucumbers to the dressing and toss to coat. Let stand while you prepare the rest of the recipe.

2 Bring a large pot of water (no need to salt it) to a boil over high heat.

3 Whisk together the peanut butter powder, soy sauce, sugar, ginger, remaining 3 tablespoons sesame oil, 3 teaspoons vinegar, 2 teaspoons sambal, ½ teaspoon salt, and 1 garlic clove with 2 tablespoons of water in a large bowl.

4 Add the fresh noodles to the boiling water; cook until chewy but not chalky, a couple of minutes (longer if using dried, of course). Drain and rinse with cold water until the noodles are cool. Add the noodles and scallions to the peanut butter mixture; toss to coat. If the sauce is too thick, add a teeny bit of warm water. Arrange the noodles in a large, shallow bowl or platter; top with the cucumber mixture (including any liquid) and the peanuts.

Super-Mushroomy Tiny Pasta
Cooked Creamy Like Risotto (but Easier)

ACTIVE TIME: 30 minutes
TOTAL TIME: 30 minutes
SERVES 4

Scott never quite mastered risotto, and mostly left it to the restaurant pros after he began cooking acini di pepe, a tiny semolina pasta shape similar in size to pearl couscous, in the risotto style, inspired by a Mark Bittman recipe of yore. The texture of the pasta here is delightfully supple. It's an easy, earthy, sophisticated main dish, perfect with a medium-bodied Italian red such as a Barbera or a Valpolicella. Add the optional marsala if you like a slightly deeper, more winey flavor.

½ ounce dried porcini mushrooms

2 tablespoons unsalted butter

½ medium onion, minced as finely as you can manage

1 cup cremini mushrooms, thinly sliced

12 ounces acini di pepe or other tiny pasta such as orzo

½ cup dry white wine

4 cups low-sodium chicken stock

1 tablespoon dry marsala wine or rich sherry (such as oloroso) (optional)

1 teaspoon chopped fresh thyme or oregano

½ teaspoon kosher salt

Freshly ground black pepper

½ cup grated Parmesan, or 1 cup super-finely Microplane-grated Parmesan

1 Chop half of the dried mushrooms into pea-size bits. Place in a small microwave-safe bowl with 1 cup of water and microwave on High for 2 minutes; set aside. Place the other half of the dried mushrooms in a mini food processor; pulverize to a powder, about 45 seconds (there will be small flecks or chunks in the powder, and that's the idea).

2 Heat a Dutch oven or a large nonstick skillet over medium heat for 2 minutes. Add the butter, swirling until it melts. Add the onion; sauté until softened and blond in color, stirring frequently, about 3 minutes. Add the cremini mushrooms and sauté until just starting to soften, about 3 minutes more. Add the soaked mushrooms with their liquid, the mushroom powder, and pasta; cook with the heat turned high enough for it to bubble energetically, stirring frequently until the liquid is absorbed, about 2 minutes.

3 This starts the risotto-style cooking process: Continue to stir, adding the white wine and then the stock a little at a time, letting the pasta absorb the liquid, before gradually adding the rest of the stock. When the pasta is almost cooked, about 18 minutes, add the marsala, if using; the thyme; and the salt. When the pasta is just al dente, correct the consistency with stock or hot water if necessary (it should be saucy, not porridge-like). Immediately portion into 4 bowls and top with a few turns of black pepper and the grated cheese.

Global Pantry Ingredients

Dried Porcini Mushrooms, *see Try This!*

Marsala, *p. 15*

Try This!
Dried Porcini Mushrooms. Dried porcini possess a concentration of rich, earthy flavor, an unmatched essence of mushroom that's released when soaked or powdered in a chopper. Look for American or European versions in supermarkets, Whole Foods, and online, in one or two-ounce packets.

Timing Tip
Cook Just Until Almost *Done.* The size and brand of the pasta, and how vigorously you cook it, will vary the cooking time quite a bit. To avoid mush, stop when it's just reaching the al dente stage—it will continue to cook as you add the cheese and serve. The consistency should be a bit saucy, not like seized-up porridge. Slightly larger pasta such as orzo will likely take a bit longer.

Global Pantry Ingredients

Mustard Powder, *see* Try This!

Panko Breadcrumbs, *p. 17*

Turmeric, *p. 24*

Try This!

Mustard Powder. Eaten straight, pure mustard powder is a wasabi-like nasal-passage gunpowder, but stirred into many savory dishes, it adds depth without the vinegar of prepared mustard, and the bitterness vanishes. Look for Colman's mustard powder, in the bright yellow tins, in supermarkets; for the S&B brand in Japanese and pan-Asian stores; or for mustard powder in Indian shops.

Shopping Intel

Large Elbows Are a Must. We cannot stress this enough: Large elbow macaroni makes for a much better dish than the standard weensy size. The noodles get softer and silkier, boosting the creamy effect, while the small ones tend to absorb more water, overthickening the sauce. If you can't find big macaroni, swap in shells or cavatappi. We've also had good results from Tinkyáda brand large brown-rice macaroni from the gluten-free section.

Easy, Creamy One-Pot Mac and Cheese
with Crunchy Pecorino Panko

ACTIVE TIME: 28 minutes
TOTAL TIME: 28 minutes
SERVES 6

Except for the last-minute broil that browns the crust, this is a fuss-free, one-pot stovetop mac and cheese that does not ask you to make a separate sauce to attain intense but creamy cheesiness. Mustard amplifies the cheesy notes, and turmeric adds the brilliant color we love in this dish (especially important if you use white Cheddar). If you already have our garlic panko breadcrumbs (see page 17) on hand, the recipe is even easier—just stir the Pecorino into those and omit Step 1.

---

4 tablespoons unsalted butter

2 cloves garlic, minced

1 cup panko breadcrumbs

⅓ cup grated Pecorino Romano cheese

1 teaspoon kosher salt

12 ounces uncooked large elbow macaroni (see Shopping Intel)

1 cup evaporated milk

2 teaspoons cornstarch

1 teaspoon mustard powder

¼ teaspoon ground turmeric (optional)

8 ounces sharp Cheddar cheese, preferably orange, shredded

1 Heat a 10-inch cast-iron skillet (with a lid) or other ovenproof skillet over medium heat. Add 2 tablespoons of butter to the pan and swirl until it melts. Add the garlic; cook, stirring constantly, until the garlic is very fragrant and barely beginning to brown, 30 seconds to 1 minute. Add the panko; cook, stirring frequently, until evenly golden brown, about 3 minutes. Pour the breadcrumb mixture into a bowl; stir in the Pecorino Romano. Rinse out the skillet and pat it dry with paper towels.

2 Add 3 cups of water, the remaining 2 tablespoons butter, the salt, and pasta to the skillet. Bring to a boil over medium-high heat. Cover and reduce the heat to low or medium-low, enough to maintain a steady simmer. Cook, uncovering the pan to stir the pasta occasionally, until the pasta is tender, 8 to 10 minutes. It's OK if there's still a little water in the pan.

3 Preheat the broiler to low with the oven rack placed about 6 inches from the top.

4 Whisk together the evaporated milk, cornstarch, mustard powder, and turmeric (if using). Stir the milk mixture into the pasta mixture; cook over medium heat until the sauce bubbles and thickens, 2 to 3 minutes. Remove the pan from the heat. Gradually add the Cheddar, stirring until it melts. Sprinkle the panko mixture over the top. Broil until lightly browned, about 2 minutes.

A Gorgeous Platter of Indonesia's
Happiest Noodles

ACTIVE TIME: 24 minutes
TOTAL TIME: 30 minutes
SERVES 4

If you're an 11-year-old kid from *Saskatchewan*, of all places, suddenly living in Indonesia and set free by your parents to eat your way through the night markets . . . well, eyes are opened. That's what happened to Scott when he discovered mie goreng. This recipe is our homage to the noodle classic, sweet-spicy and filling. It has fried goodness from the wok, gloss and umami from kecap manis, moderate heat from chiles, crunch from cabbage, and a seafood bonus from shrimp. Kids will gobble this dish up and demand more, more, more.

1 teaspoon shrimp paste

2 large shallots, peeled

2 large cloves garlic, peeled

¼ cup neutral oil (such as canola)

14 ounces dried Chinese wheat noodles (see Shopping Intel)

1 pound large or jumbo peeled and deveined US-caught shrimp, thawed or fresh, cut into large chunks and dried with paper towels

1 cup finely chopped green or napa cabbage

1 Fresno red chile or small hot red chile, seeded and cut into very thin rings

5 tablespoons kecap manis

2 teaspoons soy sauce

2 teaspoons sambal oelek (optional)

1 bunch scallions, greens thinly sliced

1 Place the shrimp paste, shallots, and garlic in a mini food processor (or mortar and pestle) and process to a uniform paste, about 30 seconds on high. You may need to add some neutral oil, a teaspoon at a time, to bring it together into a paste.

2 Bring a large pot of lightly salted water to a boil over high heat. Add the noodles and cook, stirring occasionally to prevent sticking, until the noodles are almost done, still a bit al dente. (Note that the cooking time will vary widely by the type of noodle; use the package directions as a loose guide and cook until almost done but still chewy and a bit starchy.) Drain the noodles and toss them in a large bowl with 1 tablespoon of neutral oil to prevent sticking.

3 Turn the vent fan on high. Heat a wok over medium-high heat until the air above the wok shimmers, then add the remaining 3 tablespoons oil and fry the shallot paste for 1 to 2 minutes, breaking it up with a spatula. It will turn toasty brown and smell, well, fishy-fragrant; don't let it burn. Add the shrimp and stir-fry, stirring constantly, until the shrimp are almost cooked, about 2 minutes. Increase the heat to high, add the cabbage and chile, and stir-fry 1 minute more. Add 4 tablespoons of kecap manis, the soy sauce, sambal (if desired), and noodles; stir-fry, constantly tossing, until the noodles are evenly brown and glossy from the kecap manis, 1 to 2 minutes. Remove to a serving platter, drizzle with the remaining 1 tablespoon kecap manis, and garnish with the scallions. Serve immediately.

Global Pantry Ingredients

Kecap Manis, *p. 13*

Sambal, *p. 21*

Shrimp Paste, *p. 11*

Soy Sauce, *p. 22*

Shopping Intel

The Noodles You Can Use. Look for Chinese-style dried wheat noodles about the width of spaghetti but often, in the package, kinked or curled into bundles. Some are yellow from egg; some white from lack of egg. Many good supermarkets will have them, and of course there are scads of varieties in Asian food stores. For the right texture, you'll cook them to al dente in water, then finish in the sizzling wok.

Flavor Cue

Why Bother Frying the Paste First? Frying the mixture of shallots, garlic, and shrimp paste is a first and essential step to producing a rich, surprisingly mellow final flavor. The funky shrimp paste converts to a fantastic supplier of depth. If you don't have a powerful vent over the stove, proceed with caution, and throw open doors and windows: The shrimp paste has a pungent fragrance in this early stage. Barring that, you can fry it in a pan on an outdoor grill.

Pantry Tactics

Improvising Is Fine. If you don't have capers for a briny hit, substitute chopped, pitted kalamata olives. If you don't have Calabrian chiles, crushed red pepper flakes will do. The parsley can be replaced with some chopped scallion greens. But do take time to make our garlic panko breadcrumbs.

Prep Tip

Get Your Mise en Place On. This is a very simple dish to cook if you place all the chopped ingredients by the stove before adding the pasta to the boiling water—what chefs, as we all know now from the cooking shows, call mise en place (things in their place).

Emmy's Big Bowl of Pasta
with Breadcrumbs

ACTIVE TIME: 20 minutes
TOTAL TIME: 30 minutes
SERVES 4

The first time Scott cooked for his future stepdaughter Emmylou, she was 5, had a raspy voice like a tiny Kim Carnes, and was only slightly less fierce than Conor McGregor. In short, an intimidating little girl, and hilarious. Serving a version of this dish proved a breakthrough diplomatic event. The Sicilian starch-on-starch combination of breadcrumbs and pasta is an example of *la cucina povera*—inspired Italian cooking from cheap ingredients at hand. The texture is somewhat dry rather than sauced. This version, with pine nuts and capers, is less authentically povera, but it's punchy and delicious, no matter who you're trying to impress.

12 ounces uncooked spaghetti

2 tablespoons extra-virgin olive oil

1 medium onion, finely diced

2 large cloves garlic, finely chopped

1 cup cherry tomatoes, squeezed of seeds and chopped

½ cup chopped flat-leaf parsley

3 tablespoons salt-cured capers, rinsed well, drained, and patted dry with paper towels

2 teaspoons Calabrian chiles in oil, chopped

6 anchovies in oil, chopped

⅓ cup toasted pine nuts (see page 26)

1 cup Toasty Garlic Breadcrumbs (page 17)

1 Bring a large pot of salted water to a boil over high heat. Add the pasta and cook until just al dente, about 8 minutes.

2 While the pasta cooks, heat the oil in a large skillet over medium heat for 1 minute. Add the onion and sauté until soft, stirring frequently and being careful not to brown it, about 5 minutes. Add the garlic and sauté until fragrant, about 1 minute. Add the tomatoes, parsley, capers, chiles, and anchovies and cook until the tomatoes start to soften, about 3 minutes. Reduce the heat to low.

3 When the pasta is done, increase the heat for the skillet to medium. Reserve 1 cup of pasta water and drain the pasta. Add the pasta to the skillet and stir until well combined, adding the pasta water as needed to moisten, but don't make the mixture soupy, just glistening. Add the pine nuts and breadcrumbs and toss. The pasta should be dry-ish but not seized up. If it is too dry, drizzle in a bit more pasta water. Serve immediately from the pan.

Rigatoni

with Rich, Beefy Onion Gravy

ACTIVE TIME: 30 minutes
TOTAL TIME: 1 hour 40 minutes
SERVES 6

La Genovese—Genoa sauce—
is actually from Naples but Scott
first had it in Brooklyn when a friend
cooked her nonna's specialty: melty-
sweet onions flavored by beef, a
sauce as delicious as any virtuoso
Bolognese. In that version, a large
chunk of tough meat was slow-cooked
all day with onions until tender, then
served sliced as a second course after
a primo bowl of pasta sauced with
the oniony liquor. It's pure comfort
cooking. This version seriously tinkers
with tradition in search of a quicker
hit of beef-onion majesty through
the power of the pressure cooker and
some flavor-building ingredients from
the global pantry, namely oyster sauce
and marsala. There's also a Dutch oven
variation on the following page if you
have a few extra hours for slow oven
cooking. We call the sauce "gravy"
because we've always been charmed
to hear certain Italian Americans in the
Northeast use that term.

1 pound good, fatty beef chuck eye steak,
   cut into 2-inch cubes

2 teaspoons kosher salt

2 tablespoons olive oil

2½ pounds onions, thinly sliced

1 stalk celery, diced

1 carrot, diced

¼ cup dry marsala or dry white wine

1 cup unsalted beef stock

2 tablespoons oyster sauce

1 tablespoon double-concentrated
   tomato paste

1 teaspoon minced fresh rosemary

1 pound uncooked rigatoni

2 tablespoons cornstarch

1 cup shredded Pecorino Romano or
   Parmesan

1 Season the beef with 1 teaspoon of salt.
Set an Instant Pot to Sauté. Add the oil and
the beef to the pot and brown, turning every
few minutes, for about 8 minutes; the pieces
need space between them, and if there's
crowding, brown them in 2 batches. Remove
the beef from the pot with a slotted spoon.
Add the onions, celery, and carrot to the
pot; cook, stirring occasionally, until just
starting to soften, about 3 minutes. Add the
wine, scraping the bottom to deglaze the
pot, then stir in the browned beef, ¾ cup of
beef stock, the oyster sauce, tomato paste,
and rosemary.

Global Pantry Ingredients

Marsala, *p. 15*
Oyster Sauce, *p. 16*

Flavor Booster

Get Your Brown On. We cut
the beef into chunks and then
aggressively brown the meat
on all sides to extract maximum
goodness from the Maillard
reaction—the umami-building
crust that forms under high heat.

Texture Strategy

A Bit of Thickening at the End.
Depending on the water content
of the onions, the sauce may not
thicken as much in the sealed
Instant Pot as it does in the
oven. We add a bit of stock and
cornstarch at the end.

2 Turn the pot off. Secure the lid in place and set the steam valve to Sealing. Set to Manual and cook at high pressure for 50 minutes. When the cook time is over, allow the steam to release naturally for 15 minutes, then quick-release any remaining pressure.

3 When the cook time is down to about 10 minutes left, bring a large pot of salted water to a boil. Add the rigatoni and cook until al dente, about 12 minutes. Drain the pasta and return to the pot.

4 Use a spoon or fork to shred the beef into the sauce, working directly in the pot. Bring the sauce to a bubble using the Sauté setting. Whisk the cornstarch into the remaining ¼ cup stock; add the stock/cornstarch mixture to the sauce and cook to thicken, 1 minute. Stir in the remaining 1 teaspoon salt. Pour the sauce into the pot with the pasta; toss well to combine. Let the pasta mixture stand to soak up some of the sauce, 5 to 10 minutes. Sprinkle with the cheese at the table.

When buying marsala, seek a dry, real Italian variety.

Dutch Oven Method

ACTIVE TIME: 30 minutes
TOTAL TIME: 4 hours 30 minutes

1 Preheat the oven to 275°F with the rack placed in the lower third. Season the beef with 1 teaspoon of salt.

2 Heat a Dutch oven (or sturdy, heavy-bottomed oven-safe pot with tight lid) over medium-high heat for 4 minutes. Add the olive oil and beef and sauté the beef as described in the main recipe, then sauté vegetables, then deglaze and add the remaining ingredients as described. The liquid will not cover the ingredients, but turn up the heat and bring the liquid to a boil. When it's boiling, cover the Dutch oven and put into the oven. After 30 minutes, check to make sure the liquid is gently bubbling. If it's boiling hard, reduce the heat to 250°F.

3 Cook, covered, for 3½ to 4 hours. After 1 hour, and each hour thereafter, check to make sure the onions are not sticking (onions should release enough liquid to keep things gently bubbling). Add the remaining 1 teaspoon salt and stir the mixture. If the onions are sticking, add ½ cup of stock, cover, and continue cooking. Remove from the oven when the meat is falling-apart tender, and shred the beef using a spoon or fork. The sauce is very thick, like stewed onions. There should be no need with the Dutch oven method to thicken the sauce with cornstarch.

Shrimp Scampi Vermicelli
with Garlicky Miso Butter

ACTIVE TIME: 20 minutes
TOTAL TIME: 20 minutes
SERVES 4

Global Pantry Ingredient

Miso, *p. 16*

Don't you just love it when a quick, easy dinner is also one you're proud to serve to guests? This garlicky pasta adds a touch of miso to a white-wine base for extra briny depth. The convenience factor goes way up if you keep a bag or two of peeled and deveined shrimp in the freezer for quick meals. There's no searing the shrimp or other fuss: They cook to a lovely, delicate state in just a couple of minutes. Plus, they thaw in a snap if you forget to defrost ahead of time.

---

8 ounces uncooked vermicelli (thin spaghetti)

3 tablespoons unsalted butter

2 tablespoons extra-virgin olive oil

6 cloves garlic, minced

⅔ cup dry white wine

¾ teaspoon kosher salt

¼ teaspoon crushed red pepper flakes

3 tablespoons white miso

1 pound large shrimp, peeled and deveined (see Shrimp Intel, page 203)

¼ cup chopped fresh parsley (optional)

1 Bring a large pot of water to a boil. Add the pasta; cook until al dente, 7 to 8 minutes. Scoop out and reserve ½ cup pasta water. Drain the pasta.

2 While the pasta cooks, heat the butter and oil in a large skillet over medium-high heat until the butter melts. Add the garlic; cook 1 minute, stirring constantly. Add the wine, salt, and red pepper flakes; cook until reduced by half, about 3 minutes. Whisk in the miso. Add the shrimp to the pan; cook, flipping the shrimp halfway through the cooking time, until the shrimp just turn pink and opaque, 2 to 3 minutes.

3 Add the pasta and ¼ cup reserved pasta water to the skillet; toss well to coat. Add additional pasta water as needed. Sprinkle with parsley, if desired.

Flavor Booster

A Savory Sauce with Sticking Power. Whisking white miso into the sauce not only adds salty umami to contrast the sweetness of the shrimp, it also thickens the sauce for better pasta-clinging performance.

Avoid This Mistake

Skip the Seawater Tip. Common cooking advice tells you to salt your pasta cooking water heavily, even until it tastes like seawater, but not here. Because you'll be adding some pasta water to the already-salty, miso-enriched sauce, salted water might tilt the dish toward salt-lick territory.

Anchovies, *p. 8*

Real Caramelization

Slow Is the Journey to the Righteous Onions. Although a shortcut hack involving baking soda can cut the time it takes to caramelize onions, we don't much like the texture. With a large quantity like this, the cooking can be an hour and demands periodic stirring. To achieve a bit of superhot pizza-oven char in the final product, we scorch a small amount of the onions at the end of the caramelizing.

Eye Relief

Cutting-Edge Kitchen Style. If you have an old pair of ski goggles around, they can help reduce the tears when cutting this many onions. You'll look like an idiot. Or at least Scott does.

Pacing the Dough

Keep Your Cool. Instant yeast tends to be *very* active, so we use cool water, not warm, and let the dough rise at no more than a cool room temperature, about 68°F, if possible.

Pizza-ladière

ACTIVE TIME: 40 minutes
TOTAL TIME: 3½ to 4½ hours
SERVES 6

This recipe combines two things we absolutely love: the French caramelized onion and anchovy tart known as pissaladière—a sweet-salty explosion of umami—and an easy Sicilian-style thick, crunchy-edged pizza crust made with high-gluten bread flour, whose dough rises in the sheet pan that it will cook in. Serve a bright, uncomplicated red wine with this—from Provence or Sicily—along with a salad. Please add more anchovies if you're mad for the salty fish fillets.

1¼ cups room-temperature water

1 teaspoon instant active dry yeast

3¼ cups bread flour (about 15 ounces)

½ cup plus 1 tablespoon extra-virgin olive oil

2 teaspoons kosher salt

4½ pounds yellow or white onions (not Vidalia or "sweet" onions)

3 tablespoons unsalted butter

24 anchovy fillets in oil

18 pitted oil-cured black olives or pitted kalamata olives, halved

1 To prepare the dough, in a food processor fitted with the standard blade or a plastic dough blade, add ingredients in this order: water, yeast, flour, 2 tablespoons of olive oil, and the salt. Process until the dough clumps together around the blade, then continue to mix for 30 seconds as the dough spins.

2 Put ¼ cup of olive oil into an 18 × 13-inch half-sheet pan and use your hands to oil the bottom and sides. Turn the dough out onto the pan (the dough will be sticky) and rotate several times so that it is completely covered in oil. Flatten the dough with your fingers and palms and gently press it toward the four corners. It will not stretch all the way—that comes later. Cover with plastic wrap and place in a room-temperature place (but not in direct sunlight) for 3½ to 4 hours. As it rises, it will push against the plastic and begin to sprawl toward the edges.

3 Meanwhile, peel the onions and halve them vertically, from stem to stern (not around their equator), and slice into thin half-moons; separate these into strips. Halfway through this tearful chore, heat a Dutch oven or other large, heavy pot over medium heat. Add 2 tablespoons of the oil and 2 tablespoons of butter to the pan. When the butter has just melted, add the onions and use tongs or a big spoon to toss and coat. Reduce the heat to medium-

low and cook, turning the onions every 10 minutes or so. You don't want them to burn and stick. As their natural moisture evaporates, the onions will begin to turn blond. Add the remaining butter and oil, if necessary, to lessen sticking. (You can also add 1 to 2 tablespoons of water.) Continue cooking for about 60 minutes, until well caramelized: blond to tan in color, and soft. Remove all but 1 cup of the onions from the pan. Turn the heat to high under the remaining onions and stir until the onions scorch here and there into a deep mahogany hue, about 5 minutes. Mix the scorched onions thoroughly with the rest. For convenience later, line up your anchovies and halved olives at this point.

4 One hour before eating time, preheat the oven to 550°F (or 500°F, if that's the max) with the rack placed in the lowest position. About 30 minutes before eating, remove the plastic wrap from the dough and gently work the dough so it reaches all edges of the pan. The dough will deflate during this process, so be gentle. Perfect evenness is not necessary. Spread the onions on the dough with your hands, then add the anchovies and olives in whatever pattern strikes your fancy.

5 Bake the pizza until the bottom of the crust (lift it with a fork or spatula) is nicely browned and the top of the crust is, too, 11 to 15 minutes. Brown, not blond, is the goal here. Remove to a cutting board, cut into 12 pieces, and serve immediately. If you need to wait a few minutes, put the pizza on a rack with air beneath it. It's delicious served warm as well as piping hot.

The sweet onions are offset by lots of salty anchovies, which can bake up a little crisp in the oven.

Korean Fire Chicken Pizza

ACTIVE TIME: 27 minutes
TOTAL TIME: 45 minutes
SERVES 4

Living in the South, Ann had plenty of experience with chiles before going to Seoul, the huge and vibrant capital city of her mother's home country of Korea. But she was nonetheless astonished by the love of huge amounts of fiery foods washed down with copious pourings of vodka-like soju. In typical pan-global mash-up fashion, mozzarella cheese often appeared in these dishes, to temper the flames. Buldak, or fire chicken, is one such dish in Korean restaurants and bars—very spicy, saucy chicken under a blanket of gooey mozz. Here, we use it as a topping for a crispy-crusted pizza. It's not as hot as in Korea, but still packs plenty of punch, which is why we say two slices are plenty—an entrée rather than an entire meal. Serve it with a spinach salad with citrus and a splash of Korean toasted sesame oil in the dressing, such as our recipe on page 73.

2 tablespoons gochugaru
(see Chile Substitution)

1½ tablespoons gochujang

2 tablespoons honey

1 tablespoon soy sauce

1 tablespoon Korean toasted sesame oil

1 teaspoon grated peeled fresh ginger

2 cloves garlic, grated on a Microplane

9 ounces boneless, skinless chicken thighs
or breasts, cut into small bite-size pieces

All-purpose flour for dusting the pizza peel
(optional)

12 to 13 ounces pizza dough, at room
temperature (see Pre-Prep Tip)

8 ounces low-moisture mozzarella,
shredded

2 tablespoons sliced scallions

1 Place a pizza stone, baking steel, or heavy sheet pan in the oven. Preheat the oven to 550°F with the stone/steel/pan in the lower third of the oven. (If your oven doesn't go to 550°F, heat it to the highest temperature it will go, at least 500°F.) After the oven reaches temperature, heat the stone/steel/pan for 20 more minutes to ensure it's super-hot.

Global Pantry Ingredients

Gochujang, *p. 13*

Korean Toasted Sesame Oil, *p. 14*

Soy Sauce, *p. 22*

Pre-Prep Tip

Ready Your Dough. We've had very good luck with store-bought refrigerated pizza dough (Whole Foods is one reliable supplier, and even better if you find a non-chain pizza shop to sell some). But make sure to get it home or out of the fridge in time for it to come to room temperature so that it relaxes, stretches, and stays thin. Remove from the plastic wrap an hour before baking; place the dough on a well-floured board, and cover with a clean towel or napkin. It can easily take 30 minutes or more to get to stretchable temperature.

Chile Substitution

No Gochugaru? Fire chicken sauce combines gochujang (page 13) and gochugaru, a coarsely ground Korean red pepper, for its distinctive mix of sweetness and fruity, slightly bitter heat. If you don't have gochugaru, don't substitute a ground chile pepper—too much fire. Instead, try 2 to 3 tablespoons of ground Aleppo or piment d'Espelette pepper.

2 Stir together the gochugaru, gochujang, honey, soy sauce, oil, ginger, and garlic in a medium bowl. Add the chicken; toss well to combine.

3 Heat a small or medium skillet over medium heat. Add the chicken mixture to the pan and stir in ¼ cup water. Cook until the chicken is done and the sauce thickens to a ketchup-like consistency, stirring frequently, 6 to 7 minutes.

4 If you have a pizza peel, put a liberal amount of coarse cornmeal on it so the dough will slip off the peel. If you don't, cut a piece of parchment paper about 12 inches square; lightly dust the paper with flour. Place the pizza dough on the paper and lightly dust the top of the dough with flour. Dimple the dough with your fingertips all over to start spreading the dough over the paper. Continue dimpling and patting the dough to shape it into a 12-inch circle.

5 Spoon the chicken mixture evenly over the dough, leaving a ¾- to 1-inch border. Sprinkle the pizza evenly with the cheese. Place the pizza, with the parchment paper, onto the back of a sheet pan, and slide the pizza (still on paper) onto the hot stone/steel/pan. (If you have a peel, use it to transfer the pizza to the hot stone/steel/pan.) Bake until the crust is browned and the cheese is bubbly and browned, 8 to 10 minutes (10 to 12 minutes if baking at 500°F). Top the pizza with the scallions; cut into 8 wedges.

Korean gojuchang is a great pantry staple for sweet, medium heat.

Global Pantry Ingredients

Benton's Bacon, *p. 9*

Panko Breadcrumbs, *p. 17*

Timing Tip

A Proper Soak. For a custardy interior, the bread needs to really absorb the milk-egg mixture, but not to the point of falling apart.

Shopping Intel

Grade B is A1. Maple syrup graded B is less expensive and usually darker in color than grade A, and we prefer its more intense maple flavor.

Thicker Bread Is Better. A white supermarket loaf works best, but buy a thicker, sturdier variety, sometimes called "artisan" or "farmhouse."

Crunchy Panko Pain Perdu
with Bacon Ketchup and Bacon Maple Syrup

ACTIVE TIME: 37 minutes
TOTAL TIME: 37 minutes
SERVES 4

Here's a terrific weekend breakfast or brunch spectacular, sure to wow. French toast is called *pain perdu* in France and often eaten as a savory dish. Growing up in Saskatoon, Saskatchewan, Scott almost always ate French toast with ketchup, later discovering in America that this is often seen as insane. But it's not! Our amped-up riff swings both ways: Pain perdu is made crunchy on the outside by panko, but remains custardy within, then is served with a smoky bacon-infused ketchup or, for those who prefer a sweeter touch, a maple syrup dotted with bacon bits. Try one of each for the full experience.

---

2 slices Benton's bacon, or other very smoky, salty bacon

⅓ cup Heinz ketchup, or your favorite

½ cup maple syrup

4 large eggs

1¼ cups whole milk

¼ teaspoon kosher salt

1⅔ cups panko breadcrumbs

4 tablespoons salted butter

8 slices firm, thick white sandwich bread

1 To prepare the bacon ketchup, chop the bacon into small bits by cutting narrow strips lengthwise with a sharp knife, then crosscutting into bits. Put the bits in a sturdy, microwave-safe bowl, cover with a paper towel, and microwave on High until crisp bits reside in a pool of melted bacon fat, 3 to 4 minutes.

2 Drain the fat through a fine-mesh strainer into a small bowl. Place the ketchup in a small bowl and whisk 1 tablespoon of the bacon fat into it until glossy. (Reserve any remaining fat for another use, such as sautéing onions or adding smoky goodness to a spaghetti sauce. It will keep in an airtight container in the refrigerator for a couple of months.)

3 To prepare the bacon syrup, place the maple syrup and bacon bits in a small saucepan and bring to a boil over medium heat; lower the heat a bit and bubble the mixture away energetically for 2½ minutes, being careful not to let it boil over. Set aside to cool and infuse with flavor while you make the pain perdu.

4 To prepare the pain perdu, whisk the eggs in a large bowl until no signs of white remain, then whisk in the milk and salt. Set the bowl beside the stove. Sprinkle the panko on a large plate or in a pie plate, spread to make it even, and set the pan beside the bowl.

5 Heat a large skillet over medium heat for 2 minutes, then add 1 tablespoon of butter. As the butter melts, begin soaking the bread using the following method: Place a slice of bread in the milk mixture and gently press with your fingers, then flip the bread over and gently press. Repeat this four or five times until you feel the bread is soaked through yet still holds together. Lift the slice out and gently place on the panko, then turn over to coat with crumbs on the other side.

6 Place the bread in the sizzling butter and repeat the soaking and coating with 3 more slices (if your pan is big enough for 4 pieces). Cook each slice for about 2½ minutes, until deep brown on one side. Remove the bread to a plate, cooked side down. Scrape out any panko crumbs from the pan (they might burn). Add 1 tablespoon of butter to the pan, and swirl until the butter melts. Return the bread to the pan, cooked side up. Cook until deep brown on the other side, about 2½ minutes.

7 Repeat the process with the remaining butter and bread slices. Serve with the bacon ketchup and bacon syrup.

The microwave makes quick, crunchy bits out of smoky Benton's.

Quick Moroccan-Inspired
Lamb Flatbreads

ACTIVE TIME: 24 minutes
TOTAL TIME: 24 minutes
SERVES 4

Years ago, Scott ate a mind-blowing b'stilla in Marrakesh, Morocco—a pie of phyllo-like warqa pastry that included bits of pigeon, eggs, onions, spices, and nuts, the whole thing topped with a matrix of powdered sugar and cinnamon. The dish obliterated the line between sweet and savory like nothing he'd had before.

B'stilla is a national dish of celebration in Morocco, and it's a boxcar full of work to make. Here we import some of its flavors to a flatbread, which is much easier. Ground lamb is fried with onion, garlic, raisins, and spices, then layered on store-bought flatbreads for a quick broil. At serving, a sugar-cinnamon mix is rained down for those wishing to have their paradigm shifted. For those not wishing, the dish is delish just as it is.

½ cup golden raisins

Hot or boiling water for soaking

1 tablespoon extra-virgin olive oil

1 pound ground lamb

2 medium onions, finely chopped (about 2½ cups)

2 cloves garlic, thinly sliced

1 tablespoon ras el hanout

½ teaspoon kosher salt

Dash of saffron (optional)

4 naan or other flatbread

¼ cup toasted pine nuts or sliced almonds (see page 26)

1 tablespoon powdered sugar

¼ teaspoon ground cinnamon

1 Place the raisins in a small bowl and cover with hot or boiling water to soak.

2 Heat the oil in a large skillet over medium heat. Crumble the lamb into the pan in pieces as small as you can manage. Sauté the lamb, using a wooden spoon to break it up further, until the meat is lightly browned, about 5 minutes. With a slotted spoon, remove the lamb to a bowl. Add the onions and garlic to the fat in the pan; sauté until translucent but not brown, about 6 minutes. Drain the raisins and add them to the pan, along with the ras el hanout, salt, and saffron, if using, stirring until very fragrant, about 2 minutes. Add the lamb back to the pan, stirring for another minute, and set aside.

3 Place the oven rack 6 inches below the broiler and preheat the broiler on low. Arrange the naan on a sheet pan or rack and spread the meat mixture evenly over the flatbreads. Broil, watching like a hawk, just until the edges of the naan are nicely browned and the meat is sizzling, 2 to 3 minutes.

4 Cut the naan into serving-size pieces and sprinkle with the nuts. Combine the sugar and cinnamon in a small bowl. Bring the sugar-cinnamon mixture to the table with a small strainer and dust the servings of those who wish to try it.

Global Pantry Ingredients

Pine Nuts, *p. 19*
Ras El Hanout, *p. 20*
Saffron, *see* Try This!, *p. 107*

Shopping Intel

Do Try This at Home. For details on buying a good commercial version of the national spice mix of Morocco, ras el hanout, see page 20. If your local grocery stores don't carry ground lamb, you can very finely chop pieces of lamb shoulder removed from the bone, or seek out ground lamb at better meat counters.

Easy "Pizza"
in the Style of a Tlayuda

ACTIVE TIME: 14 minutes
TOTAL TIME: 30 minutes
SERVES 4

Tlayudas—large, handmade grilled white- or blue-corn tortillas with various toppings—are a favorite street food in Oaxaca, but we'll confess that we haven't had them in situ, only in stateside restaurants. This riff on the concept yields a terrific, quick dinner—neither taco nor burrito, deliciously different from both, aromatic from the Mexican chorizo and cumin—with a side salad and Mexican beer.

---

2 tablespoons olive oil

2 cloves garlic, minced

1 can (15 ounces) black beans, drained and rinsed

1 teaspoon ground cumin

1 teaspoon ground chile pepper

1 large (15- to 16-inch) tlayuda shell or large white or blue corn tortilla, or 4 mini tlayuda shells, naan, or other flatbreads

1 medium onion, minced

1 cup Mexican chorizo (about 8 ounces)

1 cup shredded Oaxaca cheese (or cotija cheese, sliced thin and crumbled)

1 cup fresh pico de gallo

2 avocados, pitted, peeled, and sliced

1 cup shredded lettuce or green cabbage

1 Preheat the oven to 350°F with the rack placed in the center.

2 Heat 1 tablespoon of oil in a large skillet over medium heat. Add the garlic and cook, stirring frequently, until softened, 1 to 2 minutes. Add the beans and cook for 3 minutes. Add the cumin, chile pepper, and ½ cup water and continue to cook, mashing the beans with a spatula to break them up (but leaving some beans almost whole), 2 minutes. Add more water if the mixture thickens too much—it should be loose but not watery. When done, turn off the heat.

3 Arrange the tlayuda shell(s), tortillas, or flatbreads on a wire rack set into a sheet pan, or put them directly on the oven rack. If using tlayuda shell(s), bake until recrisped, 3 to 5 minutes. If using tortillas or flatbreads, bake until beginning to crisp, about 10 minutes.

4 Meanwhile, in a second large skillet, heat the remaining 1 tablespoon oil over medium heat for 1 minute. Add the onion and cook until golden, about 5 minutes, stirring occasionally. Add the chorizo, crumbling the meat in with your hands, and continue to break up the mixture until mixed. When the meat is cooked, 4 to 5 minutes, turn off the heat.

5 Spread the bean mixture evenly over the tlayuda shells, followed by the chorizo mixture and the cheese. Place on a sheet pan and bake until everything is nice and hot and the cheese is melted (if using Oaxaca), 8 to 10 minutes. Remove to the counter and top with pico de gallo, avocado slices, and shredded lettuce.

Global Pantry Ingredient

Mexican Chorizo, *p. 15*

Supermarket Substitutions
Tortillas, Cheese, Etc. When we can't find large corn tortillas or pre-crisped tlayuda shells (often available at Mexican markets), we use smaller corn tortillas (a bit fussier) or even supermarket flatbreads or whole wheat tandoor naan. Cheesewise, if you can't find softer, mozza-like Oaxacan cheese, substitute drier cotija. Look for pico de gallo, a chunkier fresh salsa, in the refrigerated part of most supermarket produce sections.

Where to Cook?
Grill vs. Oven. To keep this quick, we've precrisped the tortillas and cooked the assembled tlayudas in the oven, but you can grill them outdoors, too, flipping them until crisp. Then add toppings, reduce the heat, and finish with the lid down.

Anchovies • Yuzu • Black Walnuts • Wondra • Sumac • Calabrian Chiles • Sorghu
Millet • Tabasco Sauce • Coconut Milk • Roasted Hazelnut Oil • Curry Leaves •
Sauce • Shrimp Paste • Worcestershire Sauce • Furikake • Sriracha • Saffron • Bany
Vinegar • Gochujang • Harissa • Marmite • Kecap Manis • Chili Crisp • Freeze-Dr
Strawberries • Tajín • Kimchi • Korean Toasted Sesame Oil • Dulce de Leche •
Sauce • Lemongrass • Whole Wheat Pastry Flour • Pomegranate Molasses • Mexi
Chocolate • Smoked Paprika • Chipotles in Adobo • Shichimi Togarashi • Makrut Li
Leaves • Crema Mexicana • The Many Masalas • Capers • Mexican Chorizo • Mir
Oyster Sauce • Panko Breadcrumbs • Ras El Hanout • Andouille Sausage • Marsa
The Many Sambals • Benton's Bacon • Miso • Stone-Ground Grits • Tahini • Ghee • P.
Sugar • Ají Amarillo Paste • Thai Curry Paste • Mustard Powder • Turmeric • Cultu
Butter • Kashmiri Mirch • Dried Porcini Mushrooms • Sweetened Condensed Mi
Anchovies • Yuzu • Black Walnuts • Wondra • Sumac • Calabrian Chiles • Sorghu
Millet • Tabasco Sauce • Coconut Milk • Roasted Hazelnut Oil • Curry Leaves •
Sauce • Shrimp Paste • Worcestershire Sauce • Furikake • Sriracha • Saffron • Bany
Vinegar • Gochujang • Harissa • Marmite • Kecap Manis • Chili Crisp • Freeze-Dr
Strawberries • Tajín • Kimchi • Korean Toasted Sesame Oil • Dulce de Leche •
Sauce • Lemongrass • Whole Wheat Pastry Flour • Pomegranate Molasses • Mexi
Chocolate • Smoked Paprika • Chipotles in Adobo • Shichimi Togarashi • Makrut Li
Leaves • Crema Mexicana • The Many Masalas • Capers • Mexican Chorizo • Mir
Oyster Sauce • Panko Breadcrumbs • Ras El Hanout • Andouille Sausage • Marsa
The Many Sambals • Benton's Bacon • Miso • Stone-Ground Grits • Tahini • Ghee • P.
Sugar • Ají Amarillo Paste • Thai Curry Paste • Mustard Powder • Turmeric • Cultu
Butter • Kashmiri Mirch • Dried Porcini Mushrooms • Sweetened Condensed Mi
Anchovies • Yuzu • Black Walnuts • Wondra • Sumac • Calabrian Chiles • Sorghu
Millet • Tabasco Sauce • Coconut Milk • Roasted Hazelnut Oil • Curry Leaves •
Sauce • Shrimp Paste • Worcestershire Sauce • Furikake • Sriracha • Saffron • Bany
Vinegar • Gochujang • Harissa • Marmite • Kecap Manis • Chili Crisp • Freeze-Dr
Strawberries • Tajín • Kimchi • Korean Toasted Sesame Oil • Dulce de Leche •
Sauce • Lemongrass • Whole Wheat Pastry Flour • Pomegranate Molasses • Mexi
Chocolate • Smoked Paprika • Chipotles in Adobo • Shichimi Togarashi • Makrut Li
Leaves • Crema Mexicana • The Many Masalas • Capers • Mexican Chorizo • Mir
Oyster Sauce • Panko Breadcrumbs • Ras El Hanout • Andouille Sausage • Marsa
The Many Sambals • Benton's Bacon • Miso • Stone-Ground Grits • Tahini • Ghee • P.
Sugar • Ají Amarillo Paste • Thai Curry Paste • Mustard Powder • Turmeric • Cultu
Butter • Kashmiri Mirch • Dried Porcini Mushrooms • Sweetened Condensed Mil

Easy Vegetables and Starchy Things

Farmers Market Bonus

Sweet Onion Alert. Leeks are a year-round fallback, but if your farmers market has young, plump bulb onions (not scallions) in the spring, use those, trimming off the hairs but keeping all the tender green parts intact. You should halve or quarter them, depending on size, but can skip the blanching.

Pantry Substitute

Other Nuts Are Optional. Pine nuts are superb here, but in a pinch, toasted skinless almonds will work, or even skinless, roasted hazelnuts.

Planning Tip

Make-Ahead Option. When the blanched leeks are room temp and the sauce base is processed, everything can be put on hold for 2 to 3 hours. Pop the drained leeks in the fridge; keep the sauce covered at room temp.

Broiled Leeks
with Toasted Pine Nut Sauce

ACTIVE TIME: 30 minutes
TOTAL TIME: 40 minutes
SERVES 6

In a tiny village outside Barcelona, Scott was blessed to attend a traditional *calçotada*, in which springtime onions were grilled and served with a zingy romesco sauce that was vinegary, nutty, peppery, and slightly chewy. Here, we simplify the romesco so the pine nut flavor can shine, with just a bit of vinegar to elevate the flavors.

---

6 medium leeks

1 cup toasted pine nuts (see page 26), plus extra for garnish

5 tablespoons extra-virgin olive oil

1 teaspoon Banyuls or sherry vinegar

¾ teaspoon kosher salt

1 large clove garlic, pressed or grated with a Microplane

¼ teaspoon freshly ground black pepper

1 Fill a large pot three quarters full with salted water and set over high heat. Place a large bowl or casserole pan beside the stove and fill it halfway with water and ice, making sure there will be enough room to submerge the leeks later.

2 Cut the green ends off the leeks, 1 to 2 inches above the whites. Trim off any remaining coarse green bits, and cut away any rootlets, but keep as much of the white intact as you can, so the leeks will not fall apart. Cut in half lengthwise and run the leeks under cold water, gently pulling the leaves away from the core and dislodging any dirt with your fingers.

3 When the pot of water is boiling hard, add the leeks with tongs, pressing them down to submerge. Cover the pot until the water returns to a boil, then reduce the heat and simmer, covered, until the leeks are just tender when pierced by a knife, but not falling apart, about 3 minutes. Use tongs to lift the leeks out of the pot and submerge them in the ice water bath to cool.

4 As the leeks cool, make the pine nut sauce base. Combine the nuts, 2 tablespoons of olive oil, the vinegar, ½ teaspoon of salt, and the garlic in a small food processor and process on "puree" until the mixture resembles a loose, chunky peanut butter—don't puree until smooth. Use a silicone spatula to scrape every bit of this precious sauce into a small bowl. Cover, and set aside.

5 Preheat the broiler to high, with a rack placed 6 inches below the heat. Brush a broiling pan or broiler-safe casserole dish big enough to accommodate the leeks with 1 tablespoon of olive oil. Arrange the leeks in the pan with cut sides up, then brush the leeks liberally with the remaining 2 tablespoons olive oil. Sprinkle with the remaining ¼ teaspoon salt, and the pepper. Broil the leeks until the edges are charred on top, about 7 minutes.

6 Just before serving, whisk 1 tablespoon of very hot or boiling water into the pine nut sauce base to loosen it, and continue drizzling water until the sauce will just pour off a spoon—but don't make it thin. Drizzle the sauce over the leeks. Garnish with a few pine nuts.

Roasted Asparagus
with a Savory Butter Sauce

ACTIVE TIME: 5 minutes
TOTAL TIME: 25 minutes
SERVES 4

This is the type of dish that highlights one of our main techniques in this book: Adding a little bit of a highly flavorful global ingredient can take a dish from "fine" to "wow" without confusing the general idea; in this case, the global pantry star is oyster sauce, sweetly savory. Roasted asparagus is bathed in a two-ingredient sauce that elevates it to repeat-appearance status (Ann's family now requests this dish on the regular). Try it on other green veggies, too—green beans, broccoli, and bok choy in particular.

2 pounds medium-thick asparagus spears, trimmed

1 tablespoon olive oil

½ teaspoon kosher salt

¼ teaspoon freshly ground black pepper

2 tablespoons unsalted butter

1½ tablespoons oyster sauce

1 Preheat the oven to 425°F with the rack placed in the center.

2 Place the asparagus on a sheet pan; drizzle with the olive oil and sprinkle with the salt and pepper. Toss gently to coat. Roast until crisp-tender, about 12 minutes.

3 Meanwhile, melt the butter in a small skillet over medium heat. Continue cooking, whisking frequently (this cuts down on sputtering), until deeply toasty-fragrant and about the color of light brown sugar, about 3 minutes. Pour the butter into a small bowl and cool for 2 minutes. Whisk in the oyster sauce.

4 Arrange the cooked asparagus on a platter; drizzle with the sauce.

There are many good oyster sauces, but read the shopping tips on page 16 to find the best.

Global Pantry Ingredient

Oyster Sauce, *p. 16*

Flavor Booster
Savory Backbone. Browned butter is a great way to finish simply cooked vegetables, and when you add a little oyster sauce, you create so much more depth. If you'd like to keep it meat-free, there is, in fact, a vegetarian oyster sauce.

Avoid This Mistake
Tame the Heat. Don't be tempted to stir the oyster sauce into the skillet when the butter is browned to your liking. We learned the hard way that this burns the oyster sauce, whereafter it seizes into clumps and refuses to incorporate into the butter. So we let things cool a bit.

Coconut Milk, *p. 10*

Fish Sauce, *p. 11*

Peanut Oil, *p. 18*

Sambal, *p. 21*

Thai Curry Pastes,
see Try This!, p. 56

Shopping Intel

Global Pantry Essentials.
With the exception of the tofu puffs, this recipe can be sourced in some good supermarkets. But this is a perfect excuse for a visit to a local Asian food store, where prices on pantry staples like fish sauce, coconut milk, curry paste, fried shallots, less-refined peanut oil, and sambal are usually lower—and the selection can be vast. This is where you are quite likely to even find laksa curry paste, which you should substitute for Thai yellow curry paste if you can find it.

Even the Tofu Skeptics Love These. Bean curd fries up into golden sponges—aka tofu puffs—that bear almost no resemblance to tofu; they're almost like chewy fried crullers. Sold in the refrigerated section of Asian food stores, they come in several shapes and sizes. We like the little cubes, about an inch square (25 or so in a 7-ounce package), but you can cut the bigger pieces down to size. Tofu puffs freeze well, so buy extra and add to any saucy stir-fry, spicy soup, or Southeast Asian curry.

Singapore-ish Succotash

ACTIVE TIME: 25 minutes
TOTAL TIME: 25 minutes
SERVES 6

This is a total—and delicious—global mash-up. Succotash, the iconic Southern-harvest vegetable fest, dances to the coconut-curry vibe of an iconic Singapore comfort curry-soup called laksa, the *nyonya* version of which was pretty much Scott's favorite treat when he visited Singapore as a kid. Nyonya cuisine is a proud result of the intermingling of Chinese immigrants and Malay people over the centuries on the Malay peninsula, with special reference to the women who led the flavor evolution in their kitchens ("nonya" is a term of great respect not quite captured in English by its usual translation as "Mrs."). We swapped out lima beans in favor of edamame, dropped the okra, added some tofu puffs (see Shopping Intel)—they're optional, but the way they soak up the coconutty goodness of the sauce deserves a Nobel prize. It's a big platter of richly sauced—not quite soupy—goodness. Serve with rice and, for a full feast, our fried catfish and cornbread on pages 159 and 259.

2 tablespoons peanut oil or neutral oil
   (such as canola)

1 tablespoon minced peeled fresh ginger

3 cloves garlic, minced

1 medium onion, finely diced

2 tablespoons The Best Sambal Is Your Own
   Sambal (page 21) or 2 teaspoons sambal
   oelek, plus extra for serving

3 tablespoons laksa curry paste or
   1 tablespoon Thai yellow curry paste

1 tablespoon fish sauce

1 can (13.5 ounces) coconut milk
   (warm the can and shake before opening)

3 cups fresh corn kernels (about 2 large or
   3 medium cobs)

2 cups cherry tomatoes, halved

15 small fried tofu "puffs," cut in half
   (optional) (see Shopping Intel)

1 bag (12 ounces) frozen shelled edamame

1 cup fried shallots or crispy fried onions

1 Heat a large skillet or Dutch oven over medium heat. Add the oil to the pan and swirl to coat. Add the ginger, garlic, and onion; gently sauté until translucent and soft, about 6 minutes, stirring often and reducing the heat if things start to brown. Turn the heat up a bit, add the sambal and laksa paste, and sauté until fragrant, about 2 minutes. Stir in the fish sauce and coconut milk, mix thoroughly, and let the sauce thicken over medium-high heat as it bubbles vigorously, stirring frequently, about 4 minutes. (At this point, you can turn the heat off, cover the pan, and let the mixture stand for up to an hour.)

2 A few minutes before serving, bring the sauce to a simmer over medium heat. Add the corn, tomatoes, tofu puffs, and frozen edamame. Cook until everything is thoroughly heated and the corn is cooked, about 5 minutes. Put the succotash in a serving bowl and sprinkle the fried shallots over the top. Serve with some sambal on the side for those who want more heat.

Shopping Intel
Go for the Regular Beans.
Old-school standard green
beans are what you want for
this recipe. Slender haricots
verts (French green beans)
are too delicate.

Prep Pointer
Get Squishy. To seed tomatoes,
cut away the stem bit and then
cut the fruit in half crosswise—
across their equator. Hold them
over the sink or a bowl and
push your fingers into the holes
as you squeeze the tomato to
get the seeds out.

Tomato-Rich Green Beans
Cooked Beyond Where You'd Usually Cook Them, Deliciously

ACTIVE TIME: 20 minutes
TOTAL TIME: about 1 hour
SERVES 4

This recipe is submitted to prove the
case that beyond the crisp stage so
long in vogue for green veggies lies a
supple, silky, flavor-infused perfection.
Green beans bubble away in the
simplest sauce of tomato (both fresh
and slow-roasted) and garlic for more
than half an hour (!), for a comforting
side dish that's perfect with roast
chicken, hamburger steaks, or pork
chops. They're great hot from the pan
but might be even better at room
temperature—and hold up beautifully
the next day if you want to double the
recipe.

6 tablespoons olive oil

1½ cups thinly vertically sliced yellow onion

8 cloves garlic, thinly sliced

1½ cups chopped, seeded fresh tomatoes

1 cup Very Slow Tomatoes (page 25),
    finely chopped or pureed

1¼ teaspoons kosher salt

½ teaspoon freshly ground black pepper

1 sprig (6 inches) oregano or rosemary
    (optional)

1½ pounds green beans, trimmed

1 Heat a large sauté pan or skillet over
medium heat. Add the oil to the pan and
swirl to coat. Add the onion and garlic;
cook until softened, for about 5 minutes,
stirring occasionally.

2 Add ¼ cup water, the fresh tomatoes,
Very Slow Tomatoes, salt, pepper, and herb
sprig, if desired. Cook until saucy, about
5 minutes. Add the green beans; cover,
reduce the heat to medium-low, and cook
until the beans are very tender but not
mushy, 35 to 40 minutes. Note: If the
beans seem to be running dry after 15 or
20 minutes, add ¼ cup water or more as
required, and keep an eye on the beans
until done.

Green Beans
in a Rich Coconut Milk Gravy the Indonesian Way

ACTIVE TIME: 20 minutes
TOTAL TIME: 35 minutes
SERVES 6

This dish is so rich and flavorful that, on rice with a cucumber salad or such, it can be a satisfying meal. It's based on the iconic Indonesian dish called sambal goreng buncis. A spicy gravy, built on a fundamental flavor-development method and enriched with coconut milk, enfolds tender green beans. The coconut milk is added near the end lest it inhibit the cooking of the beans and stretch out the stove time Jurassically.

1½ pounds green beans, trimmed

2 tablespoons minced, peeled fresh ginger or, if frozen, grated

2 teaspoons palm sugar, shaved or minced

5 cloves garlic, peeled

4 medium shallots, coarsely chopped

2 Fresno red chiles, seeded

1 hot green chile (such as bird's eye), minced

1 stalk (6 inches) trimmed lemongrass, cut into ¼-inch pieces (if using frozen lemongrass, zap for 30 seconds in the microwave first)

¼ cup hot water (optional)

2 tablespoons peanut oil or neutral oil (such as canola)

1 teaspoon shrimp paste

½ teaspoon kosher salt

1 can (13.5 ounces) coconut milk (warm the can and shake before opening)

1 tablespoon sambal oelek

½ cup fried shallots or fried onions

1 Bring a large pot of salted water to a boil over high heat. Add the beans and cook until tender, 7 to 9 minutes; drain.

2 While the beans cook, place the ginger, palm sugar, garlic, shallots, chiles, and lemongrass in a mini food processor or blender and blend until you have a thick paste. Add the hot water to facilitate the pasting, if necessary.

3 Heat a heavy-bottomed pan or large skillet over medium heat for 1 minute. Add the oil and heat for 1 minute, then add the shrimp paste (with stove vent on high!) and sauté, breaking it up with a spoon or spatula, until very fragrant and slightly brown but not burnt, 1 to 2 minutes. Add your spice paste and sauté until browned and very fragrant, 4 to 5 minutes, stirring constantly. Add the cooked beans and ¾ cup water; cover, and cook until the beans are thoroughly heated and have become softer, about 10 minutes, adding more water if it cooks off. When the beans are done, remove the lid and let the water mostly cook off.

4 Reduce the heat to low. Add the salt, coconut milk, and sambal, letting the mixture gently simmer with the lid off until the milk is slightly thickened, about 5 minutes. Sprinkle with the fried shallots or onions.

Global Pantry Ingredients

Coconut Milk, *p. 10*

Lemongrass, *p. 14*

Palm Sugar, *p. 17*

Peanut Oil, *p. 18*

Sambal, *p. 21*

Shrimp Paste, *p. 11*

Cooking Step

Making Rempah. Rempah is the paste of spices, shallots, and other aromatic things that provides the foundational flavor of many Indonesian dishes. The traditional method involves a mortar and pestle, and some will warn against using a food chopper, but we go with the whirring blade here for satisfying results. Make a double batch of rempah and use it as the base of a curry or stir-fry, or rub it onto meat bound for the barbecue. It will keep in a tight jar for a week or two, much longer in the freezer.

Kitchen Smarts

Vent On! Frying the shrimp paste is essential to this dish, but it is a very pungent process, so you'll want to do it in a well-ventilated space (or on an outdoor grill). The resulting powerful sea funk magically melts into the spices, and the final dish is a fantastic, complex alchemy. Skip neither the shrimp paste nor its toasting!

Roasted Squash
Anointed with Ghee and Garam Masala

ACTIVE TIME: 6 minutes
TOTAL TIME: 36 minutes
SERVES 4

Global Pantry Ingredients

Ghee, *p. 12*
Masala Spice Blend,
   p. 15

We love acorn squash for its less-sweet and more-earthy flavor among the winter squashes. Here it roasts to beautiful caramelization on the outside and lovely creaminess within. For years we roasted squash with good olive oil, but ghee, with its slightly funky, beefy aroma and flavor (despite being vegetarian), takes things to a new level and marries perfectly with the robust punch of the garam masala.

Cooking spray

1 acorn squash (1½ pounds)

2 tablespoons ghee, gently melted

1 teaspoon garam masala

1 teaspoon honey

½ teaspoon kosher salt

¼ teaspoon freshly ground black pepper

1 Preheat the oven to 425°F with the rack placed in the center. Coat a sheet pan with cooking spray or line it with parchment paper.

2 Cut the squash in half lengthwise; scoop out and discard the seeds and membranes. Cut each squash half into 4 wedges to yield 8 total. Arrange the squash on the prepared pan, skin side down so they rest like boats (for more even seasoning).

3 Combine the ghee, garam masala, and honey in a small bowl; brush liberally over the flesh sides of the squash wedges. Sprinkle the salt and pepper over the squash wedges. Now lay the squash wedges flat, cut side down, on the pan.

4 Roast the squash until starting to brown, about 15 minutes. Turn the squash wedges over, and brush with any excess ghee on the pan. Roast until browned and tender, about 15 more minutes. Serve directly from the pan or arrange on a platter.

Simple Sub

Other Orange Veggies Work. The flavor combo here is great with winter squash, so you could also sub in sweeter butternut, or try it with sweet potatoes. For either swap, use cubes (even convenient precut ones) and roast at the same temp for the same time, stirring halfway through.

Super-Buttery, Super-Simple
Irish Cabbage

ACTIVE TIME: 16 minutes
TOTAL TIME: 16 minutes
SERVES 6

This simplest-possible recipe illustrates the power of the best butter to elevate a vegetable that, until recently, was neglected or overcooked. It's a riff on a side dish that Scott ate at a small seaside restaurant in Northern Ireland with dear friends. One bite rocked his cruciferous world. It was sweet, slightly al dente, and infinitely buttery. This will convert cabbage haters and reform cabbage skeptics. We use even more butter than some traditional recipes— because butter. Serve with a roast or stew; it would be delicious with Chuck Roast with Root Vegetables and Oyster Sauce Gravy (page 101) or Deeply Rich Beef and Marsala Stew with Dijon Mustard (page 95).

---

1 head Savoy cabbage
   (about 1¾ to 2 pounds)

6 tablespoons cultured unsalted butter,
   such as Kerrygold

1 teaspoon kosher salt

Freshly ground black pepper

1 Cut the cabbage in half vertically, so that the stem and core are visible in both halves. Cut the core out with a sharp knife, pulling out a triangular piece. Then place the halves cut side down and slice into ½-inch chunks that will pull apart into ribbons.

2 Place 4 tablespoons of butter in a Dutch oven or other large, heavy pot with a lid. Melt (but do not brown) the butter over medium heat. Add the cabbage to the pan and drizzle with ¼ cup water; using tongs, toss the cabbage until coated. Cover and cook until softened slightly, about 3 minutes. Tong and toss the cabbage again, cover, and cook until the cabbage is glossy and al dente but not crunchy, about 3 more minutes. Remove to a platter and dab with small bits of the remaining 2 tablespoons butter; sprinkle with the salt, grind some pepper over the top, and serve immediately as the butter melts.

Crispy-Crusty Roast Potatoes

Fragrant with Ghee and Aromatic Spices

ACTIVE TIME: 30 minutes
TOTAL TIME: 1 hour 30 minutes
SERVES 6

Global Pantry Ingredients

Curry Leaves, *p. 11*
Ghee, *p. 12*

Avoid This Mistake
Go Whole. Make sure to use whole coriander seeds and cumin seeds to infuse the ghee in Step 1. Ground spices are likely to burn, and even if they don't, the flavor would be too musty-intense with them.

Our friend Simon D'Arcy, a brilliant cook of global pedigree, introduced us to the British business of roughing up boiled potatoes in a colander or bowl so that the edges get fuzzy before a hot roast crisps them up. Simon sometimes uses duck fat—goose is also traditional—but we've taken a turn toward India with ghee and spices. Ghee contributes a funky, beefy sort of flavor (and doesn't run the risk of burning like butter would), coriander and cumin seeds add earthiness, and curry leaves lend remarkable toasty fragrance and flavor. The result is our go-to side for roasted meats or even a curry.

½ cup ghee

2 teaspoons coriander seeds

1 teaspoon cumin seeds

15 curry leaves (optional)

4 pounds russet potatoes, peeled and cut into small wedges

¼ cup fine cornmeal or fine semolina (not corn flour)

Freshly ground black pepper

½ teaspoon kosher salt

1 Heat the ghee in a small skillet or saucepan over medium heat for 2 minutes. Add the coriander, cumin, and curry leaves, if using, and fry until fragrant and beginning to brown but not burn, 2 to 3 minutes. Strain the ghee through a fine-mesh strainer into a bowl or measuring cup; drain the spices on paper towels.

2 Place a sheet pan on the center rack of the oven and preheat the oven to 425°F.

3 Place the potatoes in a Dutch oven or other large pot and add salted water just to cover. Bring to a boil, and cook until almost done, 8 to 9 minutes; they should still resist a knife but just barely. While the potatoes boil, crush the spice mixture in a mortar and pestle or with a small spice grinder.

4 Carefully remove the hot sheet pan from the oven and pour in the ghee; place the pan back in the oven and let the ghee heat for 5 minutes. While it heats, drain the potatoes into a large colander; toss the potatoes over the sink vigorously so that they jostle and begin to get nicely fuzzy about the edges. Arrange the fuzzy potatoes in the sheet pan, sprinkle with the cornmeal, and stir to coat with the ghee. Roast for 20 minutes. Stir and turn over the potatoes, and roast until almost perfectly browned and crisp, about another 20 minutes. Stir again and roast until crispy and browned, 5 to 8 minutes.

5 To serve, place the potatoes in a large bowl or platter. Dribble any pan ghee over, sprinkle on the spice mixture, top with a few turns of a pepper grinder, and sprinkle with the salt. Toss and serve.

Potato Variations

Alt Spuds. If you can't find the baby red potatoes, larger ones cut into quarters after cooking will work, as will Yukon Golds.

Shopping Intel

Tangy, Mouth-Popping Mustard. Whole-grain mustard often has a zippier, slightly sweeter profile than Dijon or yellow German mustard, and the little grains of mustard add texture. Widely available American-made Inglehoffer is a nice choice.

Warm Potato and Leek Salad
with Smoky Bacon and Preserved Lemon

ACTIVE TIME: 20 minutes
TOTAL TIME: 40 minutes
SERVES 6

This bowl of starchy comfort was inspired by the sweet/tangy approach of mayo-free South German potato salad. But we wanted to spike the taters with a bouquet of exuberant pantry flavors—so there's smoky richness from the Tennessee bacon and a double hit of acid zing from Banyuls vinegar and preserved lemon. Think of it as comfort food with a bit of global boogie.

1½ pounds baby (or petite) red potatoes

1 teaspoon kosher salt

3 slices Benton's bacon or other very smoky, long bacon

1 fat leek (2- to 2½-inch diameter)

3 tablespoons preserved lemon, chopped to relish texture

1 tablespoon Banyuls or sherry vinegar

1 tablespoon whole-grain mustard

½ teaspoon sugar

⅓ cup chopped fresh flat-leaf parsley

Freshly ground black pepper

1 Place the potatoes and salt in a Dutch oven or large saucepan and add water to cover. Bring the water to a boil and cook until the potatoes are tender, 25 to 28 minutes from a cold start. When done, drain and let stand for 3 minutes. Cut the potatoes in half or, if you've used bigger spuds, quarters.

2 While the potatoes cook, cut the bacon lengthwise in half, then cut crosswise into ¼-inch-wide pieces. Place the bacon pieces in a microwave-safe baking dish or pie plate; microwave on High until crisp, 3 to 4 minutes. Remove the bacon from the dish with a slotted spoon; drain on paper towels. Pour the drippings into a small bowl.

3 Cut the roots off the leek and trim the leafy end so you have about a 6-inch length of white and pale green leek. Cut in half lengthwise and wash out all dirt, using your fingers to separate the leaves and remove any grit, then cut crosswise into 1- to 2-inch strips. Put the leek pieces on the counter and press down with paper towels to extract any water.

4 Heat 2 tablespoons of bacon drippings in a large skillet over medium heat; add the leeks and sauté until soft, about 4 minutes. Add the preserved lemon, vinegar, mustard, and sugar; stir until well combined, about 30 seconds. Remove the pan from the heat, add the potato halves, and stir to coat; stir in 1 more tablespoon of bacon drippings. Pour the potato mixture into a serving bowl; stir in the parsley and bacon and top with 3 turns of black pepper. Note that the salad can happily sit for an hour, covered, developing flavors (just stir in the parsley shortly before serving).

Slow and Custardy Sweet Potatoes

with Melted Butter and a Tangy Sorghum Sauce

ACTIVE TIME: 10 minutes
TOTAL TIME: 2 hours 40 minutes
SERVES 4

Sweet potatoes roasted for more than two hours at low temperature gain an almost custard-like texture, filling the kitchen with sugary aromas. Their candy sweetness is cut with butter and a dead-simple sauce of aromatic Banyuls vinegar that's enriched with the lovely tang-and-caramel notes of American sorghum syrup. These beauties match nicely with stews, roast meats, and even salmon, but with a green salad alone this makes a satisfying meal. Serve in the skins, because the skins are delicious.

---

4 medium sweet potatoes
   (about 8 ounces each)

1 tablespoon neutral oil (such as canola)

½ cup sorghum syrup

1 tablespoon Banyuls or sherry vinegar

¼ teaspoon kosher salt

3 tablespoons cold unsalted butter,
   cut into 8 thin slices

Kosher or fancy finishing salt to taste

1 Preheat the oven to 275°F with the rack placed in the center. Rub the potatoes with the oil, put in a roasting pan, and bake for 2½ hours or so, until the potatoes are soft—when you press the skins, they will give easily. Remove to a cooling rack.

2 Combine the syrup, vinegar, and salt in a small saucepan; heat over medium-low heat until blended, about 2 minutes. Create a pocket in each sweet potato, starting a cut an inch from one end and cutting until an inch from the other end. Slip 2 pieces of butter in each pocket and drizzle 1 tablespoon of the sorghum sauce both in the pocket and zigzagged across the top. Sprinkle with salt and serve.

Sorghum is more complex and tangy than molasses.

Global Pantry Ingredients

Banyuls Vinegar, *p. 9*
Sorghum, *p. 22*

Shopping Intel

Not the Same as Yams. Sweet potatoes present with various colors and flavor profiles, from creamy yellow to orange to reddish, but are not the same as yams, which tend to be drier, starchier, and more potato-like (and not to be used in this recipe).

Flavor Booster

Old-School "Original Recipe" Flair. You might think we use too much of the spices in the flour mixture—but a heavy hand with garlic powder, onion powder, paprika, salt, and black and cayenne pepper is what creates the fried chicken effect.

Prep Tip

Let the Logs Rest. After going through the three-step breading process, the wedges should rest for a few minutes before their hot-oil swim. This helps to set or "glue" the breading onto the potatoes.

Make-Ahead Tip

Bake in the Morning, or the Day Before. You can bake the potatoes a day or two ahead and have them waiting for you in the fridge. That'll shave off two hours from this recipe.

Chicken-Fried Mississippi Potato Logs

(aka Mississippi Party Potatoes)

ACTIVE TIME: 30 minutes
TOTAL TIME: 2 hours 30 minutes
SERVES 8

As a kid in Mississippi, Ann adored potato logs—thick wedges of baked potato that are battered and fried like chicken, often found at gas stations or grocery store delis. When Scott made this version, a family member immediately anointed them Party Potatoes. By any name (apparently in the Midwest they're called Jojo Potatoes or just Jojos), the flavor and crunch of brown-fried, highly seasoned flour takes russets to a whole new level. We serve them with a chili crisp mayo, whose spicy-salty edge pairs well with the highly seasoned potatoes, but you can also dunk them into ketchup (try them with our Smoky Bacon Ketchup, page 208).

FOR THE POTATOES

4 russet potatoes (8 ounces each)

1 cup (4½ ounces) all-purpose flour

2 teaspoons garlic powder

2 teaspoons onion powder

2 teaspoons paprika

1½ teaspoons kosher salt

1 teaspoon freshly ground black pepper

¾ teaspoon cayenne pepper

½ cup whole buttermilk

1 large egg

4 cups canola oil

FOR THE CHILI CRISP SAUCE

6 tablespoons mayonnaise

1 tablespoon chili crisp

1 teaspoon rice vinegar

1 Preheat the oven to 400°F with the rack placed in the center.

2 To prepare the potatoes, prick them several times with a fork and place them directly on the oven rack. Bake until tender, about 1 hour. Cool on a rack at room temperature for 30 minutes, then place on a plate to cool in the refrigerator for 30 minutes.

3 Combine the flour, garlic powder, onion powder, paprika, salt, black pepper, and cayenne pepper in a large ziplock plastic bag. Whisk together the buttermilk and egg in a shallow bowl. Place a wire rack in a sheet pan. Line a platter with paper towels and place it near the stove.

4 Pour the oil into a Dutch oven. Heat the oil over medium-high heat until it reaches 360°F on a frying thermometer.

5 Cut each potato lengthwise into 4 wedges. Place 4 wedges in the bag with the flour mixture and shake gently to coat. Remove from the bag, shaking off the excess flour. Dip the potato wedges in the buttermilk mixture, turning to coat. Return the potato wedges to the bag and shake gently to coat. Place the breaded potato wedges on a wire rack. Repeat the process in batches with the remaining potato wedges, flour mixture, and buttermilk mixture. Let the breaded potato wedges stand on a wire rack for 5 minutes.

6 Carefully lower 6 potato wedges into the hot oil. Fry until the potato wedges are deeply browned, 3 to 4 minutes. Adjust the heat to maintain the oil temperature at 350°F to 355°F. Remove the potatoes from the oil and drain on paper towels. Repeat the process in 2 batches.

7 While the potatoes fry, prepare the sauce by stirring together the mayonnaise, chili crisp, and vinegar. Serve the sauce with the potatoes.

The hot crunch of chili crisp makes for a more dynamic mayo.

Ultimate Killer Cornbread
with Flaky Salt–Sorghum Butter

ACTIVE TIME: 15 minutes
TOTAL TIME: 35 minutes
SERVES 10

Here's the cornbread that embodies all the cornbread lessons Ann has learned during her life in the South. First, of course, you must make it in a cast-iron skillet, and heat that skillet so that the batter sizzles when it goes into the pan. Second, no added sugar; as chef Hugh Acheson says, that's *cake*. Third, a combination of medium-grind cornmeal and rustic stone-ground grits yields the best texture. (If you use only medium-grind cornmeal, the cornbread doesn't have enough grit. But if you use all coarsely ground cornmeal, the result lacks moisture and can be a little too hearty.) The right ratio is moist but deliciously gritty. Finally, a game-changing trick passed on from Josh Miller, a food writer and editor: Sprinkle some salt in the hot skillet before you add the batter so the crust is extra savory. When Ann's husband, who also grew up in Mississippi and has eaten cornbread all his life, tasted this version, he declared it "positively f***ing awesome." We serve it with a sweet butter made wonderfully tangy from sorghum syrup that has crunchy bits of flaky salt added.

FOR THE CORNBREAD

1¼ cups (6 ounces) whole-grain, medium-grind cornmeal (such as Bob's Red Mill)

1 cup (4½ ounces) all-purpose flour

⅓ cup (2 ounces) stone-ground grits

1½ teaspoons baking powder

1¾ teaspoons kosher salt

½ teaspoon baking soda

1½ cups whole buttermilk

¼ cup canola oil

2 large eggs, lightly beaten

¼ cup (½ stick) unsalted butter, cut into 4 pieces

FOR THE SORGHUM BUTTER

½ cup unsalted butter (preferably cultured), at room temperature

2 tablespoons sorghum syrup

½ teaspoon flaky sea salt

1 Place a 10-inch cast-iron skillet in the oven on the center rack and preheat the oven to 450°F. If you haven't softened the butter (for the sorghum butter), cut it into pieces and set it out now.

2 To prepare the cornbread, whisk together the cornmeal, flour, grits, baking powder, 1½ teaspoons of salt, and the baking soda in a large bowl. Whisk together the buttermilk, oil, and eggs in a medium bowl.

Global Pantry Ingredients

Cultured Butter, *see* Try This!, *p. 123*

Sorghum, *p. 22*

Stone-Ground Grits, *p. 23*

Flavor Booster

Browned Butter Is Better Butter. Many cornbread recipes require that the cook melt some butter in the hot skillet and then stir that hot fat into the batter. Here, also: But we don't just melt the butter— we brown it for those irresistible nuts-and-caramel notes.

3 Once the oven is preheated, stir the buttermilk mixture into the cornmeal mixture to form a smooth, thick batter; bring the batter bowl over to the oven. Carefully add the butter pieces to the hot skillet and return the skillet to the oven until the butter has browned, about 2 minutes. Carefully pour the browned butter into the batter. Place your oven mitt or a pot holder on or around the skillet handle. (Trust us; we've learned this trick after catastrophically grabbing a hot handle more than once.) Sprinkle the remaining ¼ teaspoon salt evenly over the bottom of the skillet. Stir the browned butter into the batter, and immediately pour the batter into the hot skillet. Bake until the cornbread is browned and set, about 20 minutes.

4 While the cornbread bakes, prepare the sorghum butter. Mix the room temperature butter and sorghum together in a small bowl until smooth. If the butter is soft enough, you can do this with a small silicone spatula. If not, you can use a hand mixer to get the mixture smooth, or just work the cool butter and syrup with your hands, then finish with a fork. Stir in the flaky sea salt.

5 As soon as the cornbread is done, carefully turn it out onto a wire rack so the crust side is up. (If you leave it in the pan, that gorgeous crust will get soggy.) Serve the cornbread hot or warm with the sorghum butter.

Only the best butter for the best cornbread.

Global Pantry Ingredient

Cultured Butter,
see Try This!, p. 123

Shopping Intel

Shuck Your Own. Avoid that shrink-wrapped preshucked corn. The longer that ears are naked, the more they trade sugar for starch. Choose cobs with firm husks and the least-withered silks you can find.

Prep Tip

Preventing Kernel Chaos. We've seen all kinds of hacks for keeping corn kernels from flying all over your counter as you cut them from the cobs. It's always a little bit messy, but here's the simplest, least-chaotic method: Stand the corn cob up in the middle of a large sheet pan. Using a sturdy knife, cut from the *middle* of the cob down. Flip the cob and repeat.

Buttery Creamed Corn

ACTIVE TIME: 18 minutes
TOTAL TIME: 18 minutes
SERVES 4

This six-ingredient side dish is all about the sweet pop of fresh summer corn and has its roots in Native American cuisine. No starch thickeners here, nor added sugar—proper corn won't need it. We finish it with a little butter for creamy richness. Not just any butter, though. We use cultured butter here because it makes the same sort of difference that using buttermilk (instead of milk) makes for pancakes—more richness, more depth. In a recipe this simple and with so few ingredients, this ingredient choice is key. This is a kids' favorite; Scott's 2-year-old next-door neighbor went bonkers for it during testing.

---

4 large ears fresh yellow or bicolor corn, shucked

3 tablespoons unsalted cultured butter

½ cup chopped scallions

½ cup half-and-half

½ teaspoon kosher salt

½ teaspoon freshly ground black pepper

1 Cut the kernels from corn cobs as described (see Prep Tip); you should get about 4 cups, maybe a little more. Using the dull side of your knife blade, scrape the milk and remaining pulp from the cobs onto the sheet pan. Place the corn pulp and 3 cups of kernels (reserve the remaining kernels) in a food processor; process until you get a chunky puree, about 1 minute, stopping to scrape down the sides of the bowl as needed.

2 Melt 2 tablespoons of butter in a medium skillet over medium heat. Add the whole corn kernels and the scallions; cook 2 minutes, stirring frequently. Add the corn puree, half-and-half, salt, and pepper. Reduce the heat to medium-low, and cook until thickened, about 3 minutes. Top with the remaining 1 tablespoon butter and allow it to pool and melt on top.

Anchovies • Yuzu • Black Walnuts • Wondra • Sumac • Calabrian Chiles • Sorghu
Millet • Tabasco Sauce • Coconut Milk • Roasted Hazelnut Oil • Curry Leaves •
Sauce • Shrimp Paste • Worcestershire Sauce • Furikake • Sriracha • Saffron • Bany
Vinegar • Gochujang • Harissa • Marmite • Kecap Manis • Chili Crisp • Freeze-Dr
Strawberries • Tajín • Kimchi • Korean Toasted Sesame Oil • Dulce de Leche •
Sauce • Lemongrass • Whole Wheat Pastry Flour • Pomegranate Molasses • Mexi
Chocolate • Smoked Paprika • Chipotles in Adobo • Shichimi Togarashi • Makrut L
Leaves • Crema Mexicana • The Many Masalas • Capers • Mexican Chorizo • Mir
Oyster Sauce • Panko Breadcrumbs • Ras El Hanout • Andouille Sausage • Marsa
The Many Sambals • Benton's Bacon • Miso • Stone-Ground Grits • Tahini • Ghee • P
Sugar • Ají Amarillo Paste • Thai Curry Paste • Mustard Powder • Turmeric • Cultu
Butter • Kashmiri Mirch • Dried Porcini Mushrooms • Sweetened Condensed Mi
Anchovies • Yuzu • Black Walnuts • Wondra • Sumac • Calabrian Chiles • Sorghu
Millet • Tabasco Sauce • Coconut Milk • Roasted Hazelnut Oil • Curry Leaves •
Sauce • Shrimp Paste • Worcestershire Sauce • Furikake • Sriracha • Saffron • Bany
Vinegar • Gochujang • Harissa • Marmite • Kecap Manis • Chili Crisp • Freeze-Dr
Strawberries • Tajín • Kimchi • Korean Toasted Sesame Oil • Dulce de Leche •
Sauce • Lemongrass • Whole Wheat Pastry Flour • Pomegranate Molasses • Mexi
Chocolate • Smoked Paprika • Chipotles in Adobo • Shichimi Togarashi • Makrut Li
Leaves • Crema Mexicana • The Many Masalas • Capers • Mexican Chorizo • Mir
Oyster Sauce • Panko Breadcrumbs • Ras El Hanout • Andouille Sausage • Marsa
The Many Sambals • Benton's Bacon • Miso • Stone-Ground Grits • Tahini • Ghee • P
Sugar • Ají Amarillo Paste • Thai Curry Paste • Mustard Powder • Turmeric • Cultu
Butter • Kashmiri Mirch • Dried Porcini Mushrooms • Sweetened Condensed Mi
Anchovies • Yuzu • Black Walnuts • Wondra • Sumac • Calabrian Chiles • Sorghu
Millet • Tabasco Sauce • Coconut Milk • Roasted Hazelnut Oil • Curry Leaves •
Sauce • Shrimp Paste • Worcestershire Sauce • Furikake • Sriracha • Saffron • Bany
Vinegar • Gochujang • Harissa • Marmite • Kecap Manis • Chili Crisp • Freeze-Dr
Strawberries • Tajín • Kimchi • Korean Toasted Sesame Oil • Dulce de Leche •
Sauce • Lemongrass • Whole Wheat Pastry Flour • Pomegranate Molasses • Mexi
Chocolate • Smoked Paprika • Chipotles in Adobo • Shichimi Togarashi • Makrut Li
Leaves • Crema Mexicana • The Many Masalas • Capers • Mexican Chorizo • Mir
Oyster Sauce • Panko Breadcrumbs • Ras El Hanout • Andouille Sausage • Marsa
The Many Sambals • Benton's Bacon • Miso • Stone-Ground Grits • Tahini • Ghee • P
Sugar • Ají Amarillo Paste • Thai Curry Paste • Mustard Powder • Turmeric • Cultu
Butter • Kashmiri Mirch • Dried Porcini Mushrooms • Sweetened Condensed Milk

Seductive Sweets and Frozen Treats

Flavor Booster
The Best Palm Sugar. See notes on Indonesian palm sugar on page 17—the only kind to use here. And it must be fresh and moist from an airtight package to be crumble-able.

Don't Sweat It
Gooey, Sugary Ooze. It's tricky to get all the sugar lumps out when you mix the dough, so don't: The sugar bits will ooze out as the cookies bake, creating crunchy-chewy "hangers-on." They're delicious.

Chewy-Fudgy Almond Butter and Palm Sugar Cookies

ACTIVE TIME: 12 minutes
TOTAL TIME: 50 minutes
MAKES 32 COOKIES

These cookies are modeled after the mind-blowingly good, absurdly easy Salted Peanut Butter Cookies recipe from New York's Ovenly bakery. We've changed up the five ingredients, fiddling with ratios to showcase the intense, deep-caramel and almost tangy deliciousness of palm sugar and the natural sweetness of almond butter. They're chewy and fudgy, with bits of crunch about the edges, naturally gluten-free by dint of being flourless, and almost chocolaty—without containing any chocolate!

---

12 ounces Indonesian palm sugar (gula jawa)

1 teaspoon vanilla extract

2 large eggs

2 cups smooth almond butter

½ teaspoon flaky sea salt

1 Crumble the sugar into a large bowl. (If it's very firm but moist, place it on a cutting board and use a heavy knife or cleaver to carefully break it into small bits, then continue chopping with a rocking motion until you have a crumbled heap, then put it in the bowl.) Add the vanilla and eggs; whisk until the mixture is relatively smooth (as noted, don't stress if there are a few lumps). Add the almond butter and stir with a sturdy silicone spatula until well combined (the mixture should look like thick brownie batter with bits of sugar in it). Chill the dough for 30 minutes.

2 Preheat the oven to 350°F and place an oven rack in the lower third of the oven and another rack in the upper third. Line 2 sheet pans with parchment paper. Check the texture of the dough; you want it to be like miso. If it's not there yet, chill it for a few more minutes.

3 Scoop the dough with a 2-tablespoon cookie scoop onto the prepared pans, 16 per pan. Sprinkle evenly with the salt. Bake until set, about 12 minutes. Cool the cookies on the pans for 3 minutes; transfer to a wire rack to cool.

Mexican Chocolate Brownies

Stuffed with Dulce de Leche

ACTIVE TIME: 18 minutes
TOTAL TIME: 50 minutes
MAKES 16 BROWNIES

We think brownies should be dense, fudgy (never, ever cakey), intensely chocolaty, and crowned with a sugar crust. To get there, we use a good bit of butter, two kinds of sugar, and *no leavening*. Mexican chocolate lends a faint whiff of cinnamon. A layer of canned dulce de leche is the final glory, a gooey bonus (make sure to layer the dulce as described, don't swirl it in). Enjoy these brownies warm or at room temp if you have the willpower to wait.

Cooking spray

½ cup (1 stick) unsalted butter, cut into 4 to 6 pieces

2 pucks (3.17 ounces each) Mexican chocolate, chopped

½ cup granulated sugar

⅓ cup packed brown sugar

½ teaspoon kosher salt

2 teaspoons vanilla extract

2 large eggs

⅔ cup (3 ounces) all-purpose flour

⅓ cup unsweetened cocoa powder

⅔ cup prepared dulce de leche

1 Preheat the oven to 350°F and place the rack in the center. Line an 8-inch square baking pan with aluminum foil; coat the foil with cooking spray. Alternatively, use nonstick aluminum foil and omit the cooking spray.

2 Place the butter and chocolate in a medium, heavy saucepan. Heat over medium-low heat until the butter and chocolate melt, stirring frequently, 7 to 8 minutes. Remove the pan from the heat; whisk in the sugars and salt. Add the vanilla and eggs and whisk until well blended. Spoon the flour and cocoa into a fine-mesh sieve set over the pan; shake the sieve to sift the mixture into the pan. Fold in the flour mixture.

3 Place the dulce de leche in a small microwave-safe bowl. Microwave on High until warm and slightly melted, 30 to 40 seconds. Spread half of the brownie batter in the bottom of the prepared pan; drizzle the dulce de leche over the batter. Dollop the remaining brownie batter over the dulce de leche and gently spread to cover.

4 Bake until the top is slightly crackly and a toothpick inserted in the center comes out with a few moist crumbs, about 30 minutes. Using the foil, lift the brownies (with foil) out of the pan and place on a wire rack. Cut into 16 squares before serving.

Global Pantry Ingredients

Dulce de Leche, *see* Try This!
Mexican Chocolate, *see* Try This!

Try This!

Dulce de Leche. Heated milk and sugar brown via the Maillard reaction to produce dulce de leche (literally, candy from milk). It's beloved in many parts of Mexico, Central America, and South America. One Mexican version, cajeta, involves goat's milk, sometimes with added cinnamon. Nestlé's version of dulce de leche is in most Latin and canned-milk sections of supermarkets. You'll find cajeta in Latin food stores and online. Spanish dulces work well, too. We also like Fat Toad Farm's goat-milk caramel from Vermont.

Mexican Chocolate. Some have an interesting gritty texture, and may be flavored with cinnamon—the type we like here. Look for Ibarra in Latin foods stores, or American-made Taza (the cinnamon version), which is sold at Whole Foods and elsewhere, and online.

Prep Tip

Stop the Sticking. These brownies love nothing more than to stick to a naked greased pan and will even cling to parchment paper. The solution is to line your pan with a) nonstick aluminum foil or b) foil coated with cooking spray.

Essential Fats

Butter and Oil for the Win. We use a combination of butter and canola oil here. The butter gives the cake great flavor and richness, and the oil ensures moisture and a tender crumb.

Pan Prep Pointers

For the Clean Release. To ensure your Bundt cake comes out of the pan perfectly, do two things. First, coat the pan generously with a baking spray that includes flour (such as Baker's Joy), or, after spraying with unfloured oil, sift flour into the pan, shaking to distribute into all nooks and crannies, then tap the pan to release excess flour. Second, run a thin offset spatula or thin knife around the edges of the cake (especially the inner ring) before inverting.

Lemon-Turmeric Company Cake
with a Proper Cake Soak

ACTIVE TIME: 20 minutes
TOTAL TIME: about 2½ hours
SERVES 12

Turmeric has been fashionable in smoothies and such for its antioxidant qualities, but we wanted to feature both its color and its faintly peppery, earthy, almost haunting flavor in a satisfying dessert. Hence, this sunny yellow cake, sophisticated enough to serve with a cup of good tea when the royals drop by, and deliciously moist and sweet enough for kids to happily munch on.

FOR THE CAKE

Baking spray with flour (such as Baker's Joy)

2⅓ cups (10½ ounces) all-purpose flour

2 teaspoons ground turmeric

1½ teaspoons baking powder

¾ teaspoon table salt

½ teaspoon baking soda

12 tablespoons (1½ sticks) unsalted butter, at room temperature

⅓ cup canola oil

2 cups granulated sugar

2 tablespoons grated lemon zest (about 2 large lemons)

3 tablespoons freshly squeezed lemon juice

5 large eggs

½ cup whole buttermilk

FOR THE CAKE SOAK

6 tablespoons granulated sugar

3 tablespoons freshly squeezed lemon juice

FOR THE GLAZE

1½ cups powdered sugar

2 tablespoons whole buttermilk

1 tablespoon freshly squeezed lemon juice

1 To prepare the cake, preheat the oven to 350°F. Generously coat a 10-cup Bundt pan with baking spray or use the spray-and-flour method described in Pan Prep Pointers.

2 Whisk together the flour, turmeric, baking powder, salt, and baking soda in a medium bowl. In a large bowl, combine the butter and oil; beat with a mixer at medium-low speed until well blended, about 2 minutes. Add the sugar; beat until fluffy, about 2 minutes. Add the lemon zest and juice; beat just until combined. Add the eggs, 1 at a time, beating at medium speed until well blended. Beating at low speed, alternately add the flour mixture and buttermilk (a little at a time), beginning and ending with the flour mixture.

3 Scrape the batter into the prepared Bundt pan. Bake until a skewer inserted in the center of the cake comes out clean, 50 to 55 minutes.

4 Meanwhile, to prepare the cake soak, combine the sugar, lemon juice, and 2 tablespoons water in a small microwave-safe bowl; microwave on High for 30 seconds. Stir until the sugar dissolves.

5 When the cake is done, immediately poke the cake (still in the pan) all over with a skewer. Brush half of the cake soak over the top (which will eventually be the bottom) of the cake. Cool the cake in the pan for 10 minutes. Run a thin offset spatula or knife around the edges of the cake. Place a cooling rack on top of the pan, and swiftly but carefully invert the cake onto the rack. Immediately poke the cake all over (top and sides) with the skewer. Brush the remaining cake soak all over the cake. Cool the cake completely, about 1 hour.

6 To prepare the glaze, in a medium bowl, stir together the powdered sugar, buttermilk, and lemon juice. Drizzle over the cooled cake. Let stand until set, about 10 minutes.

Turmeric adds surprising flavor and lovely color to this cake.

Technique Tip

Quicker Batter. The snack-cake approach used here whisks things together quickly, with much less beating and aeration than in a conventional cake batter. The result, aside from time saved, is a cupcake that's a bit more substantial in texture, well matched to the creamy icing up top.

Super-Fruity
Strawberry-Rosé Cupcakes

ACTIVE TIME: 20 minutes
TOTAL TIME: 1 hour 20 minutes
MAKES 12 CUPCAKES

Not your grandma's cupcakes! Rosé wine deepens the clean, tart strawberry flavor that suffuses both cake and icing. That flavor comes from one of our favorite high-tech pantry items, freeze-dried fruit. And if you use a rosé of strong character, the cupcakes take on a lovely winey flavor as well. This is an adaptation of a snack-cake recipe, yielding cute and welcome portion control.

FOR THE CUPCAKES

1 ounce freeze-dried strawberries (such as Target's Good & Gather brand)

1 cup plus 2 tablespoons (4¾ ounces) all-purpose flour

⅔ cup granulated sugar

1½ teaspoons baking powder

¼ teaspoon table salt

½ cup rosé wine

¼ cup canola oil

1 teaspoon vanilla extract

1 large egg, lightly beaten

FOR THE FROSTING

¼ cup (½ stick) unsalted butter, at room temperature

4 ounces cream cheese, at room temperature

¼ teaspoon table salt

2¼ cups (8¼ ounces) powdered sugar

1 teaspoon rosé wine

Small fresh strawberries, halved (optional)

1 Preheat the oven to 350°F with the rack placed in the center. Line a 12-cup muffin pan with paper or foil liners.

2 To prepare the cupcakes, place the freeze-dried berries in a mini food processor. Process until finely ground, about 1 minute. (Allow the dust to settle before opening!)

3 Whisk together the flour, sugar, baking powder, and salt in a medium bowl. Whisk in 2½ tablespoons of the pulverized berries (reserve the remaining berries for the frosting). Make a well in the center of the mixture; add the rosé, oil, vanilla, and egg. Whisk until well combined. If the batter is very thick, add an extra tablespoon of wine. Divide the mixture evenly among the muffin cups.

4 Bake until the cupcakes spring back when lightly touched in the middle, 17 to 19 minutes. Cool in the pan for 5 minutes, then remove to a wire rack to cool completely (about 30 minutes).

5 To prepare the frosting, place the butter, cream cheese, and salt in a large bowl; beat with a mixer at medium speed until smooth, about 1 minute. Gradually add the powdered sugar, beating at low speed until well combined. Add the remaining pulverized strawberries and the rosé; beat until well combined. Spread the frosting evenly over the cupcakes. Garnish with fresh berries, if desired.

Mango Meringue Pie
with Chile-Lime Flourish

ACTIVE TIME: 35 minutes
TOTAL TIME: 4½ hours
SERVES 8

We took Ann's pie to our favorite French cook in the world, who was battling breast cancer at the time. She described it as "very, very, very, very, VERY good," promptly eating two pieces, and if that's not a *très bien* endorsement, we don't know what is. In one pie you get salty-buttery crunch, tangy fruit, and a cloud of luscious sweetness. The crust is made from crumbled saltine crackers mixed with butter, a signature of Atlantic Beach Pie, a North Carolina classic made famous by chef Bill Smith in Chapel Hill. The piled-high Italian meringue nods to lemon meringue pie, but it's stable (you can make it days ahead) and creamy instead of airy-ephemeral. Sweetened condensed milk makes for a wonderfully sweet, silky-dense fruity filling in much the same way that it does for your favorite Key lime pie. And the mango-Tajín combo at the heart of things is a delightful Mexican fruit cart standard.

FOR THE CRUST

1½ sleeves saltine crackers with salt (64 crackers, 6⅜ ounces)

¼ cup sugar

½ cup (1 stick) unsalted butter, at room temperature

2 tablespoons unsalted butter, melted

FOR THE FILLING

4 large egg yolks

1 can (14 ounces) sweetened condensed milk

⅓ cup freshly squeezed lime juice

1 package (14 ounces) frozen mango pulp (about 1⅔ cups), thawed

FOR THE MERINGUE

3 large egg whites (about 6 tablespoons)

¾ teaspoon vanilla extract

½ teaspoon cream of tartar

¼ teaspoon table salt

¾ cup sugar

3 tablespoons water

FOR FINISHING

1½ tablespoons Tajín seasoning

1 Preheat the oven to 350°F with the rack placed in the center.

2 To prepare the crust, crush the crackers by hand into small pieces over a medium bowl; you want some texture here instead of finely ground crumbs. Stir in the sugar. Add the softened butter and knead lightly with your hands until the crumbs almost hold together. Drizzle the melted butter over the mixture and toss well to coat. Pat the mixture firmly into the bottom and up the sides of a 9-inch pie plate (no need to coat with cooking spray). The crust will be thick, and you will be glad as you eat the pie. Place the unbaked crust in the freezer to firm up, 10 minutes.

Flavor Booster

Frozen Fruit Is Easier, Better. Our first testing used fresh puree made by blending chopped mango with lime juice, but the fruit flavor was too mild. Solution: the frozen *fruta* section in larger Mexican supermarkets, which sell packets of mango, guava, soursop, and many more pulps, all delicious for drinks and sauces. Thawed, mango pulp has the texture of thick orange juice and a concentrated mango flavor that makes for a much better filling.

Avoid This Mistake

Don't Taint Your Egg Whites! For voluminous meringue, you must use pristine egg whites with no trace of yolk. Use the three-bowl separation method: Crack the egg over bowl #1; hold the yolk in the fingers of one hand, separate your fingers a bit, and let the white fall down into the bowl. If the white separates cleanly, transfer it to bowl #2. Drop the yolk into bowl #3. Repeat with remaining eggs, collecting the "clean" whites in bowl #2 (and note that you only need 3 whites for this recipe). For any whites with traces of yolk, save them to make scrambled eggs or an omelet.

3 Bake the chilled crust until golden brown, about 15 minutes. Remove the crust from the oven; keep the oven on.

4 To prepare the filling, whisk the yolks in a medium bowl until well blended. Gradually add the sweetened condensed milk, whisking until well blended. Whisk in the lime juice and mango pulp. Pour the mixture into the warm crust. Bake until the filling is almost set, 22 to 25 minutes; the filling should seem firm around the edges but still jiggle in the middle when you shake the pie. (If the middle is still too loose, continue baking.)

5 Cool the pie on a wire rack at room temperature for 30 minutes. Chill until fully set, about 3 hours.

6 Meanwhile, to prepare the meringue, combine the egg whites, vanilla, cream of tartar, and salt in a large bowl. Beat with a mixer at medium speed until soft peaks form.

7 Place the sugar and water in a small, heavy saucepan; stir just to moisten the sugar. Bring to a boil over medium-high heat. Cook, without stirring, until the sugar syrup reaches 250°F on a candy thermometer, 4 to 5 minutes. With the mixer on medium-low speed, carefully pour the sugar syrup in a thin stream down the side of the bowl into the egg white mixture. Increase the mixer speed to medium, and gradually increase up to high. Beat until stiff peaks form.

8 Sprinkle about 1 tablespoon of Tajín around the outside edge of the filling to form a chile-lime "necklace." Spoon the meringue into the middle of the pie, spreading to the Tajín necklace and making dramatic swoops as desired. Sprinkle the remaining Tajín over the meringue.

VARIATION: Passion Fruit Meringue Pie: Passion fruit lovers can omit the mango puree and substitute frozen passion fruit pulp (also sold in Mexican markets); the result is tangy and fragrant. You may need to bake longer to get to the jiggly state described in Step 4.

A bit of chile-lime heat from Tajín is a final flourish on this sublime pie.

Scott's Mom's
Sweet and Tangy Butter Tarts

ACTIVE TIME: 28 minutes (not including making the pastry)
TOTAL TIME: 1 hour
MAKES 18 TARTS

These are superstar pastries. Classic Canadian butter tarts are like tiny pecan pies for people who find pecan pie too cloyingly sweet. The secret, in Scott's mom's 60-year-old recipe, is the addition of vinegar to the gooey filling, which magically lifts the flavor. Corn syrup is the traditional liquid sweetener, but substituting the molasses-y depth of American sorghum syrup takes things to an even more wonderful place. Use your favorite piecrust recipe, of course, but Scott's mom's version on page 120, with lard as the fat, is supremely flaky and adds savory undernotes like those in a mince pie.

Cooking spray

1 cup packed light brown sugar

½ cup sorghum syrup, or substitute ½ cup dark corn syrup

1 tablespoon white vinegar

1 teaspoon vanilla extract

2 large eggs

½ cup (1 stick) salted butter, melted

¾ cup golden raisins

½ cup chopped pecans or walnuts (optional; if you use nuts, reduce raisins to ½ cup)

1 piecrust, suitable for a 9-inch two-crust pie (⅓ of Scott's Mom's Super-Flaky Pie Pastry, page 120)

Whipped cream or vanilla ice cream, for serving (optional)

1 Preheat the oven to 375°F with the rack placed in the center. Coat 18 cups from 2 standard-size muffin pans with a liberal amount of cooking spray and set aside. Nonstick pans work best with this sticky filling.

2 In a large bowl, briefly mix the brown sugar, sorghum syrup, vinegar, vanilla, and eggs with a spoon, then pour in the melted butter and stir vigorously until it looks like a rich, smooth caramel sauce. Stir in the raisins and, if using, the nuts.

3 Roll the pastry out on a floured surface to the same thickness you would use to make a pie, or slightly thinner, about ⅛ inch. Use a large glass to cut the dough wide enough for the muffin pans. You may need to experiment with the size of the glass: You want the dough to come all or most of the way up the sides of the cups (4-inch circles tend to work well). You can dip the lip of the glass in flour to prevent sticking. Gently press the dough into the cups, being careful not to tear it. If you do tear, patch by pressing in a little bit of spare dough. You'll have scraps of dough left after the first pass; simply knead the scraps together gently until uniform, then roll out again and cut.

4 With a ladle or spoon, fill each pastry cup about three quarters full. The filling will puff a bit during cooking before settling, and you don't want it to spill over the edges. Use a bit

Global Pantry Ingredient

Sorghum, *p. 22*

Avoid This Mistake
Be Vigilant About Sticking. If you overfill the tarts, the mixture will bubble up and stick to the pan. Even properly filled, there will be sticking, so it's critical to pry the tarts out gently while still warm, as described. The pastry may crack a bit, but coax the tarts to their proper round shape with your fingers and they'll firm up as they cool.

of paper towel to wipe away any filling that has spilled between the cups onto the pan.

5 Bake for about 17 minutes, checking near the end: You want the pastry nicely browned but not burnt. When that happens, the filling is done—not jiggly but not dry, either. The filling will likely puff up a bit into a brown dome that will fall once taken out of the oven—that's OK!

6 Allow the tarts to cool for 15 minutes, then gently remove from the cups using a blunt dinner knife, running the knife around the edges and then lifting out with the blade.

7 Serve warm with whipped cream or vanilla ice cream if you wish, though that's kind of gilding the lily. These tarts freeze well for several weeks in a tightly sealed container (return them to room temperature before eating and/or reheat, if desired, in the microwave for about 30 seconds each or in a 300°F oven for 5 to 10 minutes).

Mixing and Rolling Pastry Dough

1. Drop the cold cubed lard into the flour mixture, quickly separating and coating each piece.

2. Work the lard into small bits with your fingers, as here, or with a pastry cutter. The lard bits should be pea- and marble-sized. Don't work too small.

3. Add the liquid mixture and quickly work into a mass with a wooden spoon.

4. Put the dough on a floured work surface and gently knead until most of the flour is incorporated, but don't overwork the dough. It may be sticky!

5. Cut the dough into 3 equal pieces, wrap well with plastic wrap, and refrigerate for 2 hours or overnight. Extra will freeze well (see page 120).

6. Shape chilled dough into a ball and begin to roll it out on a floured surface, turning the dough as needed. You can flip it, too, and add more flour to the surface.

Coconutty Banana Pudding
with Candied Black Walnuts

ACTIVE TIME: 30 minutes
TOTAL TIME: 2 hours 30 minutes
SERVES 8

When Ann served this to several Mississippi-born banana-pudding partisans (aka her immediate family), they declared it the best they'd had, which is like hearing your lobster rolls are the best in Maine from Eastport old-timers. It has all the classic spongy-creamy-soft-banana texture, but the coconut milk makes a more luxe custard, and the crunchy, earthy black walnuts take the dish over the top with bells on. Do we sound excited about this banana pudding? We are.

FOR THE PUDDING

1 can (14 ounces) sweetened condensed coconut milk

1 cup whole milk

2½ tablespoons cornstarch

½ teaspoon kosher salt

1 can (13.5 ounces) coconut milk (warm the can and shake before opening)

2 large eggs, lightly beaten

2 teaspoons vanilla extract

1 box (12 ounces) vanilla wafers (you probably won't use all of them)

3 or 4 ripe bananas, sliced

FOR THE WALNUTS

¾ cup chopped raw black walnuts

3 tablespoons sugar

1 tablespoon unsalted butter

¼ teaspoon kosher salt

¾ teaspoon ground ginger

FOR THE WHIPPED TOPPING

1 cup heavy cream

⅛ teaspoon plus a pinch of kosher salt

1 To prepare the pudding, scoop out and set aside ¼ cup of sweetened condensed coconut milk. Whisk together the remaining sweetened condensed coconut milk, whole milk, cornstarch, salt, and coconut milk in a medium, heavy saucepan. Bring to a boil over medium heat, stirring frequently; reduce the heat to low and cook until thickened, about 1 minute.

2 Place the eggs in a medium bowl. Gradually add the hot coconut milk mixture, a little at a time, whisking constantly as you go. Pour the mixture back into the saucepan. Cook over medium-low heat until thick and bubbly, whisking constantly, about 2 minutes. Remove the pan from the heat; stir in the vanilla.

Global Pantry Ingredients

Black Walnuts, *p. 9*
Coconut Milk, *p. 10*
Sweetened Condensed Coconut Milk, *p. 10*

Key Technique

Temper, Temper. The secret to a smooth custard is to temper the eggs—gradually heating them so they don't cook to scrambled bits. Here this is done by pouring the hot coconut mixture into the beaten eggs very gradually, whisking as you go. Patience pays off.

Altitude Adjustment

Caramel Before Nuts. When making the candied walnuts, Scott found that at 5,500 feet he needed to cook the sugar and butter first, adding water as needed a tablespoon at a time until the sugar was melted and light amber-colored. Then he added the walnuts and cooked for a couple of minutes until they were toasty.

3 Arrange a layer of vanilla wafers over the bottom and up the sides of an 11 × 7-inch or 2-quart baking dish. Top the wafers with a layer of banana slices. Pour half of the hot custard evenly over the bananas. Repeat with another layer of vanilla wafers, banana slices, and remaining custard. Cover and chill until cold and set, at least 2 hours.

4 To prepare the walnuts, lay a large sheet of parchment paper by the stove. Combine the walnuts, sugar, butter, and salt in a small or medium nonstick skillet over medium heat. Cook, stirring frequently, until the sugar melts, about 5 minutes. Then stir constantly until the sugar turns amber-colored, 2 to 3 minutes. Remove the pan from the heat and stir in the ginger. Immediately pour the nuts onto the parchment paper, breaking apart any clumps. Cool completely. Break apart any remaining clumps.

5 To prepare the whipped topping, pour the cream and salt into a large bowl. Beat with an electric mixer at medium-low speed just until the cream stops splattering, 1 to 2 minutes. Increase the speed to medium-high and beat until stiff peaks form, 2 to 3 minutes. With the mixer on low speed, beat in the reserved ¼ cup sweetened condensed coconut milk.

6 Uncover the pudding. Spread the whipped topping over the top, and sprinkle with the nuts. Serve right away, or cover loosely and chill until ready to serve; leftovers will keep well for a day or two.

Sweetened condensed coconut milk makes the pudding luscious, glossy, and, of course, coconutty.

Splendid Peach Sundaes

with No-Churn Coconut Ice Cream and Instant Miso Caramel

ACTIVE TIME: 22 minutes
TOTAL TIME: 3 hours 22 minutes
SERVES 6

Everyone smiles when they eat this peak-peach-season, global-flavor showstopper. Fruit of Georgia meets coconut of Thailand, and they're married by the ancient salty goodness of miso in a classic French sauce, caramel. We learned the simple trick for no-churn coconut ice cream from a South African chef at a fundraising dinner in Denver: semi-whipped heavy cream, stabilized with thick, sweetened condensed coconut milk, freezes from a sort of mousse state into an airy, creamy treat.

FOR THE ICE CREAM

½ teaspoon vanilla extract

¼ teaspoon fine sea salt

¾ cup sweetened condensed coconut milk

1 pint heavy whipping cream

FOR THE MISO CARAMEL SAUCE

4 teaspoons sweet white miso or white miso

2 teaspoons hot water

¾ cup good store-bought caramel sauce

FOR THE PEACHES

3 large peaches

1 To prepare the ice cream, stir the vanilla and salt together in a medium bowl; add the sweetened condensed coconut milk and stir until well combined. In the bowl of your stand mixer (or a large bowl), beat the cream with the whisk attachment (or beaters) at medium speed for about 2 minutes, until thick and glossy and creamy but not forming peaks (the whisk will leave drag marks, but the cream will still run off a spatula, though some will cling). Add the coconut milk mixture and stir with a spatula until thoroughly mixed. Cover the bowl and put in the freezer until firm, 3 hours or so depending on the temperature of your freezer.

2 To prepare the miso caramel, mix the miso and hot water in a 2-cup measuring cup until you have a dissolved slurry. Add the caramel from the jar until the quantity is just over ¾ cup. Whisk until thoroughly mixed. Cover and set aside.

3 To prepare the peaches, peel, seed, slice, and put in a bowl if they're perfect; macerate if they're not (see Peaches Imperfect?).

4 Assemble the sundaes: ice cream, peach slices, then a dollop of caramel on top. (If the caramel is too thick, stir in a bit of heavy cream or warm it briefly in the microwave and stir to loosen.)

Global Pantry Ingredients

Miso, *p. 16*

Sweetened Condensed Coconut Milk, *p. 10*

Peaches Imperfect?

Juicing Up Firm Fruit. If your peaches are not quite ideally ripe—often the case if bought at a supermarket—peel, slice, and then mix in a bit of sugar in a bowl to macerate for a few minutes. This draws out the liquid for a more juicy effect. You can add a squeeze of lemon juice, too, to brighten the flavor.

Salty Tahini and Pine Nut Ice Cream
An Easy Kitchen Hack

ACTIVE TIME: 5 minutes
TOTAL TIME: 2 hours 5 minutes
SERVES 4

When Scott lived in Brooklyn, his kids called New Jersey–invented Häagen-Dazs ice cream Huggin' Dogs, and the family fashioned new flavors with the simple hack of softening the iconic vanilla variety—still the best big-company vanilla around, with only five ingredients and no stabilizers—and then working in a few big-flavor ingredients before refreezing. Chunks of palm sugar worked beautifully (the bits turn gooey in the freezer), as did Grape-Nuts that softened to a chewy-malty state. The tahini and pine nut hack offered here is a total nutsplosion, perfect with a slice of banana bread or a very crunchy cookie.

3 tablespoons tahini

¼ teaspoon kosher salt

1 pint vanilla Häagen-Dazs or other
   premium ice cream

½ cup toasted pine nuts (see page 26)

1 Mix the tahini with the salt in a small bowl.

2 Soften the ice cream in the fridge until a spoon goes in without brute force but the ice cream has not begun a serious meltdown. Squeezing the tub also works; it should give a bit but not too much. Put the ice cream in a large bowl (don't toss the container), and work in the pine nuts with a silicone spatula or wooden spoon. Pour the tahini-salt mixture over the mass, cutting it in a few times with the spatula but not overmixing; you want a ribbon effect. Return the ice cream to its container (it will bulge out the top a bit), and cover with the lid or plastic wrap. Freeze for 2 hours or until hardened but scoopable.

Pine nuts, properly toasted, have a flavor both subtle and profound.

4-Ingredient No-Churn Ice Cream
Spiked with Preserved Lemon

ACTIVE TIME: 6 minutes
TOTAL TIME: 4 hours 6 minutes
SERVES 8

Global Pantry Ingredients

Brilliant Preserved Lemons, *p. 20*
Sweetened Condensed Milk, *see Try This!, p. 286*

In this super-easy, super-creamy ice cream—imagine a lemony Creamsicle—the preserved lemon adds little hits of salty, chewy, supple peel for extra yum. The thick sweetened condensed milk combines with lightly whipped cream to create a base that preserves a beautiful texture that survives freezing—the combo is the key to keeping the ice cream soft enough to scoop. Serve some on chilled sweet melon such as cantaloupe for a stunning, simple summer dinner finisher.

¼ cup freshly squeezed lemon juice

2 tablespoons preserved lemon, chopped to a relish consistency

1 can (14 ounces) sweetened condensed milk

1 pint heavy cream

1 Combine the lemon juice, preserved lemon, and sweetened condensed milk in a medium bowl, stirring with a silicone spatula or spoon until thoroughly mixed.

2 Pour the cream into a large bowl; beat with a mixer fitted with the whisk attachment (or beaters) at medium speed for about 2 minutes, until thick, glossy, and creamy but not forming peaks (the whisk will leave drag marks, but the cream will still run off a spatula, though some will cling). Pour in the lemon juice mixture and beat on medium speed until thoroughly mixed, or simply mix vigorously by hand with a spatula—you'll see the cream change to a slightly darker, even color.

3 Pour the mixture into a loaf pan or 8-inch square baking pan. Cover and freeze until firm but not hard, 2 hours in a deep freeze or 3 hours in a fridge freezer.

Or try this hack: You can make a faster version of this by working chopped preserved lemon into a container of vanilla ice cream (preferably Häagen-Dazs) as directed on page 284.

Alt Ingredient

No Preserved Lemon?
We highly recommend having a jar of homemade preserved lemons (page 20) in the fridge at all times, but it does take 1 month to ferment after a scant 20 minutes of labor. In a pinch, use the zest of 1 lemon (chopped into tiny pieces) and add ¼ teaspoon kosher salt to the sweetened condensed milk.

Try This!

Sweetened Condensed Milk. Sweetened condensed milk, whose industrial production dates to the 19th century, is a global pantry favorite from Brazil to Vietnam, one way to stabilize dairy in hot climates. (Of course, boiled-down milk, used for centuries in India, is essential to many Indian sweets.) We love it for the body it brings to super-easy frozen desserts.

Avoid This Mistake

Work Quickly. This is an easy recipe, but when you blend the strawberry powder with the sweetened condensed milk for the filling (Step 5), add it to the whipped cream quickly, lest the powder mixture harden and become difficult to blend.

No-Churn Strawberry Ice Cream Pie
with Super-Chocolate Crust

ACTIVE TIME: 25 minutes
TOTAL TIME: 4 hours 25 minutes
SERVES 8

Our dead-simple no-churn ice cream is blended with powdered freeze-dried strawberries and put in a crust that is a double-hit of serious chocolate: pulverized semisweet wafers tossed with melted dark chocolate chips. Slices are served with a dollop of sliced fresh strawberries that have been macerated with a bit of fruity vinegar and sugar—a juicy soak that elevates the flavor of even less-than-perfect supermarket berries. Kids love this, and even jaded adults lick their plates.

FOR THE PIE

1 ounce freeze-dried strawberries (such as Target's Good & Gather brand)

1 package (9 ounces) Nabisco Famous Chocolate Wafers

4 ounces (⅔ cup) premium baking dark chocolate chips (such as Ghirardelli)

2½ teaspoons canola or vegetable oil

Cooking spray

1 pint heavy cream

1 can (14 ounces) sweetened condensed milk

1 tablespoon freshly squeezed lemon juice

¼ teaspoon table salt

FOR THE TOPPING (OPTIONAL BUT RECOMMENDED)

3 cups sliced fresh strawberries (1 pound)

1 tablespoon sugar

1½ teaspoons Banyuls or sherry vinegar

1 To prepare the pie, place the freeze-dried strawberries in a food processor or mini food processor. Process to a powder, about 10 seconds on high. Place the strawberry powder in a medium bowl. Wipe the processor bowl but don't bother washing it. Add the wafers to the processor and process to a powder rather like sand in consistency, about 10 seconds per batch (if using a mini chopper, you'll need to do 2 batches). Put the wafer powder in a separate large bowl.

2 Place the chocolate chips and oil in a cereal-size microwave-safe bowl and microwave on High for 30 seconds. Stir the chips with a fork. Repeat the 30-second cooking and stirring twice more. At this point there may be traces of unmelted chips, but if you stir the mix they should dissolve. If not, microwave an additional 15 to 30 seconds until you have smooth melted chocolate.

3 Combine the melted chocolate with the wafer powder and stir with a silicone spatula until thoroughly mixed. Coat a 9-inch pie pan (even better if it's a deep-dish pie pan) with cooking spray and pour the chocolate mixture into the pan, then press the mixture into the bottom and sides to form an even crust.

4 In the bowl of your stand mixer (or a large bowl), beat the cream with the whisk attachment (or beaters) at medium speed for about 2 minutes, until thick and glossy and creamy but not forming peaks (the whisk will leave drag marks, but the cream will still run off a spatula, though some will cling).

5 Pour the condensed milk, lemon juice, and salt into the bowl that has the strawberry powder and mix with a silicone spatula until it's an even pink color. Then use the spatula to blend the strawberry mixture with the cream until it's an even pale pink color.

6 Pour the cream mixture into the crust until it's even with the top of the crust. Unless using a deep-dish pan, you may have a cup or so of strawberry cream left; just freeze it separately "so you can test it later to prove to yourself it's good." Put the pie in the freezer on a flat surface and freeze for 3 hours or until firm enough to slice.

7 To prepare the topping, if using, combine the strawberries, sugar, and vinegar. Cover and refrigerate.

8 To serve, take the pie from the freezer and let it soften slightly, 5 to 15 minutes. Top with the strawberry mixture, if desired.

Just an ounce of freeze-dried strawberries makes the pie very strawberry-ish.

3 Creamy Global Pantry Freezer Bars

We know kids will jump and agitate for these because Scott's next-door neighbors, Virginia and Miles, then ages 2 and 5, were enthusiastic testers who made frequent follow-up comments about the urgency of getting more. But we also like to serve frozen bars to adult friends at the end of a hot-summer supper or spicy-food dinner: small, fun, easy-to-serve make-ahead desserts that make generous use of some of our global pantry favorites.

Tools and Techniques

MOLDS: Our favorite molds are the rectangular steel variety (such as Onyx), usually 6 half-cup molds plus a rack to set them in. They don't wobble when carried, unmold more easily than do the silicone variety, and require wooden sticks, which are more fun. They're also a breeze to clean. If a steel set is too pricey, there are many inexpensive 6- and 12-mold silicone sets, with plastic handles, that do the job fine if fussily. These recipes make six 4-ounce bars, depending on the size of the molds.

PREP AND FREEZING:

• Final mixing can usually be conveniently done in a 4-cup measuring cup—the spout is good for pouring into molds.

• Freezer timing of 4 hours is for a standard fridge freezer. A deep freeze gets the job done a bit more quickly.

• If the filling is thick, it's good to settle the mix by tapping the molds a few times on the counter.

UNMOLDING: Run individual steel molds under hot water for a few seconds until the bars slip out easily—don't force or a bar might break—then remove the metal top. With silicone molds, run hot water over the mold you want to work on, massage the silicone a bit until you can gently extract the bar, and move on to the next.

Indulgent Choco-Tahini Cream Bars

ACTIVE TIME: 7 minutes
TOTAL TIME: 4 hours 7 minutes
MAKES 6 BARS

One swooning taster called these "ultimate Fudgsicles." The tahini adds intriguing soul-of-sesame depth. The rich, lick-able texture derives from the Nestlé Table Cream (see Shopping Intel).

---

2 tablespoons Dutch process cocoa

¼ cup tahini

⅓ cup whole milk

¼ teaspoon kosher salt

½ cup sugar

2 cans (7.6 ounces) Nestlé Table Cream

Beat the cocoa into the tahini and milk in a medium bowl, then add the salt, sugar, and cream and stir until thoroughly mixed. Transfer to a large measuring cup or other spouted container and pour or spoon the mixture into the molds. Tap the molds on the counter several times to settle the thick mixture. Add sticks or lids and sticks and freeze for 4 hours.

Global Pantry Ingredient

Tahini, *p. 24*

Shopping Intel

A Luscious Canned Cream. Media crema, or "half cream," is a thick, unsoured product popular in Mexico (not the same as refrigerated, tart Crema Mexicana). It has a double-cream mouthfeel (partly because of stabilizers, actually, since it contains a bit less fat than regular heavy cream) and—*really*—a lovely canned flavor somewhere between that of fresh cream and evaporated milk. In the United States, Nestlé Table Cream, also called Media Crema, is the ubiquitous brand, found in supermarkets and Latin markets, usually with the condensed milks.

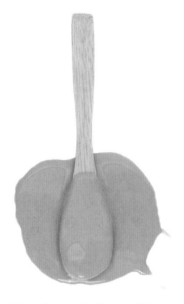

Tahini and cream make for super-rich bars.

2-Layer Key Lime Pie Bars

ACTIVE TIME: 12 minutes
TOTAL TIME: 4 hours 32 minutes
MAKES 6 BARS

Sweetened condensed milk is, in the end, more important to Key lime pie flavor and texture than the lime juice source, as long as the juice is fresh (we don't bother with the bottled key lime juice). We add sour cream and lime zest for even more tang in the dense, rich top layer of these bars. The sweet and chewy "crust" layer on the bottom has a gingery kick for even more bite.

1 cup sweetened condensed milk

½ cup light or regular sour cream

Zest of 1 lime

⅔ cup freshly squeezed lime juice
   (about 4 limes)

½ cup half-and-half

¼ cup sugar

¼ teaspoon cinnamon

¼ teaspoon kosher salt

12 gingersnap cookies (2¾ ounces)

1 To prepare the pie filling layer, whisk together the sweetened condensed milk, sour cream, lime zest, and lime juice in a 4-cup measuring cup or other spouted vessel; fill molds about three-fourths of the way up. Freeze for 1 hour and 20 minutes without adding the sticks. Then make the bottom "crust" mixture.

2 To prepare the bottom "crust" layer, add the half-and-half, sugar, cinnamon, salt, and cookies to a blender; blend on high speed until smooth. The mixture will be fairly thick. Spoon into molds, add sticks or lids and sticks, and freeze for 3 more hours.

Salty Dulce de Leche Bars

ACTIVE TIME: 6 minutes
TOTAL TIME: 4 hours 6 minutes
MAKES 6 BARS

Cans of dulce de leche are found in the Mexican or Latin sections of most supermarkets, and occasionally among other canned concentrated milks near the baking section. These bars have a small dab of dulce de leche at the top for added fun. Use Nestlé Table Cream for a rich effect, or a Mexican crema if you like a bit of sour cream tang (if using the latter, check the saltiness of the mixture before adding salt).

½ cup half-and-half

½ cup whole milk

½ cup plus 2 tablespoons prepared dulce de leche

½ teaspoon plus ⅛ teaspoon kosher salt

1 can (7.6 ounces) Nestlé Table Cream or 1 cup Mexican crema (see Shopping Intel, page 291)

Put the half-and-half, milk, ½ cup of dulce de leche, the salt, and table cream in a blender. Blend on high speed until mixed, and pour into molds, leaving a quarter-inch of room at the top. Then add 1 teaspoon of dulce de leche to each mold; it will settle to the bottom. Add sticks or lids and sticks and freeze for 4 hours.

Global Pantry Ingredient

Dulce de Leche,
see Try This!, p. 269

Salted caramel is made easy with canned dulce de leche.

Appendix:
How to Be a Canny
Global Pantry Shopper

Authenticity, Sources, Ethics

Building a global pantry is tremendous fun, a mix of food-store and market prowling, online research, label scrutiny, and taking the odd shot in the dark. We never return from H Mart or a large Latin or Indian food store without several products never before tried.

Global pantry shopping is easier today than ever before because many products simply *say* more. The foodie revolution boosted consumer interest in storytelling about the provenance and ingredients in packaged foods. That trend, plus government rules, means that the labels of most better-quality American and international pantry products provide useful although not infallible intel.

First, look for country of origin—often in tiny type. Then look for ingredient labels that list foods rather than additives. One of our favorite fish sauces, Red Boat from Vietnam, lists, simply, "anchovy, sea salt." A less tasty brand adds fructose and hydrolyzed vegetable protein. Yes, fructose is simply a form of sugar, and sugar is part of some regional styles of fish sauce (we love Megachef's sweetish sauce from Thailand), but that vegetable protein additive is more about factory methods than flavor purity.

The same rule applies to highly concocted products, such as Worcestershire sauce. The classic Lea and Perrins bottle lists only foods and extracts. A cheaper supermarket house brand includes caramel color, malic acid, and hydrolyzed soy and corn proteins. The additives are unlikely to be harmful to health, but we found them *very injurious to flavor*. When buying a complex spice mix such as ras el hanout, read up on the top-shelf spices that are traditionally used (see page 20), then look for those spices on the

label. However, the food-first ingredient rule doesn't guarantee quality: Most tahini labels list only sesame seeds, but tahini quality varies *a lot* because it's all about the sourcing of the key ingredient. That said, global agriculture is such that even very good small-production products are not necessarily made from local ingredients. Many good Korean toasted sesame oils are made from imported seeds, or even made outside Korea. As always, taste and quality are the clincher.

Price usually, but not always, correlates to quality. That's why you'll see claims about traditional methods, premium ingredients, organic production, purity, and such on the labels of better, pricier foods. If a peanut oil is cold-pressed or expeller-pressed, which a proper one should be, the label will likely trumpet that fact, and the oil will be considerably more dear than a big-factory product made using solvents. Most of these claims are not regulated, however, so the final decider must be your palate. The decades-long scandals involving false labeling of European and North African olive oil left us skeptical about quality claims pretty much anywhere. Fortunately, hanky-panky tends to be less a matter of safety than of flavor.

When possible, we seek products from food makers, old and new, who practice traditional methods and who tend to make a lot of noise about that. We love small specialty food shops run by careful curators, but we also buy online—directly or through large sellers like Amazon and Walmart—from small American producers of black walnuts, sorghum, bacon, Carolina gold rice, and the like.

Is small always better? No: Pearl River Bridge, with its old-timey labels, makes good, widely available light and dark soy sauces, particularly in the Superior and Premium Deluxe line, yet the Guangdong Pearl River Bridge Biological Technology Company claims to be the *largest* manufacturer of soy sauce in China. We've found and loved Japanese soy sauces from small, old producers, but have yet to see a kecap manis from Indonesia not made in a big factory. Sometimes food companies are big because they make good stuff.

The internet is a deep resource for global pantry sleuths. Food sellers and specialty importers evangelize the virtues of traditional foods, seeking out small, dedicated providers of ingredients, supporting artisans and farmers. The information they provide is often quite accurate. New packagers and makers and importers are constantly bubbling up in this era of great food ferment. Not everything is good, but experimenting is so much fun. Revelations follow. Recently, for example, we bought whole organic Tellicherry peppercorns from an Illinois spice importer called The Reluctant Trading Experiment, whose packages are a mix of whimsy and homages to distant growers. The texture and flavor of the peppercorns knocked our socks off, and they're now the go-to pepper in Scott's pantry. Another thought: Products from such suppliers make great gifts when we want to evangelize the global pantry to friends and cooks.

Buyer beware, of course; we've had at best mixed luck with consumer comments and online ratings of global pantry products. However, with a bit of searching you'll find that almost every product category has roundups and tasting notes from food media, bloggers, Tubers, and obsessive nerds. Look to UK and Australian sources as well. We've made good use of Google Translate on international-language producer websites.

It's hard to overstate this point: The interconnected food cultures of the world depend on the discernment and buying decisions of cooks who appreciate the traditions, expertise, craft, dedication and just plain good taste embodied in the products of the global pantry. Every cook who uses them helps to preserve them.

Sustainability, Carbon Footprints, and the Treatment of Animals

The oceans are being pillaged. Animals in factory farms are being treated, out of sight, in ways we would never treat our pets, justified because of price and efficiency. Claims like "cage free" on egg cartons are deliberately vague. Staples from Big Ag monoculture farms contribute to soil erosion and the flow of agrochemicals into waterways and the seas. And then there's the issue of your carbon footprint at the dawn of the Amazon Era. Is a jar of chili paste shipped halfway around the world a terrible indulgence? What's a global pantry cook to do? Let's take these one at a time:

Sustainable seafood: The trick with seafood is that there are often many offerings of the same species of fish—such as tuna—and only some are responsibly fished. Seafood shoppers should consult online resources such as seafoodwatch.org (which has an app for shoppers) concerning origins and species. The Marine Stewardship Council offers deep resources on species and practices, including aquaculture, and certifies products.

Seek out fishmongers and big-store fish counters whose staff seems knowledgeable about sustainability. Learn what the profusion of confusing label terms actually mean. Lean toward species that may not sound that interesting—such as tilapia—but which, properly farmed and cooked, yield delicious results.

There are also issues, in international waters, of abusive employment by fishing boat operators. There is no substitute for staying abreast of the news by seeking online information.

The carbon footprint of global pantry shipping: Given the cultural importance of the global pantry, we think it's important to support the food production of all good makers, whatever their size and wherever they may be located. As noted, most of the products we feature are concentrated and long-lasting and don't need refrigeration. That said, there are ways for a global pantry cook to cut her or his carbon footprint. When ordering online, or making a long drive to a specialty store for that matter, ganging several products can reduce the use of shipping materials or fuel (Amazon sometimes offers a wait-and-consolidate option on orders). Some online companies sell their products in compact packaging with reduced-cost or free shipping, and we hope to see more of that. Seek out local producers and support them if their products are good. Store foods properly to reduce waste. Recycle everything that can be recycled.

Climate change, politics, and global pantry production: Climate change is affecting the ability of producers to grow and make some of the great products in this book, including saffron, pine nuts, chocolate, paprika, sesame, and chiles—the list goes on and on. As consumers, there is little we can do except pressure for political action at levels that might actually effect change. Supporting small food makers probably targets people who have more reason to care about this issue at the local level. It may also support—as in the case of Afghan women who harvest saffron, at least when this book went to press—smaller communities, women, and minorities. Online, you will find companies—such as small chocolate producers and importers—that support indigenous communities and organic methods. A bit of internet research usually surfaces businesses run by people who care.

Humane treatment of animals: We try to buy eggs, dairy, and meat from companies that stress the pastured life of the animals. Yes, this costs more, sometimes a *lot* more. That's why it's safe to conclude that products that don't make any claims in this area are doing little on behalf of the animals. Alas, many claims in the United States are poorly regulated. "Cage free" doesn't mean much concerning a hen's life (and so we always buy pasture-raised, which at least generally involves the greatest amount of roaming space per hen). In the case of meat, shoppers should read up on the various certification programs and terms, consulting sites such as certifiedhumane.org, which recommends the nongovernmental programs behind the labels Certified Humane and Animal Welfare Approved. Whole Foods has a certification program about the provenance of its meat, which has been subject to unsuccessful lawsuits alleging misrepresentation, but few other large retailers have even bothered to make similar efforts. Many small, high-quality butchers purchase meat from ranchers who emphasize the diet and care of their animals, giving cattle room to roam and feeding them grasses and hay after weaning, while avoiding the brutally small pens used for pigs in many large pork operations. The truth is, however, that the United States has miles to go in this area (the word "natural" on meat doesn't have much to do with animal welfare, for example), and some global suppliers seem to care even less. One healthy solution is to cook more from the vegetable recipes in this book, less from the meat recipes.

Tools, Terms, and Techniques

A Few of Our Favorite Cooking Tools

We assume most kitchens have a good set of heavy saucepans, a blender, a food processor, a KitchenAid-style mixer, a set of both dry-food and liquid measuring cups, measuring spoons, sharp knives of various sizes, and the like. Here are a few other things that come in particularly handy for global pantry cooking.

• **A large (14 inches works for most homes) American-made carbon-steel wok**, which is sold in Chinese and other cooking shops and online by companies like wokshop.com. Once seasoned, the wok becomes a nonstick pan, conducting heat well and radiating it up the sides for more cooking surface. Home stoves, even large gas burners, don't generate the sort of rocket-engine firepower you'll see in Chinese restaurants, but a wok is still one of the finest pan-frying tools around. It holds a lot of food and allows easy stirring and flipping. Flat-bottomed woks are easiest to handle on home ranges.

• **A large (at least 12-inch) nonstick skillet.** We particularly like the recent hybrid pans, such as from HexClad, which incorporate etched steel and recessed nonstick coatings. These require less gentle handling than old nonstick, and some can go into a 500° oven, so that pan-seared things such as chops can be finished in the radiant heat of the oven. In conventional nonstick pans, we like the Tramontina Pro pan, with its long, silicone-wrapped handle.

• **A cast-iron skillet.** Indispensable for making cornbread, searing meat, pan-frying, and going seamlessly from stovetop to oven. Generally, a 10-inch skillet is the most versatile. While you could spend a lot of money on fancy cast-iron offerings, we find that inexpensive Lodge skillets are the gold standard. Almost all of them come preseasoned now.

• **Heavyweight sheet pans.** So much better than flimsy cooking sheets, which can buckle and bend during heating, when it comes to broiling veggies or meats or making cookies. Look for shiny aluminum pans, not dark or nonstick (which tend to burn your food); Nordic Ware is a great brand. Invest in a couple of half-sheet pans (measuring 18 × 13 inches) and one or two quarter-sheet pans (13 × 9 inches). While you're at it, invest in heavy cake pans and baking pans as well. They cook more evenly.

• **A few very good knives.** Scott's a bit of a Japanese-blade packrat, but all you need is a nakiri-style knife (flat-sided and tall, for thin-as-you-require slices of vegetables, fruits, garlic, and such); a strong paring knife (for finicky work, and deboning chickens); and a sturdy, pointed, tapering chef's knife for general duties. Others to consider: a thin serrated knife for delicate things (tomatoes, peaches), for which there are excellent Japanese models; and a hefty cleaver. It's also good to learn how to sharpen with whetstones—not difficult, and therapeutic.

• **An electric food chopper (aka mini food processor).** Smaller than a standard food processor, and with only one job: to reduce herbs, spices, garlic, onion, nuts, and such to paste, powder, or jumbly mixture.

• **A stone mortar and pestle.** Available at good prices in Asian or Indian food stores, these are handy and satisfying to use, when you need to quickly crush a small amount of spices or garlic, or to make salt powder for our wokcorn (see page 53). Don't buy a tiny version—it will frustrate. We like models made of rough stone.

• **A very large glass measuring cup or two.** We find four- and eight-cup Pyrex glass cups handy almost every day—not only to measure large volumes of ingredients in one go, but as backup when you need an extra bowl or two, or even as a stand-in for a pitcher.

- **An Instant Pot or similar multi-cooker.** Several recipes in this book take advantage of the ability of the Instant Pot to both sear food and then cook it quickly under pressure. A conventional pressure cooker can also be used, though we haven't provided times or settings for that (if you have one, you probably know or can seek internet counsel). However, if you don't cook under pressure, recipes can be adapted for Dutch ovens; just leave a lot more time to get to the proper state of doneness.

- **A Chinese "spider" strainer.** These cheap tools are incredibly useful for fishing food out of hot water or hot oil. They come in various sizes and fineness of the wire mesh. Available online or at any large Asian food store. If you have room, buy a small and a large.

- **A large fine-mesh strainer.** Beyond the usual draining colanders, it's nice to have a big strainer. Ours are large enough that from basket to the tip of the handle, they can straddle a sink, holding drained or washed food until it's needed (there are extendable models that work nicely for this). A large fine-mesh strainer will retain bits of food that might fall through a larger colander.

- **An electric rice cooker.** Ah . . . this one divides us. Ann has mastered stove-top rice cooking. Scott has not. Consequently, he worships his expensive Zojirushi Pressure Induction rice cooker, which turns out perfect basmati, Japanese, sticky, and brown rice every time. Much less pricey models do pretty much the same. You'll find methods for both approaches in our recipes.

- **A large, heavy Dutch oven.** There is no better tool for a good stovetop sear and a long oven simmer than this. An heirloom purchase.

- **A few ultrasharp plane-style graters** in different sizes (we like Microplane). We often use these for fresh garlic and frozen things like lemongrass, ginger, turmeric, and makrut lime peel. For larger grating—cheese, potatoes, etc.—the newer 4-side box cutters using the same very sharp blade technology work wonders (the brand we love for that is Cuisipro).

- **Tight-sealing freezer bags.** We love sturdy quart- and gallon-size bags, with their plastic zippers; you can squeeze out air around pantry products for less freezer burn, fit more bags into a freezer space than boxy containers—and wash and reuse the bags several times rather than toss.

Measurements and Weights

Measuring ingredients correctly is key to recipe success, especially when it comes to baking. Here are a few reminders:

- **Liquid ingredients:** For water, milk, syrup, or oil, use a liquid measuring cup—typically one with a spout. Make sure that, at eye level, the liquid hits the measurement mark you want. When measuring small amounts (whole or incremental tablespoons or teaspoons), use measuring spoons.

- **Dry ingredients:** To accurately measure rice, oats, cornmeal, sugar, or millet—when a more accurate weight for a baking recipe isn't required—use dry measuring cups. They typically come in a nesting set and are meant to be filled completely to the top. Spoon the ingredient into the cup until it mounds a bit, then level off the excess with the flat side of a knife. Use this same mounding and leveling method for teaspoon and tablespoon amounts. For thick, almost-solid ingredients such as yogurt, tahini, almond butter, and sour cream, we also use dry measuring cups—filling completely level to the top of the cup.

- **Weight ounces vs. fluid ounces:** In baking, it's important for key dry ingredients to be weighed. We provide the ounce weight in our baking recipes (along with the measuring-cup amount, if you don't have a scale). These weights have nothing to do with the ounce markings on liquid measuring cups, intended for fluid ounce volume measurement. Eight ounces of flour by weight is not the same as 8 fluid ounces of flour in a measuring cup.

- **Cooking times:** We show active hands-on time as well as total time. Keep in mind that stove and oven times are approximations, and take a back seat to your best judgment about doneness, texture, etc.

- **Stovetop heat terms:** Both Scott and Ann cook on mid-priced gas stovetops, nothing too fancy, but gas allows for even sautéing of onions and such over medium heat. It's the most common heat level we use in our recipes. If your cooktop's medium heat seems too cool to sauté, bump the heat up to medium-high and make a mental note that this should be your baseline adjustment. We try to give visual or other cues to help you achieve the cooking effect we intend—calling for a vigorous boil, for example (however you get there), or gently cooking at a low simmer (a medium-low or low setting, depending on the burner and the pot).

- **Serving sizes:** The serving sizes we used to determine how many people our recipes serve reflect the way we like to eat: Generous for salads and vegetables, and modest—compared with many restaurant servings—for meat dishes.

- **Altitude cooking:** Scott cooks a mile above sea level and consults published guidelines about adjusting leavening, flour, sugar, temperature, and such. One good overall guide, from Colorado State University, is at https://extension.colostate.edu /docs/comm/highaltitude.pdf. The King Arthur Baking Company publishes a very useful guide at https://www.kingarthurbaking.com/learn/resources /high-altitude-baking.

  Because water boils at well below the temperature it does at sea level, cooking times increase with altitude for tasks like boiling beans and making caramel sauce. Baking temperatures and times also change. Temperature for proper deep-frying should be lowered. Roasting times and temperatures do not change, however.

Conversion Tables

Approximate Equivalents

1 stick butter = 8 tbs = 4 oz = ½ cup = 115 g

1 cup all-purpose presifted flour = 4.5 oz

1 cup granulated sugar = 7 oz = about 200 g

1 cup (firmly packed) brown sugar = 7½ oz = 215 g

1 cup powdered sugar = 3¾ oz = 115 g

1 cup honey or syrup = 12 oz

1 cup grated cheese = 4 oz

1 cup dried beans = 8 oz

1 large egg = about 2 oz or about 3 tbs

1 egg yolk = about 1 tbs

1 egg white = about 2 tbs

Please note that all conversions are approximate but close enough to be useful when converting from one system to another.

Weight Conversions

US/UK	METRIC	US/UK	METRIC
½ oz	.15 g	7 oz	200 g
1 oz	.30 g	8 oz	250 g
1½ oz	.45 g	9 oz	275 g
2 oz	.60 g	10 oz	300 g
2½ oz	.75 g	11 oz	325 g
3 oz	90 g	12 oz	350 g
3½ oz	100 g	13 oz	375 g
4 oz	125 g	14 oz	400 g
5 oz	150 g	15 oz	450 g
6 oz	175 g	1 lb	500 g

Liquid Conversions

US	IMPERIAL	METRIC
2 tbs	1 fl oz	30 ml
3 tbs	1½ fl oz	45 ml
¼ cup	2 fl oz	60 ml
⅓ cup	2½ fl oz	75 ml
⅓ cup + 1 tbs	3 fl oz	90 ml
⅓ cup + 2 tbs	3½ fl oz	100 ml
½ cup	4 fl oz	125 ml
⅔ cup	5 fl oz	150 ml
¾ cup	6 fl oz	175 ml
¾ cup + 2 tbs	7 fl oz	200 ml
1 cup	8 fl oz	250 ml
1 cup + 2 tbs	9 fl oz	275 ml
1¼ cups	10 fl oz	300 ml
1⅓ cups	11 fl oz	325 ml
1½ cups	12 fl oz	350 ml
1⅔ cups	13 fl oz	375 ml
1¾ cups	14 fl oz	400 ml
1¾ cups + 2 tbs	15 fl oz	450 ml
2 cups (1 pint)	16 fl oz	500 ml
2½ cups	20 fl oz (1 pint)	600 ml
3¾ cups	1½ pints	900 ml
4 cups	1¾ pints	1 liter

Oven Temperatures

°F	GAS MARK	°C	°F	GAS MARK	°C
250	½	120	400	6	200
275	1	140	425	7	220
300	2	150	450	8	230
325	3	160	475	9	240
350	4	180	500	10	260
375	5	190			

Note: Reduce the temperature by 68°F (20°C) for fan-assisted ovens.

Index

Note: Page references in *italics* indicate photographs.

R

S

Acknowledgments

I owe who I am as a cook to my parents' roots—
my mother's in Korea, and my father's in the South.
—Ann

Thanks to John and Kay Mowbray, who moved overseas when I still thought
Kraft Dinner was the best thing, and took me on global food adventures
from Bali to Athens, Hong Kong to San Francisco.
—Scott

About the Authors

Ann Taylor Pittman is a longtime food writer, food editor, and recipe developer who has won two James Beard Foundation Awards: one for the feature article "Mississippi Chinese Lady Goes Home to Korea" and one, with Scott Mowbray, for writing *The New Way to Cook Light* cookbook. At *Cooking Light* magazine for 20 years, she rose to oversee all food content as well as the operation of the Test Kitchen, developing thousands of gold-standard healthy recipes for print, web, and video. At *Cooking Light*, her work was nominated for a National Magazine Award. She is also the author of *Everyday Whole Grains*. She has spoken at Southern Foodways Alliance events and IACP conferences. She now writes and creates recipes for *Food & Wine*, *Southern Living*, Weight Watchers, and Kitchn. Ann lives in Birmingham, Alabama, with her husband, Patrick, their teenage twin boys (the emo twins), one big slobbery dog, and one little busy dog.

Canadian-born **Scott Mowbray** came to the US in the early 1990s to pursue an editorial career. Since then, he has been a national magazine editor, columnist, book author, and editorial strategist. He was the editor of *Eating Well* and *Cooking Light* magazines. He has won awards from both the American Society of Magazine Editors and the James Beard Foundation. Scott lives in Boulder, Colorado, with his wife, Kate, where he feeds a large population of wild birds a luxurious diet of shelled sunflower seeds.